BLACK SANDS
and
CELESTIAL HORSES

Tracks over Turkestan

By the same author:

JAILBREAK
(A slow journey round Eastern Europe)
1998

STEPPE BY STEPPE
(A slow journey through Mongolia)
2000

www.scimitarpress.co.uk

BETWEEN THE DESERT AND
THE DEEP BLUE SEA
(A Syrian journey)
2006

www.classictravelbooks.com

www.horsetravelbooks.com

BLACK SANDS
and
CELESTIAL HORSES

Tracks over Turkestan

Gill Suttle

To Ann + Chris
Best wishes
Gill Suttle

Scimitar Press

SCIMITAR PRESS

www.scimitarpress.co.uk

A CIP catalogue record for this title
is available from the British Library

ISBN 978-0-9534536-2-7

Printed and bound by
CPI Group (UK) Ltd, Croydon, CR0 4YY

Front cover image:
Plaque in the Form of a Horseman, Kul Oba Barrow
Photograph © The State Hermitage Museum,
St. Petersburg
Photograph by Vladimir Terebenin,
Leonard Kheifets, Yuri Molodkovets

to Olga

with love

v

CONTENTS

ACKNOWLEDGEMENTS

There are so many people to whom I am indebted for their assistance in setting up and carrying out this journey, that it would be impossible to name them all. I would like, however, to give a special thank you to those without whose help it could not have happened at all.

To Sue Waldock, President of the Akhal-Teke Society of Great Britain, who put me in contact with people in Russia and Central Asia who were able to advise me; and who subsequently spent much time and trouble researching the breeding of Atamekan.

To Benedict Kolscynski and to my cousin Andrew Gummer, Russian linguists, who undertook all of my preparatory arrangements by phone.

To Yusup Annaklichev, Secretary of the Turkmen Akhal-Teke Horse Association, for underwriting my visa application and for introducing me to his many friends.

To all the good friends I made on the road through Turkmenistan, people who were ready and willing to accommodate a total stranger and a horse, without warning, and with a friendliness and hospitality which knew no bounds. If it is not invidious to single out one or two for even more gratitude than the rest, I should particularly like to thank Akhrana, who became a firm friend during my week's stay at his yard; and, most of all, Aina (Ainabat Annadurdieva), a most remarkable lady, without whose help I would have been in a nasty spot, and whose friendship I count a rare privilege.

To Djumaberdi Yazberdiev, who gave me five-star hospitality and stabling for several days at his stud-farm near Mari, and organised our transport (Kaan's, that is, and mine) back to Ashkhabad, for which we were both equally grateful.

And lastly, to perhaps the two most important people of all.

I was very lucky indeed to meet Repmurad Atalanov, a man with many talents of which only one is owning a superb string of Akhal-Tekes. There simply are not words enough to express my appreciation of his trust and generosity in allowing someone he had known for only a few hours to make off for several weeks with one of his horses.

And I was equally lucky to meet Olga Briusova and her family, who welcomed me so generously in Ashkhabad - as Olga's parents did also in Mari - and who propped me up with moral support and a bottomless teapot when problems seemed most insoluble. Olga's warmth, generosity, common sense and good humour were at times the only force that kept me from packing my bags and jumping on the next plane home; when things worked out, her pleasure on my behalf exceeded my own. She was big sister, proxy mum, best friend; her flat, my home.

So my deepest thanks of all go to Olga, Sasha, Maxim and Katya. Not forgetting, of course, Bim.

Note on terminology: Since Turkmenistan is a country peopled mainly by two very different ethnic groups, the native Turkmens and the Russians, there is an ambiguity in describing its people as "Turkmen": this could mean either a person with Turkmen nationality (Russian, Turkic or other) or one of ethnic Turkmen descent. So as to differentiate where necessary, I have used "Turkmen" for the national, and the more old-fashioned "Turcoman" for the ethnic.

These journeys in Turkmenistan and Uzbekistan were made in 1996. The resulting book has been far too many years in the preparation. The priority of other projects, the limitations of permanent ill-health - and the demands of Kaan's growing family - have all impeded it. In the intervening time, however, Turkmenistan has become ever more impenetrable to foreigners; wandering freely there, as I did, is no longer possible. It is only now, therefore, that I have come to know just how lucky I was.

overleaf:

Map 1

Western Turkestan

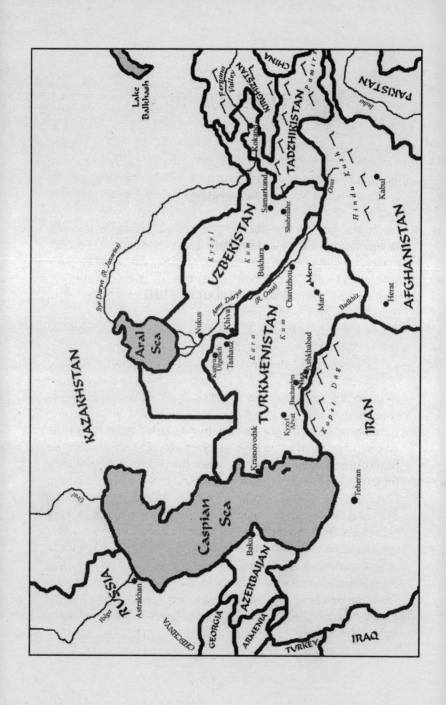

INTRODUCTION

The earthen battlements of the ancient city-mound reared above the plain. Above them in turn towered the mountains, still covered with snow, mountains that were old before the city was young.

We picked up the track in the village. Around us young women in multi-coloured headscarves fed sheep from a trough made of a hollowed tree trunk, and old men sweated in heavy Turcoman hats of black woollen dreadlocks. There was a factory of sorts, and cattle drank from a stream thick and brown with industrial waste. Some boys coming home from school ran beside the trotting horses, keeping pace bravely for a couple of hundred yards before dropping by the way, gasping.

Beyond the last house, opposite the old capital of Parthia, stood other, newer mounds: concrete bunkers covered with earth, mortal remains of the Soviet civilisation. Would travellers come to visit these in two thousand years' time?

Spring was coming. A tentative flush of green lined the verges, spotted with the blue of hyacinths. The land would be beautiful in a couple of weeks, when the colour at the willow's fingertips spread throughout the branch, and the fruit blossom, now no more than pink pinpricks, fully unfolded. We left the road and cut across farmland, riding along tracks and picking our way among the vineyards. On every corner foaming pipes spewed water on to the thirsty land, and the horses leapt the irrigation ditches barring their way. The ramparts came down off the horizon and grew to meet us, bigger now by the minute. As we gained height we could look down to where, a few miles distant, the green of the oasis gave out abruptly into the Sands, the hundreds of miles of emptiness.

With a flat half-mile remaining, Natasha threw down the gauntlet and kicked on. Three abreast, we thundered down the track towards the old city, the horses racing each other. When we hit the ramp Katya, far from slackening pace, threw her horse the reins. So we breasted the rise and entered the gates of Nisa at full gallop, like conquering nomad warriors... and riding the direct descendants of Parthian warhorses.

Part One

The Macedonian Way

I

The stillness that suddenly descended on the spectators hummed with suppressed energy. When the starting gates opened and the horses came flying out, the hum became a murmur and began to gather force. The jockeys shared its urgency; this was a seven-furlong sprint, and there could be no hanging about. As the field rounded the bend the whips were already out, and the crowd cheered the leaders up the straight with a roar disproportionate to its size. They thudded past the post in a rainbow tangle and vanished into the distance, jockeys standing up in the stirrups as they fought to pull up. The sand kicked up by their passing hung in the air, a curtain hiding them from sight.

After a few moments they returned, horses still pulling and jogging, riders jubilant or disconsolate. The winner peeled off to parade briefly in front of the stands, the owner and trainer hugging the jockey and patting the stamping, excited horse. Someone draped a Turcoman carpet over the horse's neck, and it set off at a canter towards the stables, while the jockey struggled to maintain both the equilibrium of the burden and the composure of the horse underneath it. The ceremony was over in a flash, unlike the western process of lengthy celebration in the winners' enclosure.

They do things differently in Ashkhabad. There is no pre-race parade, no lengthy inspection of runners in the paddock. The horses warm up over by the stables, as far as possible from public scrutiny. If the start is on the far side of the course, the spectators' first glimpse of them is in the last stages of the race itself. The excitement lies all in the action, in the few brief, electrifying moments when several tons of highly-charged bone and muscle whip by; and in the fun of cheering your horse home.

The crowd today was different, too. Under the tortured knot of metal that might one day grow up to be a complete roof, the watchers in the grandstand were mostly boys. The smaller ones ran around frenetically, while some of the older ones were keeping a book, passing around hundred or even five hundred *manat** notes with the dexterity of card sharpers. Not such ambitious bets; a "monkey" in manats is about ten pence. A line of military police stood, backs to the racetrack, guns at the ready, in case the festivity forgot its manners and became a riot.

Behind the stands was the nearest thing to a bar: a line of Turcoman ladies in long dresses and flowered headscarves selling *piroshki*, small flat buns. Apart from me, they were the only women present. Most people brought their own refreshments, and when the grandstand emptied at the end of the afternoon they left behind a thick dusting of sunflower seed husks, heaped in the corners like drifting snow.

There could be no finer setting for a racecourse. Across the track rose the white spine of the Kopet Dagh, the ten thousand foot mountain range that divides Turkmenistan from Iran. Its snowy backdrop relieved the intervening grey gloom of Ashkhabad's industrial suburbs, and distracted the mind from the monochrome desert sands on the other side of the Hippodrome.

But I hadn't come to look at the mountains. The next race was imminent, and I wanted a closer view of the horses. Leaving the spectators, I went down to watch from the rails. Immediately I was sent back with a flea in my ear by a military policeman.

"You must remain in the stands!"

Another distant glimpse as they cantered down; another straining, frenetic finish; another brief ceremony, before the winner disappeared with a scarf around its neck. This wouldn't do at all.

I left the side of the grandstand on the pretext of buying a piroshka, eyeing my soldier friend furtively while he eyed me openly. When he looked the other way I disappeared behind a

---

* A glossary at the end lists the commoner Turkmen and Russian vocabulary

building, keeping it between him and me as I started up the track towards the stables. Without further trouble I reached the warm-up ring, to stand enraptured as the runners passed a hair's-breadth away: tall horses, powerful but delicate, their strength softened by the lightness of their floating paces, their long ears questing forward and back like antennae above finely chiselled faces. Horses at once very similar to, yet fundamentally different from, those on other racecourses across the world.

For this was the most different thing of all about racing in Turkmenistan. The racehorses were not, as elsewhere, English Thoroughbred. They were Akhal-Teke: the rare, ancient horse that I had come three thousand miles to find.

*

"...And you mustn't miss the exciting new solar power plant in the middle of the desert. You can even stay at the factory! Only recently a party of tourists spent three whole days there, admiring the work of the Turkmen Academy of Sciences."

The two ladies had arrived unexpectedly, apparently chance guests of my host. Within a couple of minutes it had become obvious that they were tourist guides, and that their visit was anything but fortuitous.

Aksan was platinum blonde, her make-up applied with a palette knife, her long, shiny earrings hanging down to the shoulder of her dress, which was black, heavily embroidered and very short. Natasha was more down-to-earth, plump and cheerful. Because only she spoke English, and vastly better than my Russian, it was she who did most of the talking.

Enthusiastically, she passed to the subject of Ashkhabad's many carpet factories. "Even the ones that are normally closed," she promised with the air of a fairy godmother producing sweeties, "we will arrange to be specially opened for you."

I had already blotted my copybook by declaring my intention of going into the city centre - not even by taxi, but on a bus - alone, to investigate the trains to Samarkand. Now I had to destroy entirely what remained of my street cred with the two well-meaning ladies.

"I'm not a very normal tourist," I apologised. "Of course, I would be thrilled to visit technological institutions, if there is time at the end of my stay, and your carpet factories must be fascinating. But I'm interested more in people than in industry and monuments, and the very word 'organised' terrifies me."

Natasha sensed things getting out of control. "But without a guide, there are things you might miss. There are many monuments in Ashkhabad alone. You must see them all. Perhaps we could start to draw up your programme..."

"I much prefer to find my own way about," I countered. "It's terribly good of you to offer to help, but I don't need a guide, and I absolutely, absolutely don't want a programme. More than anything I want to get out on horseback and explore the countryside, talk to people, see life in Turkmenistan." Aksan's expression, which had been getting more and more glum, now glazed over entirely, and even the cheerful Natasha frowned.

"First, though, I'm going to Uzbekistan - to Samarkand, Bukhara, Khiva." Magical names, names already ancient before the Silk Road was born; these places couldn't be missed by any traveller to Central Asia. "When I come back, Yusup is going to find me a horse to hire." I had long been corresponding with Yusup Annaklichev, President of the Akhal-Teke Horse Association in Turkmenistan and my present host, about my plans. "You have wonderful horses here, and I have come to find out more about them. I want to travel some of your old trade routes, perhaps cross part of the desert, with an Akhal-Teke horse. Yusup is coming with me for some of the way.

"And I want to find out how your country has changed as a result of Independence." Turkmenistan, one of the five former Soviet Republics of Central Asia, had recently declared Independence along with the other four. These vast lands of deserts ringed by mountains and spotted with oases, with their rich history of Silk Road cities struggling continually against nomad invaders, their comparatively recent imposition of industrial and agricultural economies under Communist rule, had run through a vast range of historical and political experience. Now they were in the throes of perhaps the biggest upheaval in their history. I wanted to be a spectator, however transient, at the birth of the new era.

Aksan and Natasha brightened visibly at this appeal to their patriotism. With renewed interest, they told me how the end of Communism had changed their lives.

Both thoroughly approved of a new political and social ethos which allowed the industrious and energetic to get ahead. "Before," said Natasha - "before" and "after" were words that figured heavily in this sort of conversation, without needing to be qualified as "before what?" - "Before, getting on had nothing to do with personal abilities, but depended on loyalty to Communist doctrine and..." - the universal Open Sesame - "...membership of the Party."

And the questions, and the probing... "My grandmother," said Aksan, "was a Polish Countess, but I didn't even know. Such origins had to be kept a secret, even from one's children."

"And if you wanted to travel abroad," added Natasha, "it was all questions... Who is your neighbour, who are your brothers, who is your cousin's cousin...? 'Do you have any relatives in prison?' was always the first question. It was especially difficult for me. My mother was Turcoman, my father Russian. That way round is very, very rare. A bombshell!"

Of course, things were far from perfect now, they continued; there were many practical problems. Shortage of bread, for instance. The agricultural monoculture of cotton had been maintained by the present government, desperate for a cash crop. Wheat acreage was insufficient. But the food situation wasn't all bad. Turkmenistan grew the best grapes, the best watermelons in the world. "You should come back in summer and taste them!"

And there were no strikes, no unemployment. "Here, work is guaranteed." (Yet in actual fact, as I later discovered, this was far from the case.) Both were heartily thankful that Turkmenistan had accomplished a smooth transition to

Independence, rather than suffering the unrest and even civil war that had followed the fall of Communism elsewhere. The discussion here turned, inevitably, to Chechnya.

Yusup was utterly contemptuous. "If people have different ways, different origins, different culture, they should be free to live according to those, as they choose." The reason they couldn't, of course, was Russia's insistence on the continuing integrity of the Russian Federation largely in order to maintain her grip on Chechen oil. Here Yusup became impassioned.

"The matter should have nothing to do with oil, with gold, with money!" he raged.

There was more than a hint of "there but for the grace of God..." Turkmenistan, with its colossal deposits of oil and natural gas - the third biggest in the world - might so well have gone the same way. It was fortunate in having been only a part of the USSR rather than, like Chechnya, a province of Mother Russia herself; and too far away from Moscow for the attenuated, overstretched and underpaid Russian Army to come adventuring here.

*

On the horse front, despite my confident assertions to Natasha and Askan, things were looking pretty rocky.

Yusup, former Commercial Director of Turkmenistan's leading Komsomol Stud - now renamed the Niazov Stud in honour of the President - knew Ashkhabad's horse world inside out. Having said for over a year that he would find me a horse, and even that he would accompany me part of the way on my travels, he had been generous with enthusiasm and economical with details. In the weeks leading up to my departure for Turkmenistan I had sensed his impending cold feet. Now, it seemed, they were positively frostbitten.

My ultimate goal was to ride a stretch of the Silk Road, that between Nisa and Merv. *Merou, Shahou Jehan* - Merv, Queen of the World; the mediaeval title of this priceless gem of the Silk Road had fired my imagination for long years. To realise

10

the dream I needed a horse to borrow for a few weeks at a reasonable cost. Instead, Yusup introduced me to Aleksandr, who ran a commercial stable at American tourist prices. Aleksandr would be happy to offer me an individually tailored and escorted six-day riding holiday, with accommodation and bus excursions to tourist sites, at a price which represented more than the funds I had set aside for several weeks' horse hire.

I emphatically did not want to go pony trekking, with or without minders, and anyway the tour was far outside my low budget. But I was in a quandary.

Yusup, when I pressed him about his intentions, seemed ready to commit himself. If I would go and ride with Aleksandr, then meanwhile he would find a couple of horses so that he and I could ride to Mari, Turkmenistan's second biggest city.

This was highly promising. It meant travelling the old Silk Road route between Nisa and Merv, a course closely confined between desert and mountain and oasis, and thus as densely trodden as any path in history. And ancient Merv, ancestor of modern Mari and the goal of my armchair dreams, was only a dozen miles further. If Yusup bottled out at Mari, I would carry on alone. Even if he bottled out before leaving Ashkhabad - well, once I was mounted, I was a free agent. But first, I needed that horse. Which meant pleasing Yusup by co-operating with Aleksandr.

It was a delicate balancing act. I persuaded Aleksandr down to a two-day programme, setting points for Good Behaviour against a price which literally gave me many sleepless nights to come.

"Then will you please pay me $200 deposit now." Aleksandr's mouth stretched in a shark-like grin above a double row of gold teeth. The date was set two weeks ahead, but I would get no chance to sleep on it and change my mind. I was neatly hooked. To prevaricate would be to embarrass Yusup and jeopardise his participation in the journey. With a sick smile I handed over the money obediently. Aleksandr stuffed it into an inside pocket and punctiliously wrote out a receipt.

11

Out came the vodka, and the three of us cemented the deal in the usual fashion. Now came the double whammie. With disbelief and mounting fury, I listened as Aleksandr talked Yusup out of the plan to ride to Mari. "It would be quite impossible," he said, with a deprecating smile and generous sympathy. "You would have nowhere to stable the horses on the way. And there is no feed to be had." He was preaching to the converted. Yusup took little persuading. The bottle went round again, and the trip to Mari was off.

I couldn't help feeling neatly stitched up.

Yet, as far as feed was concerned, Aleksandr had a point. Turkmenistan was in the middle of a terrible crisis over animal feed. Barely able to grow enough grain to feed its people, it had little or nothing to spare for its horses. There had been three successive dry springs, burning off the new year's growth; spring this year was a month later than usual, and the barns had been empty for weeks. Waiting for the sun to bring on the grass, horses literally starved.

Even at the Hippodrome, some of the country's best bloodstock felt the pinch. On each Sunday's racecard the number of races, the size of the fields, and the race distances were all cut to the quick. "How can horses race when they're hungry?" exploded one breeder. In the stables, much of the hay was dried reeds or camelthorn, all that remained, and few trainers had any barley left. Yet the racehorses had the best bargain, the first bite. Elsewhere, things were much worse.

Visiting the Niazov Stud, I saw a horse which had died of starvation. The body had lain in the paddock for two days, and no-one had even bothered to move it. This was symptomatic of a deeper underlying problem: *rigor mortis* in high places.

The State reveres the Akhal-Teke horse; in theory. Is it not one of the country's national emblems? And is there not a specific Horse Minister? See how President Niazov loves the Akhal-Teke; how he has appropriated the best bloodstock for his own private stud, as well as honouring the Komsomol Stud by renaming it after himself. And look at the bronze statue of himself, together with an Akhal-Teke horse, at the Hippodrome entrance. What more proof do you need?

12

Then why had this priceless national treasure been allowed to starve? Why had an export ban prevented *all* Akhal-Teke horses, not just the prize bloodlines, from leaving the country, creating a vast surplus which could not be fed? Why had the State rejected Yusup's attempt to introduce new methods for the intensive cultivation of lucerne, a staple feed?

As people gradually became less reticent with me, the picture began to emerge. The present Horse Minister, it seemed, was a dead loss. "He is an old man," said one person tactfully. But, whatever its source, the do-nothing attitude was catching.

"No-one has to do anything; no-one's responsible; the buck doesn't stop anywhere."

"They won't let you see the real thing if you go to the Komsomol; horses standing up to their knees in shit and no-one bothering."

"No-one'll do anything without a backhander. 'You say you own this horse, but you haven't any papers. I'll give you some - for a consideration.' Suppose you want to register your horse. 'You say your horse is a pure-bred Akhal-Teke; I say it isn't. But it could become one with the right incentive.' *Korruptsia!*"

That the Horse Minister had to go was the universal opinion.

"People who don't know horses should be running hotels!"

*

Ashkhabad, the Persian-named "City of Love", was re-inventing itself, and wiping the Soviet dust off its feet in the process.

Gone were the Heroes of the Revolution, the inspiring slogans from the street nameboards, to be replaced by names more in line with local sentiment. The Street of the First of May had become Goroglya after a Turcoman hero, while the splendid Street of Fifty Years of the Turkmen Soviet Socialist Republic had been tersely relabelled *Azedi*, or Freedom.

The main thoroughfare, Prospect *Mir* (Peace), now bore the name of the Turcoman poet and philosopher Makhtum Kuli. Born in 1733 of the Göklen tribe, Makhtum Kuli was educated at the classical madrasas, or Islamic colleges, in Bukhara and

Khiva. He must have been something of a free thinker, for in him their strict dogma was moderated by the mystic influence of Sufism to a kind of Islamic humanism. His exemplar was the Sufi poet Omar Khayyam.

"Oh Turcoman people!" he wrote.

"If we could find peace and accord,

"We'd make Kulzum our home, and chain the Nile.

"Teke, Yomud, Göklen, Yazyr and Alili* -

"All five should be a single family."

More relevant today than ever before, the verse is much quoted. It even merited a hoarding above the entrance to the Hippodrome, where another quotation: "*Halk, Watan, Turkmenbashi!*" - "The People, The Land, the Turkmen Leader!" with its uncomfortable echoes of "*Ein Reich, Ein Volk, ein Führer*" - dropped from the wisdom of Turkmenistan's contemporary Hero.

Saparmurat Niazov, the country's president and *de facto* dictator, was busily establishing for himself a personality cult. He had taken the surname "Turkmenbashi", or Leader of the Turkmens, much as Mustafa Kemal of post-war Turkey styled himself "Ataturk". His slogans, like the Thoughts of Chairman Mao, sprang out at you from noticeboards and roadside hoardings. He began to style himself "the Great", aping Alexander. His portrait was everywhere, and in his latter years a golden statue of him gazed over Ashkhabad from the top of a great monument, rotating daily ahead of the sun.

Princess Diana would never have stood a chance here in the cover girl stakes. There was only one national pin-up, one supremely marketable image. Saparmurat Turkmenbashi's face adorned every newspaper, stared from the cover of every magazine, permanently occupied a corner of the television screen. It was not a memorable face; one less charismatic would be hard to imagine. Bland, with light grey hair above heavy jowls and double chin, little expression in the eyes… he was the archetypal Grey Man. Perhaps he needed to keep his face

* the principal Turcoman tribes

14

constantly in the limelight, so that his people could remember what he looked like.[*]

Is it necessary, this concentrating of patriotism into the person of the leader? To us in the West, accustomed as we are to holding our leaders mercilessly to account, sometimes treating them with contempt, and throwing them out when we have had enough of them, such hero-worship is frankly incomprehensible. Yet it is an almost universal feature of Asiatic politics; even those people who individually (and behind closed doors) disparage their leaders seem content, almost to expect, to pay collective homage.

The trappings of the State came in for similar reverence. I'd never seen anything so grand as the Cabinet Office, immaculately finished in yellow marble with Turcoman carpet patterns running in mosaic up and down the doors behind Palladian columns. Outside, two flunkeys in uniform made a show of cleaning the railings, mechanically rubbing cloths over them to little effect. It wasn't so much a job as a public statement, like so much in Turkmenistan: it must be seen that the Seat of Power was being cherished.

Lenin, still surprisingly on his pedestal in the park, also had the Turcoman carpet treatment applied to his plinth. A sort of reciprocal agreement, perhaps, for pasting his face on so many of the real things. For when the State nationalised the carpet industry, they diversified the designs. Beside the traditional patterns, which varied from tribe to tribe and were said sometimes to embody the life history of the weaver, the face of Vladimir Ilyich appeared everywhere in an affirmation of revolutionary fervour. It wasn't exactly what the Turcomans had had in mind when they coined the proverb, "Roll out your carpet, and we will see what there is in your heart."

At the further end of the park I found a small History Museum. Plenty of carpets here, too, among the social history of the Turcomans. The most breathtaking items on display, though, were in another room. A collection of ivory horns, used

---

[*] Saparmurat Niazov died shortly before the publication of this book.

in Zoroastrian rituals, had been excavated from the ancient Parthian city of Nisa, just outside Ashkhabad. Priests and worshippers, as fresh and vital as the day they were carved, led sacrificial beasts around each rim; at the base cantered lions, centaurs, griffins and other fantastic creatures, forelegs rampant, bodies tapering into the well of the cup. They gave a small breath of the brilliance, the vibrancy of the cultures that passed to and fro along the Silk Road when for five hundred years the Parthians controlled its heartlands.

All history in Central Asia, it seemed, shaped or was shaped by the Silk Road, that network of trade routes which linked the ancient world from China to the Mediterranean. All paths, physical and metaphysical, converged on its origins, its legacies, its actual tracks. And led, in turn, to the Turcoman horse.

*

More than two thousand years ago Wu-Ti, Emperor of China, was having trouble with his neighbours. To the north, the Great Wall had checked the worst incursions of the Hsiung-Nu, mounted nomad terrorists whose descendants the Huns were to sack Rome five centuries later. The western Hsiung-Nu, however, continued to harry his borders.

In 138 BC Wu-Ti sent his emissary, Chang-Ch'ien, to seek an alliance against them with a tribe now living in Khoresmia on the lower Oxus. The Yueh-Chih had good reason to dislike the Hsiung-Nu. The latter had driven them out of their lands and west across the Tien Shan mountains; in the process they had killed the Yueh-Chih Emperor and made a drinking cup from his skull, a favourite trophy of Central Asian nomads.

Chang-Ch'ien must have felt much as an astronaut would on setting out for Mars; his journey would lead him into uncharted country and probably take him several years. His mission was also likely to be considerably more dangerous than the astronaut's.

So it proved. Crossing Hsiung-Nu territory his caravan was ambushed. Chang-Ch'ien was taken prisoner, and carried off to

16

live among his captors. He did so for ten years, took a wife, raised several children - and then escaped.

With extraordinary determination he continued his journey. On finally reaching his destination he found the Yueh-Chih comfortably settled on good land, with no inclination to return to a state of war. After such trials, this must have seemed a crushing anti-climax to Chang-Ch'ien's mission. But on passing homewards through Kokand he made a discovery which excited him more than any possible alliance.

Here, on the rich pastures of the Fergana Valley, were bred horses the like of which he had never seen: tall, fast and strong. They came, he was told, from the stock of the Celestial Horses, and had an unusual trait: at speed, they sweated blood.

Chang-Ch'ien had never heard of the Sacred Nisaean Horses, as the Greek historian Herodotus described the warhorses of the Medes and Persians. He did not know that their "blood sweating" was prosaically due to a parasite under the skin. He could not anticipate that two thousand years later their descendants would be bred, having survived essentially unchanged, by the Turcomans of Central Asia, a race of people who did not yet exist. But his imagination thrilled to their potential. Such horses, he knew, could literally run rings round the small, stocky ponies used by both Hsiung-Nu and Chinese cavalry.

He was to be disappointed again, for the ruler of Kokand would not sell him even one. He did manage, though, to obtain seed of the precious lucerne, crucial to their size and strength, on which the horses were raised.

Chang Ch'ien's adventures were not over. On his way back to China, he was captured again by the Hsiung-Nu and spent a further year in captivity. But he escaped again - complete with wife, this time - and reached home. His enthusiasm was infectious, and soon the Chinese were laying plans to obtain some of the Celestial Horses for themselves. Meanwhile, the Emperor ordered his peasants to begin cultivating Chang-Ch'ien's lucerne.

Further Chinese missions went to Kokand, armed with priceless treasures to trade for the horses. But they came home empty-handed. "China can do nothing to harm us," replied the ruler. "The inestimable horses shall remain the horses of Kokand."

He was wrong. Distance notwithstanding, China could certainly harm Kokand, and sent a vast army to do so. Kokand was forced to sue for peace. A truce was negotiated, and the Chinese returned home with about thirty pure-bred and three thousand part-bred horses, and with future tribute promised of two every year.

The horses were brought to China amid scenes of great rejoicing, and the poets made a hymn to the occasion:

> The Celestial Horses are coming,
> Coming from the far west.
> They crossed the flowing sands,
> For the barbarians are conquered.
> The Celestial Horses are coming,
> That issued from the waters of a pool.
> Two of them have tiger backs;
> They can transform themselves like spirits.
> The Celestial Horses are coming,
> Across the pastureless wilds,
> A thousand leagues at a stretch,
> Following the eastern road.
> The Celestial Horses are coming.
> Open the gates while there is time.
> They will draw me up and carry me
> To the Holy Mountain of K'un Lun.
> The Celestial Horses have come,
> And the dragon will follow in their wake.
> I shall reach the Gates of Heaven,
> I shall see the Palace of God.

The Chinese had their warhorses, and duly subdued the Hsiung-Nu. But history is less interested in the proper end to the story, than in its corollary. For contact had been made between east and west, and routes opened up across the forbidding deserts and mountain ranges between. The war was over, but merchants followed in the steps of the soldiers.

And so the Silk Road was born.

II

Where had they come from, these Celestial Horses so different from those known to the contemporary world?

Horses were probably first domesticated in the fourth millennium BC, for it is from that period that their bones turn up in rubbish pits in the southern Ukraine.

They were bred to be eaten, not ridden, although a few horses were bitted - and therefore either ridden or driven - around the same time. The idea of driving horses, let alone sitting on them, wasn't to become widespread for a long time. It crept insidiously into Man's aspirations with the domestication of the donkey around 3000 BC, which opened the door to long-distance trade; while in Mesopotamia the onager, relative of the Central Asian "half-ass", the kulan, joined the ox as a draught animal five hundred years later.

But the horse, even after a thousand years or so of selective breeding, was still mostly too wild to progress from table to saddle. When the idea of riding first came to Man, he probably looked to the reindeer. For tens of thousands of years this docile beast had played a central part in primitive economies. Easily domesticated, it was pulling sledges in Siberia by 5000 BC. To this day the reindeer peoples of Siberia and northern Mongolia ride them, with saddles, as they do horses. No-one knows when men - or, more likely, adventurous children - first climbed on their backs; but almost certainly it was long before the horse had the honour.

By the second millennium BC, though, history was on the march. With some of its wildness bred out, the horse was becoming ripe for exploitation. It began to replace the slow onager in the early chariots of northern Mesopotamia. Two inventions around the same time completed the transformation of ancient warfare: the spoked wheel, allowing for faster vehicles, and the metal bit, stronger than the wood, bone or antler prototypes, giving greater control.

Such chariots must have burst on to the scene like nuclear missiles. They were the key to the balance of power, the difference between victory and defeat. From the Hurrians of northern Mesopotamia who first used them, the idea spread quickly to the Hittites, the Egyptians - and the Assyrians. When the latter "came down like the wolf on the fold" to overrun Babylonia, it was their war chariots that made them invincible.

But an even greater revolution in military technology was already under way.

The first actual proof that Man had sat on Horse comes from an Egyptian tomb dated to 1350 BC, and even this wooden figure shows only the "donkey seat", with the rider perched on the rump. But the art of riding was developing throughout the millennium, particularly in northern Iran and Central Asia. It was a process accelerated by a catalyst which we are too apt to consider the exclusive property of our own era: global warming.

As the rain-bearing winds followed the receding ice northwards at the end of the last Ice Age, the once rich grasslands of Central Asia began to turn to arid steppe and then desert. Settled farming became obsolete. The farmers of the Central Asian steppes had to move greater distances to find pasture for their animals. And the key to their mobility was the horse.

Whole communities now abandoned their farms and took to the saddle. A new way of life was in the process of evolution. From the steppes of Ukraine to the Altai mountains on the edge of Siberia, mounted nomadism became the *modus vivendi*. It gave other advantages, beyond just those of wider grazing lands. Raiding could now be conducted on a scale hitherto unknown. Those settled farmers whose land could still support them withdrew behind their fences, and braced themselves for the next attack; or upped sticks and joined the crowd.

By 900 BC, the Central Asian horsemen were banding together in federation and alliance. They had refined their technique to the point where they could shoot arrows from the saddle. They were ready to take on the big guys. From raiding, they progressed to war.

And so began the pattern of history which was to last for over two thousand years. From now on, tidal waves of nomadic peoples crashed repeatedly into the shores of the settled world. Sometimes to plunder and withdraw; sometimes to taste the softer life of civilisation, to settle themselves and absorb their conquered enemies; sometimes to evict them altogether. Thus the Hsiung-Nu terrorised the Chinese, and the Scythians harried the Assyrians and then the Persians; thus the Huns forced their way into Europe, driving the Goths before them; thus the Mongols subjugated the Turks throughout Eastern and Western Turkestan - that is, from central China to the Caspian Sea - remaining and breeding until their own blood, already half-Turkic, all but disappeared under weight of numbers, and power passed seamlessly back to the Turks.

The horse, then, represented the ultimate in military technology. The contest to breed the best, strongest, fastest horses was the original arms race. And the ultimate prize was the super-horse of Central Asia: the Sacred Horse of the Medes, the Celestial Horse of Chang Ch'ien, the ancestor of what would later be known as the Turcoman horse, and of its sub-strain the Akhal-Teke.

Did this horse spring ready-formed from the clay of the Creator, or was it the result of centuries of selective breeding by some tribe who took a head start? There are those who believe the former, that there evolved naturally on the Central Asian steppes a breed of horse finer, bigger and faster than elsewhere, ready to be tamed and used. Some, supported by recent DNA-based research, argue for man's handiwork, citing the beautiful - but much smaller - Caspian pony as the ancestor of a strain bred up to a greater height. There are even those who propose the Asiatic Wild Horse - the Przewalski Horse of Mongolia - as a forebear; although this coarse, pre-historic animal bears about as much resemblance to the Turcoman horse as does a moose to a gazelle.

Turcoman tradition ages their horses at five millennia. Archaeology goes only half as far back; but this is more than enough to confirm the antiquity of the breed.

Throughout the plains of Russia and Central Asia, excavations of the tombs below the kurgans, or barrows, of the Scythians have revealed much about the lives of these people, the most powerful and widespread steppe nomads in the first millennium BC. The richest finds of all were made around Pazyryk, where the borders of Mongolia, Siberia, Kazakhstan and China converge. Here, archaeologists investigated kurgans scattered across a hundred miles geographically and two centuries chronologically. In these latitudes, the permafrost deep-froze treasures which elsewhere had simply reverted to dust: clothing, saddlery, and the earliest known carpet.

The Scythians did not venture alone into the afterlife. They often took with them their slaves, concubines, wives even; always, their horses. Their rugs and hangings showed horses being trained to the saddle, or in ceremonious procession with stags. Two pads stuffed with deer hair and joined by birchwood arches comprised their saddles, similar to those used on reindeer. Ceremonial, antlered masks of felt and leather covered the horses' faces, turning them into griffins - or reindeer. Was this an echo of the Siberian shamanistic idea of the reindeer as a familiar spirit, bearing its rider to the spirit world? Or a vestigial collective memory of the reindeer as the earlier, and natural, mount of Man?

The horses themselves were of two distinct types: small steppe ponies like those found today in Mongolia, China and Kirghizstan; and tall, fine horses gelded for riding. Skeletal measurements and other characteristics of the latter were essentially those of today's Turcoman horse. Even the hair, preserved under the ice, showed the same metallic gold sheen that characterises the Akhal-Teke strain.

There is no doubt that the line of the Scythian horses passed, unbroken and effectively unchanged, through the hands of the Medes, Persians and Parthians, via the Turks of Western Turkestan, into the ultimate possession of the Turcomans.

23

Whether the Scythians themselves presented history with such a gift, or received it from the hands of even earlier peoples - or from nature itself - history has yet to tell us.

*

Ashkhabad's Sunday market, held at the edge of the city between the Kara Kum Canal and the desert, was like a gigantic car boot sale. Whole rows were devoted to engineering goods alone: tarpaulins strewn with fan belts, spark plugs and anonymous bits of metal, all looking as if they had been to Moscow and back several times. Next door were the builders' merchants, whose odd collections of down-pipes and U-bends might have been salvaged from the earthquake that devastated Ashkhabad in 1948.

I followed the grunts, bleats and roars to the livestock section with more than a passing interest. Might there be horses here? If so, would I be able to afford to buy, rather than hire?

There were no horses. But every other domestic four-legged beast was for sale. Pens of sheep and goats down one side, railed stalls down the other for cattle of all shapes, sizes, colours, genders and cycles of milk. And here were the camels I'd heard, hitched in bickering groups, knee-haltered precariously on the back of a truck, or - in the case of she-camels in milk - tethered singly and accompanied by woolly, doe-eyed calves.

Little forethought went into the layout. Wide spaces yawned in the middle, where no-one wanted to be; busy thoroughfares round the edge were hemmed in tightly by close-parked trucks, so that men and beasts clotted stickily in the main arteries. From time to time these cursing queues were disrupted by someone towing a reluctant sheep, or elbowing through with both hands full of live chickens tied by the legs. Once a calf ran amok, dragging its owner by the halter at frantic speed.

The animal lines were the gathering-place for the older men. Most wore the *telpek*, signature of the Tekes - the tribe whose ancestral lands centred on the Akhal Oasis. The enormous woolly hat buried the wearer, dropping black curls over the

24

forehead, looking like a dead sheep wrapped around the head. The beards and whiskers below were pale imitations, for all their luxuriant growth. And never a full set; the Teke fashion was to shave the upper lip completely, plus a safe drinking distance around the lower, then to grow the rest for all it's worth.

A hole in the wall, where bent railings increased the log-jam, gave on to the central market-square. Turcoman women in robes and headscarves of every imaginable combination of colours sat in rows a hundred yards long selling everything under the sun. Uzbek skullcaps, Chinese T-shirts, Turkish chocolate, hand-made socks and woollies, plastic tat, brilliantly embroidered dress-yokes for DIY dressmakers, Turcoman scarves, all in glorious confusion. Tough luck, if from the middle of one line you saw what you wanted over in the next; you had to push all the way down the row and back up the next, and by the time you got there it was probably sold anyway. Whereas if you were impertinent enough to step straight across...

This was obviously taboo. I tried, and a cursing Turcoman fishwife grabbed my ankle with such force that she nearly tipped me all over her goods - just the disaster she meant to prevent.

At the far end were the carpets. Acres and acres of carpets, draped over frames, hanging from the walls, spread up to three deep over the dirty sand; enough to cover a sports stadium twice over. Forget the famous Bukhara rugs; they are imports from Ashkhabad, mother of carpets. No longer made, as for centuries, in the *yurts* of the semi-nomadic Turcomans, but under efficiently regimented production in the factories. These turn out everything from tiny mats to huge living room carpets. Among the sophisticated traditional patterns were clumsy human figures and Disneyesque caricatures of cavorting bunnies.

The very centre of the pulsating square was relatively empty of people, the eye of the storm. Here, at last, I found what I was looking for. Row upon row of telpeks, spread out on the ground or perched on sticks with woolly dreadlocks dangling, like monstrous hairy spiders. Black telpeks for everyday use, white telpeks for high days and holidays. Behind each display sat a Turcoman ancient wearing his own goods; all competed with each other to see who could grow the longest beard.

Ten minutes' hard bargaining and just thirty dollars later I staggered away bearing four; two white and two black. Some nephews and nieces were in for a very unusual present.

*

To thank Yusup for his help, I had brought him a bridle from England. New tack, I reckoned, would be hard to come by in Turkmenistan. It was a lucky guess. He was delighted by the rubber-grip reins and the heavy, comfortable German snaffle.

He brought out some tack of his own to show me, tack from a completely different stable. No modern riding-gear, this, but antique Turcoman saddlery from a hundred years and more ago.

The saddles were wooden, their frames beautifully painted. Mother-of-pearl decorated the edges, inlaid like the furniture sold in the souks of Damascus. Heavy studs, embossed and engraved, secured the tooled leather lining to the seat and panel. One bore a jewelled metal strip: silver set with cornelian, trade-mark of the Turcoman horseman.

The stirrups, almost circular, were also engraved. The leathers hung from a simple hole bored in the wood, as on a Western saddle. The hook at the pommel rose to two scrolled knobs, designed to accommodate a hawk or eagle; the Central Asian Turks were noted falconers. Girths were plain webbing strips with a loop at each end, "meant to be thrown over and fastened rapidly for a quick getaway," said Yusup. "It's the same as Argentinian gauchos use."

He laid the saddles on the floor and sprawled against them, as his forefathers had done, padding his elbow with a cushion. So we passed the afternoon drinking tea out of bowls, talking of *Turkmenchilik* - the code of honour and hospitality among the Turcomans - and leisurely examining the rest of the old harness.

The bridle was also heavily decorated with cornelian, its blood-red making a dramatic contrast with the silver mounting. A breast-plate of similar design went with it; so did a couple of "choker" leathers, one attached immediately behind the bridle like an extra throat-lash and the other, lower down the neck, used for tethering. Both were encrusted with jewels.

For the horse was the chief recipient of the Turcoman's wealth, the main object of his love, above his wife or even his father. "When you rise in the morning," quoted Yusup, "greet your horse first and then your father." In such a hierarchy the wife, it seemed, came nowhere.

But then, the horse wasn't just the pride of a Turcoman; it was his wealth, too. Raiding was his way of life; and particularly slave-raiding. He might make a basic living as a semi-nomadic farmer, but it was the slave trade that made him rich. A strong young Persian from the farming villages on the edges of the Central Asian deserts, or - if the tribesmen were feeling lucky - a nice healthy Russian from the Caspian colonies, could fetch good money in the markets of Bukhara and Khiva. Such a living couldn't have been earned without the extraordinary capacity of the Turcoman horse, capable of travelling a huge distance at speed and returning carrying the double weight of rider and captive.

Much has been said - and written - about the speed and endurance of the Turcoman horses. Writing of them only a year after the crushing defeat of the Teke Turcomans by Russia in 1881, the Russian General Artishevskii desribed how, on campaign, he "had to travel 160 versts" - a hundred miles - "a day, on alternate horses; the tribesmen accompanying me... were sent on reconnaissance sorties to either side... besides rider, the horses carried huge saddlebags, clothing and various stores, a weight of not less than nineteen stone." One V. Kolosovskii wrote in 1910 of a Turcoman horse that "galloped without a break for 11 days, covering 120 versts a day" - that is, seventy-five miles. The greatest tribute of all came from a British Ambassador to Persia, who was quoted as saying that "no other horse in the world can cover such a distance so fast as the Turcoman horse... a fit Turcoman, in good training, can do 250 km in twenty-four hours."

In 1935, at a time when the Turcoman horse - by then represented largely by the Akhal-Teke strain - was in danger of dying out, a group of Turcomans set out to show the world what kind of horse they possessed. In 84 days they rode the 4,300 km from Ashkhabad to Moscow, covering the first 360 km, across waterless desert, in three days with minimal support. It was a brave adventure in more ways than one; for, in those perilous Soviet times of the mid-thirties, no-one could guess how such a non-conformist idea would be received by Stalin. "It must have been even money," commented the American writer Jonathan Maslow in his book *Sacred Horses*, "they would either be welcomed by their smiling 'Little Father' or simply arrested, taken to the edge of town, and liquidated."

The idea was revived in 1988, when recent champions of the breed repeated the Ashkhabad-Moscow marathon in an attempt to raise public awareness of the Akhal-Teke. Yusup spoke with pride of his participation in the historic event.

"You rode to Moscow?" I was duly impressed.

He looked slightly awkward. "No. But I helped to organise it." He shifted his weight against the wooden saddle, and told me stories of the 1988 *probeg* while we emptied yet another pot of tea.

It was the nearest I ever came to seeing Yusup in the saddle.

*

Aleksandr picked me up early one morning in a battered old minibus painted army green, and drove me a few miles west out of Ashkhabad to his stables at Firyuza.

It was a slightly uncomfortable ride, with Aleksandr and myself fencing in over-polite conversation. He exerted himself to be a dutiful guide, mostly pointing out the obvious while baring his expensive teeth in a wide smile. But when he gestured to the earthworks hard under the mountains, I paid attention. Nisa, city of the Parthians. The destination tomorrow of my ride, via the old tracks passing through the Kopet Dagh foothills and known, for their association with Alexander the Great, as the Macedonian Way.

Shortly after, Aleksandr turned the van off the main road and headed straight for the abrupt scarp of the mountains. They appeared solid, an impenetrable wall, but opened at the last minute to let us into a tiny crack: the Firyuza Gorge.

It was a corkscrew cleft which buried all sense of direction. The walls rose almost sheer to blot out the sun, leaving only a giddy darkness. As suddenly as it had swallowed us up the gorge spat us out again, into an open valley where houses clustered at the bottom and rose erratically up the hillside. At the centre of the village a flat space held schooling jumps. Aleksandr turned into a yard and stopped the van between two buildings.

His team came out to greet us. Katya and Natasha were like all girls around horses; neat, competent and business-like. There all similarity between them ended, although each in her way was stereotypically Russian. If our western concept of Russian women is shaped by Ian Fleming or le Carré, they would have fitted in effortlessly. Katya, with a no-nonsense short bob to her dark hair, her eyes rimmed severely with kohl, and bluntly outspoken, might equally well have been foreman on a construction site or controller of spies; Natasha, fair-skinned and delicate, her long hair elegantly plaited and caught up, her ready smile showing a flash of gold teeth, could have been cast as the bait for compromising photographs.

To my dismay, the horses were thin, like most in Turkmenistan just now. I tried to hide my concern, but Katya was watching me.

"It's the same everywhere. Look at our hay!" She held out a handful of thorns. "What rubbish! It's only fit for camels. And we've only managed to get barley twice this year... in a month, things will be better." I felt ashamed. Who was I, coming from a land flowing with milk, honey and oats, where grass grew hard for nine months of the year, to sit in judgement on this country where people strove so hard for so little? No wonder Aleksandr had been desperate for custom.

There were fourteen horses in all. Two camels, a couple of sleek dogs, a cat, a clutch of chickens and some rabbits made up the ménage. I didn't ask whether the rabbits were for cuddling or casseroling.

There was no nonsense about rushing off; this was Central Asia. We sat and drank coffee in the garden under an almond tree, and I asked Aleksandr about the riding stables.

It was a recent venture. "I only started it a few years ago. I'm really a railway engineer. The girls got me on a horse for the first time ever last year!" Not bad, at over fifty.

Staff from the various embassies in Ashkhabad provided most of his custom. But the business had been an uphill struggle. Only last year a neighbouring farmer had been careless with chemicals, poisoned the water supply, and killed most of the horses.

"I had to re-stock completely; start all over again."

I was aghast. "Couldn't you have taken him to court?"

He spread his hands in a wholly Asiatic gesture of resignation. "This is Turkmenistan." Katya, on whom resignation would have sat as easily as a second head, snorted with contempt for the system.

Poor Aleksandr. It was no longer any surprise that he had been so anxious for my dollars. I began to find myself liking him. And to feel ashamed again, for my easy disapproval.

Most of his horses were Akhal-Teke, including the little grey mare Malika whom I rode, and Katya's Masha. Natasha's Larissa was Trakehner, an East Prussian breed. How on earth, I wondered, had a Trakehner fetched up in Turkmenistan? As we set off through the village it was raining, obscuring the mountain tops and splattering the streets with blobs that were not so much mud as coagulated dust. We forded a stream and clung to the grass verge on the other side, for the horses were not shod behind.

"It's impossible to find a farrier here," Katya had explained. "Natasha and I are learning to shoe them ourselves. But it's very difficult. We're not really strong enough."

Natasha took a track leading off the road, and immediately stepped up the pace.

I hadn't realised it was possible to trot so fast. Now I understood why the Russian for "trot" is *begat roisniu*: to run at the trot. "Fly" might have been more appropriate. As Malika's feet flew back and forth beneath me, I felt as if I were riding an emu. In the end I had to beg for mercy, and the girls slowed to a walk. "We normally keep that up for ten or twelve kilometres," Natasha commented, somehow managing to keep any shade of disapproval out of her voice.

"We used to be able to ride off-road all along this valley," said Katya with a black look at the fences which herded us back on to the tarmac, "but now it's all getting bought up privately. These were children's camps, but now they're being turned into hotels. Foreign business consortia..."

Desperate for hard currency, the government could not afford to let anything stand in the way of foreign investment. This was one root cause of the feed problem.

"Cotton; all cotton," explained Katya. "Even more than under the USSR."

"And what happens to the foreign money it earns?"

"Hotels, factories, business enterprises..." And meanwhile people queued for bread, and horses starved.

A valley led off the road and into the hills, which were clearing again as the rain eased off. A ford barred our way. Malika had a minor tantrum over crossing it and then, deciding that to be left behind was too alarming but still declining wet feet, cleared it in a huge leap. We skirted two old men loading a donkey with brushwood, then cracked on once again in the same racing trot, the horses picking their way like fell runners through a litter of rough stones. My God, I thought, these horses are tough; this sort of usage would break down an English horse in no time.

The valley climbed slowly towards the high peaks of the Kopet Dagh. Now and again we passed a settlement consisting of a few sheep penned next to a rough trailer, with no vehicle to be seen. Was this all that remained today of Turcoman nomadism? Wheatears and stonechats flew from under the horses' feet. Hoopoes frivolled in pairs, twisting their heads a half-turn to watch us from the branches of tamarisk scrub; their crazy top-knots mirrored their beaks, so that you couldn't tell if they were looking forwards or backwards. A family of six buzzards lazily rode the updraughts in circles above, hunting as a pack. We turned a corner and slammed on the brakes as our path was blocked by a new-born lamb, still wet, staggering for the first time on to splayed legs.

"Better find the shepherd," said Katya, "so he can get to it before the wolves do."

"You have wolves here!?"

"And hyenas... and coyotes..."

The track rose sharply above a spring, issuing from the mountainside to feed the stream. Above it the valley was dry, and steep.

"We'll stop here," Katya decided. "There's nothing more up here except Iran."

We watered the horses at the spring which, for no other reason than that this was Turkmenistan, ran not from clean rock but from a rusty pipe covered with green slime. For all that, the water was absolutely pure, and I swallowed greedy handfuls. Loosening the girths, we grazed the horses, and Natasha fed us handfuls of raisins from her pocket.

Then it was back down the valley at the same breakneck speed, giving no quarter for the huge rocks or the gullies which split the path. Had Malika lost her footing at such speed she would have broken a leg, and I my head. But her stride never faltered, never even lost its rhythm. I began to understand more completely the dictum, "ride the horse you're on today". It was supremely relevant in this situation; you had to forget about controlling pace, balance, direction, for the horse had far more sense than you of such things. It was enough to let go and follow the movement, to keep your body fluid and your weight in the right place so as to help and not hinder. Rather, in fact, like skiing down too difficult a course: let the skis run, and take what comes. Don't try to interfere, to control, or you'll crash.

Just as we reached the road a necklace of cloud, winding around the hills behind us, breathed in deeply and rose to swallow the tops. The rain came down hard. None too soon we spotted the green van, waiting to welcome us among a huddle of tents.

*

Under a polythene awning, a huge table staggered under its weight of food. Wineglasses were set ready, and enormous casseroles bubbled and plopped on a portable stove, shielded from the rain by two candy-striped parasols. I began to understand why Aleksandr was so expensive. This was luxury tourism outside my experience. I'd expected a pot of baked beans warming on a camel-dung fire.

For the horses, there was a long paddle in the stream to ease their weary feet and drink deeply; then rugs against the rain, and a good helping of hay.

As we ate an enormous meal, the rain came down in earnest, splashing off the plastic roof well clear of the table. "It's your fault," laughed Katya. "You've brought English weather!" Though, in fact, the rain could only be welcome. Now all that was needed was a bit of sun - easily come by in a Turkmenistan spring - and perhaps the grass would begin to grow at last.

In the late evening the rain stopped, and fragile scraps of blue sky emerged. To make room for another huge meal, Katya and I climbed the nearest hill with Tanya, another of Aleksandr's team.

These were harsh, abrasive mountains, still in the process of being thrust upwards by violent forces beneath; young mountains, not flattened by time nor even softened by erosion. Slate-brown, they bore stripes of harder, grey rock at varying angles, tracing how the earth's crust had crumpled like a paper handkerchief under violent geological pressure. Was this what happened when tectonic plates collide? I had seen such formations before, and searched my memory for a reference. When I had it, it was no surprise; such were the mountains of Wadi Itm, at the head of the Red Sea Gulf of Aqaba, fingertip of the Great Rift Valley and a similarly mobile seam on the surface of our world.

Katya held out a porcupine quill. "They shed them in spring; we often find them." Tanya had a handful of what looked like seashells. "This was once under the sea," she said. But a few moments later I found one still inhabited - by a distinctly terrestrial snail, for all its exotic pointed whorls.

On the way down we talked horses. "When I was a little girl," said Katya, "I had hundreds of books on horses; zoological, technical, horsemastership... I remember meeting an old man at Ashkhabad Hippodrome, who told me how he had personally presented an Akhal-Teke stallion to your Queen of England." "Mele Kush!" I interrupted. At a similar age I'd seen the photograph in *Riding* Magazine. "The first picture of an Akhal-Teke I ever saw."

"She really loves horses, your Queen, doesn't she? And Princess Anne, too. What will happen to all the Queen's horses when Prince Charles comes to the throne? Is he interested in them?" I was humbled at how much the people of this remote country knew of our affairs, and how little I knew of theirs.

The conversation took us to the foot of the mountain, and back to the table. As we ate, a buzzard sat on the hillside counting our every mouthful; he was back again at breakfast. Two nightingales were practising their scales in readiness for full song in a couple of weeks. And by the time we slept, the frogs were singing also, a throbbing gurgle punctuated by occasional manic cackles that continued far into the night.

*

The valley was thick with tamarisk and patterned with orchards. Just now, but for the odd almond tree, the blossom was no more than a promise. I would like, I thought as we jogged gently downhill, to come back here in a fortnight.

A few miles, and the hills drew back suddenly. Ahead, the land was utterly flat, stretching away until the haze obliterated it. It was like coming between cliffs to the mouth of a river and hitting the sea; except that the beach was green oasis, and the sea itself was of sand: the Kara Kum, or Black Sands, which extend unbroken to the Kazakh steppes several hundred miles further north, and cover nine-tenths of Turkmenistan.

The girls turned right and followed the edge of the scarp across a gently sloping plain littered with rocks and seamed with gullies. At first, Malika was wary of these gullies, mincing down carefully and straining up the far side. Before long she got the idea and began to play with them, running down to get up steam then launching herself at the further bank in a series of plunges. She began to accelerate every time she saw one ahead, until my arms ached with the strain of preventing her from breaking both our necks.

Here were what could only be hut circles. Farmers settled the edges of the Kopet Dagh as early as the fifth millennium BC, while the Black Sands were still green. Was it they who had left these traces behind? Nearby, someone had erected a Mongolian-type *obo*, a cairn with a stick rising from its peak. Some atavistic offering, perhaps, to the spirits of those who had lived here so long ago.

The rain had spent itself and the weather was bright. The mountains shook off their sulks and turned crystal clear against a blue sky streaked with drifting cloud. But little grew even here in the Akhal Oasis, that strip of natural grassland which runs along the base of the mountains and is irrigated by their run-off.

"This should be all green!" said Katya, gesturing to the brown wilderness around.

In the villages, a few optimistic people were beginning to work in their gardens and surrounding fields. By the time the brown earthen hump of Nisa rose on the skyline, vineyards enclosed us, criss-crossed by irrigation channels. At these, Malika was again first cautious and then joyful, lifting cleanly off her hocks and jumping them with feet to spare. Still only four years old, she was a fast learner.

A raised iron pipe barred our way. Natasha kicked on and jumped it. I wasn't sure that I wanted to follow on a young horse who had only just mastered ditches, but there was no way round. I needn't have worried; the little horse picked up cleanly and pinged it in perfect balance. I was learning at the sharp end about the intelligence and athleticism revered by those who know the Akhal-Teke. And my prejudices about thin horses were getting hammered at the same time. When the girls stepped up the pace, Malika stuck her head out and tried to race the others. No horse that was in poor condition could run like this for two days and

35

still fight to be first. It was time I stopped judging her by the irrelevant yardstick of our well-rounded warmbloods, and started to think of her as a greyhound. Malika's ancestors had been conditioned for millennia to live on iron rations and still run for fun. Again I thought: these horses are tough.

She was still pulling as we galloped up the ramp and thundered into the city.

*

In fact there were two Nisas.

"That's Alexander's Nisa." Katya gestured to the other, smaller, mound a few hundred yards away.

Although Alexander the Great took possession of these lands on defeating Persia in 331 BC, it is doubted whether he came this far west in Central Asia. But his name has reverberated down the centuries, spoken with the reverence more commonly afforded to national heroes than foreign conquerors. So the Nisa of Media and then Persia is attributed to him, and the roads back from here through the mountains to Persia and the west are collectively referred to as the Macedonian Way.

It was to be nearly a century after Alexander before his Seleucid heirs were ousted. Their Parthian successors were a classic case of historical poachers-turned-gamekeepers. Nomads of probable Scythian descent (the Roman historian Justinian comments that "Parthi" means "exiles" in Scythian), they acquired a taste for settled living and proceeded to make an art of it, carving out an empire from the Euphrates to India and ruling it for five centuries. They won and kept it by their horsemanship. The first real cavalry tacticians, they developed the trick of feigned retreat followed by a volley of arrows released backwards, giving the idea of the "Parthian Shot" both to contemporary warfare and to modern metaphor.

The Parthians bred the famous Nisaean horses here in their thousands, in the cooler, wetter days before the desert lapped so closely at the hills. But they weren't the first to do so. While the Scythians were presiding over the distribution of their horses

36

throughout the steppes, the Medes were already introducing them to the settled lands. After the Persian Cyrus defeated the Medes in the mid-sixth century BC, he ordered a yearly tribute of twenty thousand Median horses. Such a number is scarcely believable; many times the number of their descendants today.

Parthian Nisa was well-preserved. Inside the massive earth ramparts, the mud-brick buildings were still recognisable as such, despite two thousand years of wind and weather. Katya and Natasha untacked the horses and flopped down on the grass, while I went to explore.

Restored steps led to the palace and harem complex by the west wall. Even now the rebuilding continued, and in a quiet corner workmen paddled mud with straw to make bricks. A low archway led into a labyrinth of corridors and rooms; in the Throne Room the remains of pillars broke through the crusted surface. At one end rain had washed down the open wall as down a limestone curtain, forming mud stalactites.

I rambled through the ancient rooms, peopling them in my imagination with exotic figures, forgetting the time. Katya called, upbraiding me roundly.

"Come on, eat! We must be getting on!"

Sitting down to the lunch which they had conjured from nowhere I understood, too late, their impatience. Politely, they had waited for me to return before taking a single bite themselves.

Afterwards, we left by the south gate and took a beeline for the hills. On the plain between, new buildings were going up; mostly block, unfinished, surrounded drearily by loose barbed wire. One or two older ones, mud brick, framed by vine trellis, softened the view. A tractor and trailer passed, loaded with fresh grass. Now who, I wondered, had been lucky enough to get hold of that, and where?

A steep, unclimbable gully scarred the hill. Alongside, someone had bulldozed a rough trail to plant a row of electricity pylons. Whoever had done so wouldn't be getting up there now; a rock-fall had carried away the track near the top, and it wasn't fit for the faint-hearted.

We scrambled upwards, horses sure-footed on the boulders. Malika tired at last, and I let her drop back, not wanting to ride her to a standstill. It was bad judgement. At the crux, a steep scrabble with a hundred foot drop to one side, she lost her momentum and almost stopped. Katya dismounted and ran back, cursing Malika and me alternately, driving us both to greater effort, seizing the bridle with an imperative heave. It was a bad moment, but we got there. A few more yards, then we were in safer territory, and could breathe.

"I'm sorry," I apologised. "She's very tired..."

"We're all tired!" snapped Katya, and generously said no more.

The top came as abruptly as I was learning to expect from these mountains. Suddenly the track dipped downwards. Ahead stretched rolling hills, dry and dusty, leading to the white peaks beyond. Bare, hungry hills, these, with a faint green tinge on the rainward side, dull grey-brown on the other. Yet when you looked closely the flowers were even now, even here, springing up. Tiny yellow iris with a purple collar, tulip leaves cradling embryonic buds, anemonies of glorious, deep red with the hint of yellow at the centre.

A switchback of hillocks, and we joined a broad track curving between the ridges: one of the oldest bits of the Macedonian Way. Tired as I was, goose-pimples still pricked. Perhaps Alexander himself had really come this way. Surely, it had echoed to the hooves of cavalrymen-turned-drovers, herding Nisaean horses to Persepolis, perhaps even to Macedon. A flock of sheep scratched a living on the bare hillside; the shepherd, a youth in a Teke telpek, sketched a greeting to us as we rode past. So might his ancestors have sat, in these mountains, watching other horsemen passing by.

Malika was pulling again. "*Domoi!*" said Katya. "We're going home." Soon the hills drew back and the village appeared, its outer edges glued to hillsides that towered above it like slag-heaps. Slate-grey slag-heaps, a few jagged edges protruding, crouching in cramped and ungainly postures wherever the latest shrug of the earth's shoulders had dropped them. Beyond, the last of the cloud had lifted, and an unbroken line of high peaks shone brilliantly white in the late afternoon sunlight.

Aleksandr had managed to get a small load of lucerne from somewhere for the horses. I hoped our three would get the lion's share. With fifty miles behind them, they deserved every mouthful.

Part Two

Iron Road
to
Samarkand

III

"It was all Gorbachev's fault!" Murad's anger filled the small compartment of the Tashauz Express with a tangible force. "He deliberately destroyed the Communist system!"

Surely, I thought, Communism had simply imploded; the Red Peril had become a Red Dwarf, its zealotry exhausted, its purse drained, its iron fist rusted clean away.

Murad would have none of it. "That's a lie of the West! Gorbachev was to blame! Communism collapsed because of the deliberate actions of the Government." The old cry, which had rung from one end of the Soviet Union to the other as the *Ancien Régime* gave way to Chaos: *Eto Gorbachev vinovat!*

"But why should he deliberately bring down his own country?" I persisted. The answer was uncompromising: Gorbachev had meant to pull the plug.

"Gorbachev was an agent of the CIA!" I hadn't known this, and admitted so with due humility. It seemed the only possible reply.

Murad*, a *kolkhoznik* (collective farmer), was travelling, like me, to Chardzhou on the eastern border, the nearest station to his *kolkhoz*. With him were his son Mahmoud, a shy teenage lad overawed by his extrovert father, and Murad's friend Rosie, a huge man whose butch manner dared you to mistake his name as effeminate.

Life, said Murad, had been very bad since the fall of Communism. Most people, he was sure, would like to reinstate the Soviet Union.

"Since the Russians left," he said, "we have had no tractors, no technology. There is no bread in the shops, no clothing to buy."

* not his real name

43

Perhaps, I ventured cautiously, the Russian-imposed cotton monoculture was the main reason why Turkmenistan couldn't now feed its people.

"But you can't grow wheat without tractors. Meanwhile, we must import it from Iran, from Armenia, from Turkey. We want to go back to the old ways! Write that in your book!" he added fiercely. "Write how it is for us now! - But," he added quickly, "don't write my name."

Would that still make him feel threatened, I wondered, or was his fear a hang-over from the former neurosis of Soviet times? "But there must be advantages, too. Aren't you glad, for example, that you can speak and act more freely now?"

"Rubbish! We could say whatever we liked before. Now, it's different." Murad, I learned, had been thrown off the kolkhoz committee for speaking his mind. Much as I sympathised with him, I was beginning to see why.

"Do you have any hopes for democracy?" Independent or not, Turkmenistan was still a one-party state, moving (so said the official line) towards democratic government.

It was the right button to press; he became positive at once. "Democracy would be very good for us," he replied. "But I can't see it coming for another ten years or so."

His enthusiasm for a democratic future sat very oddly with his pro-Soviet stance. Murad explained succinctly. "Democracy first, Communism second, the current situation nowhere!"

"Now there are no really poor people in Turkmenistan. But in a few more years of this, there will be. At least things were always good for the kolkhozniks under the Russians."

Now, I was on firmer ground. "Always? Not if you go back sixty years. Look how the kolkhozniks fared under Stalin." Enforced collectivisation, unattainable quotas, mass starvation.

Rubbish, he said again. "Stalin was god for everybody - kolkhozniks *and* intellectuals. He was a great chap!" Thumbs up for Stalin. Rosie joined in vigorously, prodding the air with a thumb protruding like a rhino's horn from his massive fist.

"Write!" commanded Murad, like the Angel of the Revelation. "Above all, Stalin was an honest fellow! Write that!"

He was now thoroughly away on his soap-box. Rosie seconded him enthusiastically. "Now the shops are empty! We can't even get bread!" He jabbed at the offending loaf on the seat between them; then, his excitement getting the better of him, picked it up and waved it around furiously. I thought he was going to hit me with it, as if it were all my fault. Mahmoud sat quietly beside them in the corner, now and again catching my eye with a furtive smile. He evidently knew it all by heart.

Poor Murad. He had been born into the wrong time and place. Had he lived in Russia in earlier times – 1917, for instance - he would have made an excellent Workers' spokesman, or led a miners' strike. As it was, he had only me to harangue, and was making the best of a bad job.

I thought of Natasha and Aksan, with their wholehearted approval of Independence. It was the same throughout the former Soviet Union: the intellectuals rejoicing at the opportunity to get ahead on their merits, the manual workers longing to restore the devil they knew. The Bourgeoisie stifled by Communism, the peasants getting the best of it.

But then, Lenin could have told me that was exactly how it was always meant to be.

*

Snow had been falling heavily in Ashkhabad as I prepared to ride the Iron Road to Samarkand, my gateway to Uzbekistan. Much as I would have liked to travel through Central Asia entirely on horseback, the distances involved were too great, the border bureaucracy insuperable. Besides, if not quite as ancient as the Turcoman horses, this railway had a rich history of its own.

Built to aid the final subjugation of Turkestan under the Russian Empire - and, in the minds of those with expansionist ideas, to facilitate invasion of British India - the Trans-Caspian Railway was more than a century old. The rolling stock, the samovars bubbling in the corridor of every coach, even some of the hoary old attendants looked aboriginal.

You travelled four to a compartment, with let-down bunks. Which four was negotiable; on departure, a game of musical chairs had ensued among the passengers in our coach, finally stabilising into Murad, Rosie, Mahmoud and me.

As the train rolled slowly out of Ashkhabad's suburbs on to the fringes of the desert, my first close-up glimpse of the Black Sands was a white one. If it was desert at all; within reach of the Kara Kum Canal, this could just as well be Turkmenistan's prime farmland. But there was little to see under the snow; only sad, damp trees drooping over sad, damp land. Here and there a field of dormant vines, or a geyser at the intersection of a number of dykes, gave the game away. There was plenty of time to look, as the train kept stopping for no apparent reason.

Some lads next door, who had started the journey in my compartment, invited me for supper. They produced a meal of soup, bread, oranges and cucumbers, to which I could only add a few apples. We exchanged the usual questions about life, work and the cost of living, followed by a searching enquiry about English society.

"What do you earn?" was the first question.

"When I was a teacher, my salary was about twenty-four thousand dollars a year."

Such riches were beyond their comprehension. "Here, a teacher or other professional person earns about two hundred dollars a year."

"What about unemployment?" they asked. "We've heard it is very bad in the West. Can you live if you haven't got work? Could we go to live there? How does a foreigner go about getting into Britain?"

The last was difficult; it was hard to discuss, with my limited Russian, the notion of political refugees versus economic migrants. I tried to explain that immigrants from Central Asia would only be accepted if they were in danger in their own country. Their interest subsided into universal gloom.

Back in my own compartment, I was buttonholed again by Murad. His son, he said, learned English at school. He had never heard him speak it, and commanded a performance.

46

"My name is Gill," I said obligingly to the boy and, visibly quivering with nerves, he managed a stiff, "My name is Mahmoud."

"How old are you, Mahmoud?"

"I am very well, thank you," he replied. "How are you?"

In fact, when he relaxed, he spoke very well. I put him through his paces just long enough to satisfy his father before letting him off the hook. Murad, though, was unimpressed. That his son should speak good English to a total stranger at the first attempt was no more than he expected.

"You should be proud of him!" I said reprovingly. Obediently, he beamed at the boy; then, leaning his large bulk intimately across Rosie's lap, demonstrated his approval with a huge, wet kiss on the boy's cheek.

Outside, the dreary white landscape retreated into a dreary grey. As we let the bunks down and prepared to sleep, the train ground to a halt yet again. It was definitely the Wrong Kind of Snow.

*

The last stretch of the journey to Chardzhou was across virgin desert, its drifts of sand punctuated by *saxaul* bushes and the black skeletons of last year's camelthorn. The snow had vanished as the railway veered north-east and away from the mountains. In the early morning light it took me a while to realise this; for the low sun, diffused through a filthy window, bleached the landscape like an over-exposed photograph, leaving it quite colourless.

At Chardzhou I stood on the platform watching the Tashauz Express turn off north-westwards. There was a five-hour wait for the Samarkand train. I joined the depressed, stationary queue at the ticket window and was instantly besieged by Evgeny and his friends, offering to buy my ticket for a percentage. Evgeny's mob were professional ticket buyers. They knew the ropes by cats'-cradles, the timetable backwards, the ticket clerks by name and all the tricks for avoiding the queues. So they provided a useful service for travellers prepared to pay a few extra manats

47

rather than stand for hours, and thereby scratched a living. This was the reality of "no unemployment in Turkmenistan".

I fended them off, until a Turcoman lady came over to try her luck. Gulya was about thirty, but at first glance looked older. The prematurely lined face under the flowered headscarf was streetwise but kind, and utterly straight. I surrendered at once, and she jumped the queue to get my ticket within minutes. Out of perversity, I gave her a larger tip than the boys had asked. Evgeny followed me as I left and, out of sight of Gulya, hopefully explained that there was a mistake; my ticket had actually cost a further 12,000 manats, and he would be delighted to pass this on to Gulya for me. It was, I suppose, worth a try.

Outside, bright sunlight softened the biting wind off the desert. There was little to illuminate. Chardzhou, built where the Silk Road once crossed the great river Amu Darya, existed mainly as an *entrepôt*. The town itself was a nonentity.

Even the *rinok*, or local market, had little but imported tat: sweets, cigarettes and vodka. One of the stallholders was a well-dressed, well-spoken Russian lady. Formerly a teacher, she couldn't now live on her salary and had turned to market trading. "Things are much worse here than in Russia," she said. So, beyond the capital, even the professional élite had big problems.

"Couldn't you go back to Russia?"

"Back? But I was born in Turkmenistan," she replied, "and it's difficult to change my citizenship."

Across the road from the market was a small *chai-khana*. Throughout Central Asia, whose Moslem laws long prevented the use of alcohol, society still gathers around the teapot. Much more than just a café, the tearoom is a meeting-centre, forum, resting place for weary travellers, and a mirror of Asiatic life: all the functions of an English pub, minus the beer.

To the street the chai-khana presented the usual blank, uninviting exterior. Inside was a pleasant, secluded yard, in which a vine found its way through a series of S-bends to an upper trellis where, in due course, it would open its leaves between the idlers here and the scorching summer sun. The tables were rough planks, meeting the adjoining benches with no gap for the legs; you were meant to lounge, not sit upright.

"Large or small?" asked the boy. "Large," I begged, my tongue hanging out, and greedily sat drinking dry my first pot of Asiatic green tea, until it was time for the train.

*

Gulya saw me off, fussing over me like a kindly aunt. "Watch your wallet. They're all thieves in Samarkand. And don't pay more than a hundred *sum* for a taxi." She even found a friend to change some money and give me ready cash in Uzbek currency.

As the train moved slowly eastwards out of Chardzhou I sat on the edge of my window seat, waiting eagerly for my first view of the Amu Darya. Called the Oxus by Herodotus, this is one of the great rivers of history: today the life-blood sustaining millions of people across two countries; formerly the artery feeding the ancient empire of Khoresmia and silent witness, many times over, to its destruction and reconstruction. "No river," wrote Lord Curzon, future Viceroy of India, in 1888, "not even the Nile, can claim a nobler tradition, or a more illustrious history."

It was six miles before the bridge came into sight. The shifting course of the Amu Darya, which once flowed through Chardzhou, was only one of the problems facing the engineers who first bridged it two years before Curzon's visit.

Until it reached the Oxus the Trans-Caspian Railway had met few serious engineering problems as it marched across Turkmenistan from the Caspian Sea. It had no tunnels, few cuttings, only two bridges - over the Tedzhen and Murghab rivers - and crossed an almost entirely flat landscape with no gradient steeper than 1 in 150. The worst problem was that of continually drifting sand. It was resolved by planting saxaul and tamarisk along the line, and by the use of wooden palisades, like those used against drifting snow on the Trans-Siberian Railway.

Now, however, a track had to be driven across an obstacle whose width varied from half a mile wide in autumn to five miles when swollen by spring meltwaters; whose shifting, sandy bottom gave no grip for supporting pillars; and whose fluctuating path was a matter of its own whim.

The result, completed in an astonishing 103 days, was described by Curzon. "It is an inelegant structure, built entirely of wood... and rests on more than 3,000 piles... It is constructed in four sections, there being four branches of the river at this point, separated by islands... The rails, although thirty feet above the lowest water, are only five feet above the level of the highest flood."

This stupendous achievement was immediately followed by an equally stupendous bungle. The central section, designed to swing open for the passage of the steamboat built for the opening ceremonies, was too narrow to let the boat pass. Rather than abort the ceremony, the engineers chopped down part of the bridge so that events could go ahead as planned. The structure was so weakened that it took months to return it to working order.

Despite the catastrophe, the wooden bridge lasted for twenty years before it was replaced by the structure of steel girders and granite piles that my train was now approaching. The river running below it was brown, turgid and unexciting - except that even now it spanned perhaps three-quarters of a mile. In a month or two, when the Pamirs and the Hindu Kush began to spit out some small part of their snow and ice, it would become a monstrous, thundering torrent.

On the far side the Kara Kum gave way to the Kyzyl Kum, the Red Sands of Uzbekistan. There was no visible change in colour, but the patches of irrigation that dotted its wastes became more frequent. So, too, the villages: small hamlets in comfortable harmony with their surroundings, their mud-brick blending into the landscape with the blessing of antiquity. They were, after all, nearly as old as the sands. Outside each village was a graveyard. Local styles varied: here the barrel vaults of Bukhara, there in pointed section like the upturned hull of a ship, somewhere else plain, square blocks. The only uniformity was in the cemeteries themselves: unstable-looking, crumbling mounds, heaped repositories of millennia of human bones.

The cemetery mounds outnumbered the villages. Many stood abandoned in wasteland far from anywhere. There could be no stronger reminder of the long span of history here, the intensity of human habitation over many years, than these ugly hillocks of dust and ashes. One after another, they ticked off all the long weary miles until the train rolled into Samarkand.

*

I stepped out of the compartment straight into the winter I thought I'd left behind in Ashkhabad thirty hours before. A bitter wind heaped snow in the corners of the platform, and the temperature was five degrees below.

The streets outside had never seen grit, and half an inch of ice coated them. Yet the taxi man accelerated and cornered like a rally driver. The car clung grimly to the road until he braked to pick up a couple more passengers. Then he lost control, expertly corrected the skid and immediately braked hard again. The two passengers bravely stood their ground.

Yet something about the city cheered me enormously. After the drabness of Ashkhabad, my spirits rose under the glittering, gaudy chandeliers in the station building, and the bright lights slung crazily across the streets lifted them higher. And the dingy Hotel Leningrad (no St. Petersburg nonsense here), with its friendly cockroaches in the bathroom and the familiar air of a backpackers' hotel, felt like home.

Even the staff had a welcome for jaded travellers. The luggage boy greeted me like an old friend, and the *djournaya* - not the archetypal severe, moustached Russian matron but a young, pretty girl - was touched by my gratitude for hot water. "*Bednaya, bednaya* - you poor thing," she replied as I described the long journey and apologised for my layers of grime. She shooed away the inquisitive staff who were peering into my room, and ordered them to let me rest.

After the practice on the train, my Russian was flowing a little better; and everyone here called me *devushka* - girl - which

51

did wonders for my ageing self-esteem. Samarkand, I decided, was going to be good value.

*

In the morning I caught a minibus out to Afrasiab.

At first sight there was nothing to mark this empty land of jumbled sandy hills as any different from the nearby deserts; until, climbing a low hill, I made out a truncated cone in the distance, with the remains of walls clinging to its further end. Here was the citadel of ancient Samarkand, the Maracanda of Alexander, the capital of an ancient Sogdian empire and later Persian satrapy, the thriving Silk Road city wasted by the Mongol hordes of Genghis Khan.

Afrasiab, whose name clung to the old site after Samarkand shifted to the south-west, was the legendary Sogdian wizard-king who founded the city. He is an elusive character. Historian and travel writer John Lawton quotes tradition dating him to the fifth century BC; 1930s traveller Ella Maillart confidently puts him at 1100 BC; other writers are non-committal, attributing him purely to an epic poem. Maracanda entered recorded history via a rock inscription at Behistoun in Persia, celebrating the Persian conquest; and three centuries later took centre stage.

In 329 BC Alexander crossed into Transoxiana, the Land Beyond the Oxus. His defeat of Persia had been the catalyst for her remoter satrapies to attempt secession, and he was moving to consolidate his new empire. It took five days to get his army across the Oxus, using makeshift rafts floated on inflated hides - a method still used in living memory. After such a feat, he might have expected it to be relatively easy for his battle-hardened men to take Maracanda and put down local tribal revolts from the Oxus to the Jaxartes (Syr Darya).

What seduced Alexander, already in possession of the greatest empire in the world and on his way towards the fabled riches of India, into this Central Asian excursion to subdue a few rebellious nomads? Was it the tales of glittering citadels hiding behind empty deserts; or the fascination of the desert itself, the strange magnetic pull of echoing voids that has sucked in so many lesser travellers over the ages? Or was it the recognition that these nomads were not so insignificant; that they were a serious fighting force, and as such a danger to his flank? More than a danger, a challenge: the challenge posed by their very existence to an undefeated commander, the age-old urge to take on the challenge for its own sake; "because it's there". The urge to put two extremes to the test: the agile Scythian horsemen versus the solid Macedonian phalanx.

Certainly they gave him a run for his money, for it took two campaigns to defeat them.

The Scythians, comments the Roman historian Arrian, were "always ready at a word to take part in any fighting which may be going on …they have no towns, no settled homes, and consequently no cause to fear the loss of what is dearest." And, of course, they were well mounted. "Their country," commented Herodotus, "is the back of a horse." At first, their superior horses quite literally ran rings around the Macedonian cavalry.

After one successful cavalry battle, the complete annihilation of his detachment in another and a series of brutal reprisals, Alexander garrisoned Maracanda and retired across the Oxus to winter in Bactria. A spate of insurgencies the following year brought him back to a High Noon with Spitamenes, the deposed Sogdian king, and his combined force of three thousand Massagetae and Scythian horsemen. The day was Alexander's; whereupon the retreating Massagetae, trimming their sails to the wind, "cut off Spitamenes' head and sent it to (Alexander), hoping that by this friendly act they might keep him from molesting them."

When the last insurgent, Oxyartes, had been plucked from a seemingly impregnable position on a mountaintop, peace was cemented by Alexander's celebrated marriage to Oxyartes' daughter Roxane. Said to be the most beautiful girl in Asia, she may have been the only woman to whom Alexander - whose preferences usually lay elsewhere - was ever sexually attracted. "Captive though she was, he refused to force her to his will, and condescended to marry her. For this act, I have - on the whole - " (adds Arrian in a patronising aside) "more praise than blame."

Sogdiana was finished as a military force. Yet it lived on as a nation, under Alexander's Seleucid successors and thereafter under the Parthian and Kushan empires. Its people turned their talents to trade, and until well into our era controlled the markets of the Silk Road, where their language - related to Aramaic - became a *lingua franca* far beyond their borders. Like Aramaic, it survives today in one or two remote valleys.

As for Alexander, posterity seemed to bear him no ill will for the savagery of his conquest. Rather, it remembered him generously for his great exploits, and for the chivalry and romance of his match with Roxane. Alexander Zulkurnain, the Two-Horned Alexander, entered the Central Asian pantheon. And many centuries after invading Arab iconoclasts had swept away much of local superstition, festivals in the region of Samarkand were inaugurated with a prayer to Allah and his prophet, and to two legendary heroes: Afrasiab, with his chariot drawn by the sacred bull with golden horns and silver legs - and Alexander Zulkurnain riding his mighty horse Bucephalos.

*

A sixth century BC Sogdian frieze is the showpiece of the Afrasiab museum. Depicting an embassy to King Kaganyanes, it describes the journey via exotic scenes of the foreign lands through which the messengers came to Maracanda. Towards the beginning, horsemen hunt lions with spears, and a lady is punted downriver among waterbirds... and a hippopotamus? On the centre wall, deputations of Sogdians and Koreans hold a conference; and the journey reaches its conclusion with the arrival of the ambassador and his wife, followed by respectful attendants and a flock of sacred geese. This is only a copy, but the gaps in the original are faithfully reproduced, right down to the erasing of the eyes in the human figures, scratched out by Moslem fanatics. If the other details are equally true, the intervening centuries have done little to mar the vitality of the work, or its brilliant colours; the Sea of Bliss is a scintillating blue, the ambassadorial elephant spotless white.

A little way beyond the museum, the River Siab crosses under the busy Tashkent road to penetrate the heart of Afrasiab. Could this muddy stream, I wondered, really have fed the great Samarkand? Though I was hardly seeing it at its best, for just here it watered a couple of factories, washing away their rusty and poisonous excrement.

Caves honeycombed the banks, surely longer occupied than the citadel itself. Occupied still; where the walls, part loose sand, part sandstone, were crumbling too fast, mud bricks supported the entrances, framing iron doors. It was odd to see a padlocked cave; odder still to see one with a fierce "no parking" sign.

I turned up a narrow side valley leading into the heart of the old site. Halfway up, a little garden had been levelled against the sheer side of the hill. Here onions grew in the compost of several thousand years, freshly turned. Each few feet of the bank above probably represented a millennium or so; near the bottom, perhaps, the city of Afrasiab himself, Alexander's Maracanda a few feet higher, near the top the Samarkand devastated by Genghis Khan.

And, although no longer built on, very much living and breathing. Everywhere ran the tracks of sheep. I tripped over a string and followed it to an abandoned kite, mud-soaked where it had crash-landed, its long, blue tail of knotted, torn fabric strips looking sad and dirty. A rickety iron footbridge spanned the little valley, and a goat walked over my head.

Karakul sheep grazed at the foot of the citadel. A lamb of less than a week old wore the short, tight-curled fleece so highly prized. This lamb was lucky; some are slaughtered at birth, when the curls are tightest, to produce the best quality skins. A hoarse yell sounded from above, and I turned to see the shepherd, a silhouette on the skyline, waving his staff in greeting.

The citadel falls into two parts: an outer ward consisting of a roughly circular bowl, and the main stronghold thirty feet higher at the eastern end. To the west, where it falls away almost sheer to the road a hundred feet below, are the remains of a mud-brick wall and parallel walkway. Holes pierce the wall at regular intervals, making spyholes, arrow-slits or just drainage.

I sat up here until the sun dropped, washing with pink the snow-capped mountain rib behind the city. A row of crows, a hundred or more, settled down for their night's rest along a nearby ridge, crammed shoulder to shoulder like spectators at a football match. When the afterglow had almost gone, the thin sliver of a new moon rose over the hillside.

The daytime noise of the road had died away, and time became meaningless. The moment could have belonged to any one of the past heroes who had walked where I sat now.

*

A couple of hours' drive south of Samarkand is the birthplace of the mediaeval Emperor, Timur Leng[*], formerly the town of Kesh but renamed by him Shakhrisabz, the Green City. It has a couple of mausolea and the remains of Aksaray, the White Palace built for the Emperor. It was mainly for the journey, though, that I went there; for in the way lie the Fan mountains.

The bus takes the long route, in a four-hour slog round the end of the ridge. So I hired a car to take me directly over the Tashtakaracha Pass.

We left Samarkand by the back roads, bouncing over potholes and swerving to avoid a pile of concrete blocks in the middle of the street. "Are the roads this bad in England?" asked the driver.

The fields bordering the road sprouted already with spring wheat. "They plant potatoes after," said Osman. Evidently fertile soil, this, fine silt brought down from the mountains, giving quick growth. But vulnerable to the wind; old electricity pylons stood high above the plain on eroded mounds, all that remained of a higher ground level. The topsoil was washing or blowing away faster than the mountain run-off could replenish it.

The long line of hills encroached on the farmland and began to squeeze the road. We drove through a hollow grassy bowl, a landscape reminiscent of Mongolia. Suddenly even more so; for we passed a group of horsemen jogging down the verge.

[*] Timur-i-Lenk, Timur the Lame or Tamerlane

56

Half a mile further on, I hollered for a halt. On an open field below the farm terraces, horsemen were gathering.

The horses they rode weren't just farm animals carrying their owners to market. Many were high-bred. Obviously, they were central to this gathering. I went to find out more.

There were to be *skatchki* - races - said a friendly Uzbek in skullcap and long coat. They would start in an hour or so and continue into the afternoon.

He was older than the riders, maybe the father or uncle of a competitor. Seeing that my interest was more than skin-deep, he asked, "Would you like to ride?"

My face answered him, and in a moment he had jocked off a teenager from his horse and put me up. I took a turn about the field, stopping to chat to spectators and ask about their horses. As I dismounted and returned the horse to his owner, I noticed the friction marks at the shoulder that come from wearing a rug - an unusual luxury, surely, for the horse of an Uzbek villager. These men must rate their horses highly.

If we didn't hang about, we could get to Shakhrisabz and back in time to watch the races. A pity the weather was so bad; the bitter wind had blown itself out to give a couple of days of pleasant warmth, but today the sun was definitely sulking. As I climbed back in the car the heavens opened, and the mountains hunched themselves deep into their cloud covering like a cold old man into an overcoat. Osman searched his pockets for cigarettes, looked hopefully at me, and finally resorted to a small tin which he took from his breast pocket.

He put a pinch of dark green powder straight into his mouth and began to roll it round his teeth. "*Nas*," he explained. "Better than vodka." The speedometer needle began to climb steadily. Things looked promising for the hairpin bends up to the pass.

Until now, Osman had been monosyllabic. But the nas loosened his tongue.

He was an Uzbek who had lived all his life in Shakhrisabz, except for his military service. At twenty-three he had been called up and sent to Afghanistan; and scarcely knew what had hit him.

"A bad business. The Uzbek people had no interest whatever in Afghanistan, or what happened there. It was the government that sent us. The Russians."

He was stationed in Kandahar, where he saw many of his friends die. "The rebels had American automatic weapons," he said simply, as if that explained everything.

"You mean, they were better equipped than you?"

"No," he corrected me hastily, uneasily. "Of course the Soviet weapons were superior. But they were fighting for their homeland..."

After two years he took a shrapnel wound in the hip and was invalided out, left with a permanent limp; luckier than many. He was forty, and looked sixty.

The hills closed in and the road began to climb. A pebbly stream alongside ran turquoise with spring meltwater, the only splash of colour anywhere that day. Mud-brick villages straggled up the hillside below craggy outcrops. There was virtually no other traffic - just a donkey, tottering under such a load of brushwood that even its head was sheltered from the rain; and later a bulldozer, shovelling a landslide off the inside of the bend and dropping it on the outside for the river to carry away. Right and proper, for it is river silt which fertilises these valleys, and the workmen were just giving the process a helping hand.

The rain turned to snow in thick wet flakes that exploded as they hit the windscreen. Near the top of the pass, snow still lay in the gullies and outlined the terraces where, even up here, someone scratched a few crops from grudging soil. At the summit Osman leaned from the window and spat out his nas; it spurted from his mouth in a green jet, as if he were being horribly sick. Better out than in; for the road down was spectacular, hugging an almost sheer mountainside in a giddy series of ledges, one below the other. In the improving visibility of lost height Shakhrisabz appeared, materialising silently from the mist as if conjured by djinns.

Just near here one of the twentieth century's great adventurers met his end. Enver Pasha, Turkey's Minister of War, had been disgraced and then arrested at the end of the First

World War. Escaping into exile, he offered his services to Lenin to help pacify Central Asia, which was proving curiously reluctant to embrace Bolshevism. Quickly proving his credentials by putting down an anti-Soviet insurrection at Tedzhen in Turkmenistan, he persuaded Lenin to adopt his master plan of uniting the warring Turkic peoples of Central Asia, with the ultimate aim of turning them against Afghanistan and British India.

But Enver had his own agenda. His secret dream was no less than a pan-Turkic state, centred on Bukhara - and headed by himself. He turned his coat to attack the Bolsheviks in Bukhara with a force of 6,000 recruited from the *Basmatchi* - the freedom fighters he had been engaged to destroy. Early successes gave him control of a large part of the Emirate of Bukhara.

Yet the writing on the wall was in Cyrillic. Infighting arose among Basmatchi leaders jealous of Enver's ambitions, just as Red Army reinforcements arrived. With his partisans reduced by degrees to a small band of followers, Enver was tracked down to Deh-i-Nau by the Cheka, forerunners of the NKVD and KGB. In the ensuing skirmish he was decapitated with a sabre.

Small cells of the Basmatchi fought on. But without a charismatic leader, they were doomed. During Ella Maillart's visit to Samarkand the last of them were rounded up and imprisoned in the Sher Dor Madrasa, before trial in the public square of the Registan. She didn't record their fate, but it isn't hard to guess.

When we reached Shakhrisabz, Osman carried me off to his house for tea. Like most houses here, his was dingy and unattractive from the outside, but opened on to a pleasant courtyard where a vine rambled among trees and rose bushes. Osman's wife appeared, looking rather cross at having to entertain a visitor without warning. He had had four wives, he said as he introduced us. "All at the same time?" I teased. He was not amused, and looked primly away.

The house was cheerful with bright furnishings, and immaculate. Centrepiece of the guest room was a glass chest, with a fine display of carefully stacked china, and the family photographs. Potted geraniums sat demurely behind lace curtains. An Arabic primer lay on the table, the homework of Osman's third daughter Dlafus. Religion wasn't taught in schools, he said, but Arabic had replaced Russian at the local school since the reinstatement of Islam and re-opening of the mosques. Osman himself, formerly atheist, had been glad to embrace Islam. "At first, only the old women attended the mosques, but now the faithful are returning in large numbers."

Osman's wife brought tea, *sumala* - apricot puree - and, now, a welcoming smile. His eldest daughter followed, just home from work. A nurse, she worked only one day in four. "It's normal, here." So much, again, for full employment. Meanwhile, Osman had disappeared. "Gone shopping". I was getting twitchy; much later, and I might miss the races. I was on the point of going to look for another driver when he reappeared. He dutifully handed over a bag of fruit and vegetables to his wife, but the real object of his errand lay on the car seat beside him: a bottle of vodka.

Little remains in Shakhrisabz of Timur's palace; only a monumental gateway bristling with scaffolding. It wasn't officially open, so we hopped over the gate, Osman's limp much in evidence, and walked briefly among the rubble. An inner door was ajar, and I climbed a steep, dark stair to the top of the arch. But there was little to see except a close-up view of metal rods, caked with rust, and a huge crack from top to bottom of the opposite pillar. It was hard to imagine that there could have been a swimming pool up here; but Osman insisted it was true. At the bottom was a brass plate. "Aksaray: 1380 - 1404," it read. "The monument iz guard by the state. The disturber will be hand to justice."

I arrived back at the car to find Osman taking a furtive swig from his bottle. It was already half empty. Before returning to the mountain road, I bought a bag of apples in the local market, where ladies from the villages stood behind mounds of fruit and vegetables, and ancient Uzbeks in quilted jackets chaffered over the price of fish. Nas was on sale among the sacks of herbs and spices.

60

As we hit the road again, I began to feed Osman a steady stream of apples. I didn't want him to tackle that hairy road after half a pint of vodka on an empty stomach. There was some spectacular overtaking, but we made it in one piece, and the races were still in progress. Only it wasn't races at all.

It was *buzkashi*.

*

At the centre of the field a dense knot of horsemen heaved and surged. In the mud under the frenzy of stamping hooves, looking like a filthy piece of wet sacking, was the prize they struggled for: the headless corpse of a goat. A rider who had forced his way with fist and whip to the heart of the struggle lunged downwards, one foot hooked over the saddle bow, risking his head among the straining tangle of horses' legs; only to be forced aside by a violent thrust from his neighbour. Now and again a horse reared to its full height, momentarily clearing a yard of space around itself, only to be enveloped by a fresh wave of tumult a second after it came back to earth. A great cloud of steam rose from the cauldron of bodies, steam made from the sweat of man and horse, and the reek of sweat mingled with the smells of wet leather and of blood.

Suddenly a cheer went up from the spectators. A rider had grabbed the goat and slipped the pack. Another pursued him, clutching at a dangling hoof, and a tussle ensued at full gallop. A few of the pack peeled off and thundered in pursuit, while the cannier sat resting their horses, waiting for the game to return their way; as it must long before it ended.

This was buzkashi in the raw, the savage game said to have been brought here by the armies of Genghis Khan, and which encapsulated all the innate violence expressed in Central Asian history. There were no rules; it was dog eat dog, or rather, horse eat horse. For if your horse kicked or bit your rivals, so much the better, and those that reared were trained to it for advantage in the scrum. Whips were carried to be used on man or horse, and more than one rider had blood running down his face under

61

his cap, the leather soldier's helmet left over from the Afghan war.

There was little structure to the game. The headless corpse must be carried on a prescribed route, usually round two poles planted widely apart, though no merit attached to the rider who did so. All that mattered was the goal, and the horseman who finally threw the goat into the Circle of Justice was the one who gave the victory cry.

Still less was there a defined "field". If the spectators were in the way, you simply galloped over them. So, apart from the wealthy few who brought trucks and tractors for a makeshift grandstand, the watchers gathered on the cultivation terraces marching up the hill above the winner's circle, scene of the fiercest action. Only the brave watched from the non-existent touchline of the lowest terrace; for more than once the chase passed along these very ledges. The further complication that two games were in progress at once increased the fun; you sometimes had to stand teetering on the brink while a single-file, full-gallop pursuit crashed past behind, knowing that the least slip would throw you under more pounding hooves six feet below. It gave a whole new meaning to the idea of Saturday afternoon on the terraces.

As the afternoon wore on, riders detached themselves from the game in ones and twos, to rest their horses or make for home. A young man stood near me with a grey horse, a rug thrown over its sweat-soaked back, their day's sport over. I asked if I might look at his saddlery, and he was ready to chat.

Saifi was older than he looked, being a twenty-nine-year-old father of two. But domestic responsibilities couldn't keep him from his sport. There was a game somewhere most weekends throughout the winter, he said, and some sort of local league. It was about the nearest buzkashi came to resembling village cricket.

"Would you like to ride?" he asked. So for the second time that day, I found myself circling the field on horseback; and keeping a wary eye out for high-speed collisions.

Saifi's saddle was of the old wooden Central Asian type that Yusup had shown me, with a high pommel and cantle. The girths wrapped right round, the stirrups hung from a hole bored in the wooden skirts. The *luka*, or hook, on the pommel, enabled the buzkashi rider to hook his leg over while performing acrobatic feats near the ground.

Not that they called it buzkashi here, Saifi corrected me. That was the Afghan word. The Uzbek name was *kubkari*, while in Turkmenistan it was known as *baigha*. But the victory cry was the same in any language.

IV

Today was National Day, and Uzbekistan was making holiday. The wide street, closed to traffic, heaved with people. Many of the women and most of the children wore national dress: knee-length robes, heavy with embroidery, over close-fitting trousers. Speakers harangued the crowd from vantage points, and smoke from the *shashlik* barbecues filled the air. It was a double shock to emerge from the seething mass of humanity into the silence, and the immensity, of the Registan.

"Painted minarets trembling in the blue astringent light and the great Madonna blue domes of mosques and tombs shouldering the full weight of the sky..."* So Laurens van der Post described this extraordinary square in 1964. Curzon, eighty years earlier, was almost humbled: "I know of nothing in the east approaching it in massive simplicity and grandeur... No European spectacle indeed can adequately be compared with it, in our inability to point to an open space in any Western city that is commanded on three of its four sides by Gothic cathedrals of the finest order."

Samarkand's Registan - literally, "Place of Sand" - was a market-place already old when in 1420 the scholar-king Ulug Beg built the *madrasa*, or religious college, that bears his name. It was two hundred years before two more madrasas followed, in quick succession. Three sides of the square are thus defined by the towering façades of the three colleges, their great arched doorways flanked by soaring minarets. Behind lie the quadrangles of teaching and living accommodation; the same pattern as that adopted by western universities during and after the Renaissance.

* from *Journey Into Russia*, by Laurens van der Post. Copyright © 1964 Laurens van der Post. Reproduced by kind permission of Island Press, Washington, D.C.

The scale is vast, the architecture grandiose; but it is the decorative tilework which takes your breath away. Every inch of the clay brick is covered with colour, in a bewildering variety of materials, of patterns, of shades. Whole tiles, faience mosaic, glazed brick; calligraphic, geometric, floral, Arabesque; ultramarine, turquoise, white, gold... Blue most of all; for the spreading, flat tops of the minarets were so designed to hold up the heavens, and it was right that I shouldn't be able to tell where the one ended and the other began.

Major rebuilding closed off the courtyard of Ulug Beg's madrasa. Squinting through the honeycomb lattice of a window I saw a hive of activity, with workmen crawling over the scaffolding against two walls. The heavy, carved doors of the main entrance were locked against entry. Thwarted, I ran my hands over the ancient door knockers, their engraved whorls worn almost smooth by centuries of human hands, their grooves etched in green where the copper in the bronze had oxidised.

Turning to look across at the Sher Dor Madrasa opposite, I saw a near copy. The outline is similar, and the crazily leaning minarets at each corner, tilted by time and earth tremor, virtually identical; but the two fluted domes at either side of the façade break the pattern. Intentionally; for a perfect image would offend the laws of Islam.

Yet these laws are brazenly flouted by the representations of animals above the arched doorway. The lions which give the Madrasa its name - "Lion-bearing" - chase a pair of deer among stars, and carry human faces, the ultimate heresy, on their backs. Around them run Arabic inscriptions. "Never in all the centuries," says one, "will an artist, thought's acrobat, even with the bow of fantasy, scale the forbidden peaks of this minaret."

Framed by the splendour of these two madrasas, the youngest of the three, the Tilla Kari ("Gilded") Madrasa, seems almost modest in scale. The minarets at either end are barely half the height of the others', and the façade avoids pure architectural fantasy to embrace a double row of galleries. Here the students' cells give on to balconies, via carved wooden doors under a hexagonal lattice arch. Small men, these students; the doors are less than five feet high.

I set my shoulder to a creaking wooden door and entered a courtyard shelving gently down to a central garden. Vines climbed a trellis above beds filled with roses, the famous roses of Samarkand. Another doorway on the left brought me into the mosque, and I stood transfixed.

Over deep blue paintwork the walls and dome dazzled with gold. Gold flowers and vines wound their way up the panels, Aryan style geometry described gold right-angles into the corners among gold Arabesque and swirls, praises to Allah rang out in gold Kufic inscription over the arches. Gold flowers and tendrils spiralled into the roof, growing smaller towards the centre to give to a plane surface the skilful illusion of a dome. It would have shattered Islamic law by its perfection, but for two parallel flaws: two cracks across the centre of the structure, where two large staples fought the earth tremors that had striven to pull it apart. Doves cooing on the roof sent strange, distorted voices down among the vaults, celestial voices reaching to the mortals below.

*

Long stripped of their sanctity and no longer houses of prayer, these temples have their own tables of those who sell and buy. The students' cells, in both the Tilla Kari and the Sher Dor, nowadays house vendors of all kinds of goods: carpets, books, jewellery, Uzbek skullcaps. These more properly belong in the nearby Chorsu, the old covered bazaar that was once a caravanserai. But it was still early for tourists, and the chorsu today was as dull as ditchwater, with just a couple of half-empty tables rattling in the corners. The most interesting thing about it was its guttering system: down-pipes, topped with crown-like heads, running about halfway down the length of the walls before stopping in mid-air, their ends considerably angled outwards for maximum soaking of passers-by.

The wind was bitter. I was wearing every piece of clothing I had, and still shivered. Across the square was a chai-khana, the angle of its wall offering shelter. I huddled over a teapot and sat looking back at the Registan through clouds of smoke rising from the kebabniks' grills. Mynah birds, looking like large piebald jackdaws, stalked among the tables filching leftovers, or sidled up to the vendors of *lepioshki* - round loaves - who stood on the street corners.

Most of the young people in Samarkand gather around the shashlik grills, or the street vendors of alcohol, or the cheap restaurants playing cheap pop music. The chai-khanas belong to the elders, who sit for hours around their bowls of green tea putting the world to rights. I sat watching one old man with the most splendid set of teeth, the top row all of gold and the bottom of silver. To my embarrassment, he caught me staring. Unoffended, he waved me over to join his group.

Sulaiman had a round, rosy face like an apple, and the eyes that peered out from underneath the thick Russian fur hat twinkled merrily. He smiled most of the time; and with such an expensive smile, who wouldn't? His companion, an elderly Uzbek with beard and skullcap, was a retired university lecturer who had written textbooks on economics. It being proper to talk politics in a chai-khana, I asked them of the political situation since Independence.

Powerful forces were at work in Western Turkestan. Poised on the edge of the post-Communist vacuum were two movements, probably (though not necessarily) mutually exclusive, each with a strong pull on the traditions and sympathies of the Turkic race.

The first was Pan-Turkism, an idea which might be expressed as anything from a feeling of solidarity between the Turkic peoples to the aspiration towards a political federation of Turkic states, depending on your viewpoint.

The Turks, one of the world's most successful races, inhabit a vast area. In four of the five Central Asian republics Turks predominate; that is, Kazakhs, Kirghiz, Uzbeks and Turcomans. The Azeris of Azerbaijan, and the Uighurs of eastern China - that is, of Chinese Turkestan - are Turkic peoples, as are the Yakuts of Siberia. Turkey, whose Seljuk, then Ottoman, settlers represented the last push westward of the Turks in the Middle Ages, lost no time in extending the hand of friendship to the natural allies so long cut off from her by Communism. Her desire to exert political influence had so far expressed itself mainly in financial help, in particular with large investment programmes in those countries willing to co-operate politically and economically. This was especially true in Turkmenistan, poorest state in Central Asia, where most new factories and many other development programmes used Turkish finance. The reception in Uzbekistan, though, had so far been cool.

The Uzbeks might not find themselves with the same degree of choice when it came to the second force. The wind of Islamic fundamentalism blowing from Iran had earlier fanned civil war in neighbouring Tadzhikistan, whose people are not ethnically Turkic but Persian. Some feared that the remaining states of Central Asia, long spiritually starved and now returning to the Islamic fold with fervour and gratitude, might topple like dominoes to the new totalitarianism of an Iranian-type regime. If so Uzbekistan, with its large population percentage of ethnic Tadzhiks, and the holiest cities of Islamic Central Asia within its borders, could be the first to fall. This was the possibility that I hoped to learn more about from Sulaiman and his friend.

The Professor was reassuring. "Not here," he said. "We have had what we wanted - free religion - since the time of Gorbachev." Earlier, of course, faith had been a secret and private affair. "If Lenin and Stalin had had their way, all the religious buildings here would have been levelled."

He was satisfied with the fact that, under the new "Democrats", Uzbekistan had been formally declared an Islamic country. And popular response to this had been enormous.

"There are now ten million Muslims in Uzbekistan. And, although religion is still not on the school curriculum, the young are turning to Allah." His own children, a product of the modern age and respectively a doctor and an engineer, had been brought up as good Muslims and remained so. Faith, he implied, had never disappeared from the country; its open expression now was a welling up into the daylight of what had always existed, not an unstable, knee-jerk reaction to sudden freedom. Uzbekistan didn't need fundamentalism to be reassured of its Muslim identity.

The relative unimportance of the Islamic party was a case in point. "We have three main parties," said the Professor. "Communist, Islamic, and Democratic. So, yes, we have free elections." Not so free, I discovered later. The Democratic Party leader and President, Karimov, was universally considered a dictator, with a policy of exile for any leader who started to inch up the popularity ratings. The very legitimacy of the Islamic party, therefore, indicated its political impotence thus far. Not until it was formally banned need anyone fear for the stability of Uzbekistan.

*

A little way up the street, the largest crane I'd ever seen was dwarfed by an even bigger mass of scaffolding. Behind the planks and bars a great wall of crumbling brick was just visible, its drabness in contrast with the shimmering blue dome behind.

Entry was surely Forbidden? Even outside this colossal building site, the notices of Officialdom threatened unmentionable horrors for anyone daring to throw rubbish in the building trench. But today was a public holiday; perhaps I could slip in unnoticed. Just by the gate, a shabby little man approached me; he would be happy to let me in for a hundred *sum*. Funny, I answered, when even the Registan only cost thirty. Yes, of course he meant thirty, he said quickly. Private enterprise, it seemed, was alive and well here.

He went away dejected, and I entered the courtyard; and once again stood rooted by the immensity of the complex, the height of the portal overlooking it. From here I could see its face; not after all blank brick, but spotted with blue stars representing, they say, the Milky Way. The opposite wall was over a hundred yards away.

Surely the biggest mosque in Asia, this was built for his favourite wife, Bibi Khanum, by Timur Leng. Having won himself a great empire, Timur had set about making his capital, Samarkand, the most beautiful city on earth. In his old age, mindful perhaps of the measure of his years, he had built with

increasing frenzy, demanding the impossible of his workers -
and getting it. What Timur decreed, lesser mortals performed.

Five hundred labourers built the Bibi Khanum Mosque,
working under two hundred architects and other craftsmen, and
using ninety-five elephants to transport materials. One observer
described how Timur supervised the project from his litter,
throwing coins and scraps of meat at the workmen to encourage
them. Perhaps he was keeping an eye on more than just their
diligence. Persian chroniclers tell of the chief architect who fell
in love with Bibi Khanum, leaving the mark of a kiss on her
cheek. Enraged, Timur sent his guards to pursue the man.
Escaping to the top of the highest minaret, the resourceful
architect sprouted wings and flew home to Mecca. A different
version appears in Timur's official biography, which says that
the lover was caught and hanged.

Thrown together at colossal speed, the mosque began to
collapse even before the first earthquakes tore at its fabric.
Falling masonry threatened the faithful like bolts from heaven,
and reluctant worshippers drifted away elsewhere. The huge
entrance gates, made from an amalgam of seven metals, were
filched by a greedy Emir and melted down for coinage, and a
Russian shell made a hole in the dome. It was eventually
abandoned, and by the start of the twentieth century its
courtyard had became a cotton market.

*

Timur was born in Kesh in 1336, supposedly of the line of the
Mongol Emperor Genghis Khan, and his career mirrored that
of his fearsome ancestor. Like Genghis, Timur was the self-
made son of a minor chieftain, and experienced penury and
captivity on the road to power; like Genghis, he had first to unite
the tribes of his homeland into a single army before setting out
to conquer the world. And like Genghis, he was known for the
brutality of his conquests, and a trail of pyramids made from
human skulls marked the passage of his armies.

His pride in descent didn't stop him from attacking his
Mongol neighbours. Among the first dynasties he overthrew

were the Mongol Ilkhans of Persia; then the Golden Horde of southern Russia, domain of Genghis' grandson Batu and his heirs. Next, he successfully invaded India and Georgia, then Mesopotamia and Syria, dispossessing the powerful Egyptian Mamelukes. Finally, he turned on the biggest force in the near east. Beyazit the Thunderbolt, Emperor of the Ottoman Turks, had just dismissed the Last Crusade at Nicopolis on the Danube. Now he was encroaching on Timur's lands in Armenia.

The preliminaries to this clash resembled the build-up to a world championship boxing match. "An ant should not go to war with an elephant," wrote Timur to Beyazit. "Oh ravening dog named Timur..." replied the Emperor. The elephant won the match, smashing the Ottoman army at Ankara in Turkey, and Beyazit was carried off in a cage. Afterwards Timur took the long way home, extending his conquests to the Mediterranean with the sack of Smyrna.*

The time he could spare from slaughter and rapine Timur devoted to making Samarkand into the most beautiful city on earth. This contradictory man, illiterate but a formidable chess player, seemed as much at home raising mosques and mausolea of staggering beauty as he was building piles of his enemies' bones. And there was ample provision of talent, for he had carried off to Samarkand craftsmen of every description from the ends of his empire. As with the Bibi Khanum Mosque, he often demanded that his projects be carried out with frantic haste.

Dissatisfied with the mausoleum he was having built for his grandson Muhammad Sultan, he ordered that it be torn down and re-erected within ten days. For his next project, the construction of a bazaar running from one end of Samarkand to the other, he added the ruthlessness of town planner to the threats of a tyrannical slave driver. All houses in the way were to be demolished, the market erected and the merchants open for business within twenty days. The other alternative being too dire to contemplate, the workmen finished on schedule. "Getting the builders in" would never be a problem for Timur.

* present-day Izmir

71

Don Ruy de Clavijo, a Spanish ambassador to Timur's court who gave history the account of Timur's bizarre schedules, also left a description of the man himself.

"He was sitting on the ground, but upon a raised dais before which there was a fountain that threw up a column of water into the air backwards, and in the basin of the fountain were floating red apples. His Highness had taken his place on what appeared to be small mattresses stuffed thick and covered with embroidered silk cloth, and he was leaning on his elbow against some round cushions that were heaped up behind him. He was dressed in a cloak of plain silk without any embroidery, and he wore on his head a tall white hat on which was displayed a balas ruby, the same being further ornamented with pearls and precious stones. As soon as we came in sight of His Highness, we made our reverence... His Highness, however, commanded us to arise and stand close up to him that he might the better see us, for his sight was no longer good, indeed, he was so infirm and old that his eyelids were falling over his eyes, and he could barely raise them to see..."

Scorning such intimations of mortality, Timur rode to war again early the following year. He set out to conquer China but died on the way; thus, unwillingly and for the last time, imitating his ancestor Genghis Khan.

They buried him in the mausoleum he had built for his grandson, beneath the biggest lump of jade in the world, sent from Chinese Turkestan by a Mongolian princess. "After he was buried," recorded a courtier, "the priests that served the temple heard Timur howl every night for a year. Finally, they went to his son and begged that he set free the prisoners taken by his father in other countries, especially those craftsmen he had brought to his capital to work. He let them go, and as soon as they were free Timur did not howl any more."

Other legends surround his grave. Long spoken of was a protective curse, said to be engraved on the underside of his tombstone. "He who disturbs this grave," ran the warning, "will bring down upon his country an invader more terrible than me." It didn't stop the Russian anthropologist Mikhail Gerasimov from opening the crypt and examining the remains on 22nd June, 1941. On the same day, Hitler invaded Russia.

*

The jade tombstone is in two parts now, broken by Persian invaders. It was also, just now, buried under scaffolding, like so much else in Samarkand.

"*Perestroika*," the street-vendor commented, jerking his thumb towards the Gur Emir, the Ruler's Tomb. The word was so familiar that it took me a moment to remember its basic meaning: "rebuilding".

Much of the mausoleum's brickwork, once tiled, was quite bare; much of it was brand new. Piles of glazed tiles lay in a doorway, waiting to be fitted. The azure dome, its colour still intact, hovered under a jungle of scaffolding. Scaffolding rambled over the inside, too, dwarfing the piece of dark jade and the six marble tombstones, of Timur's family and close friends, that surround it. I half expected a grim shade to rise up and decree terrible torments for those who had disturbed its rest with hammer and chisel.

The dome above, dimly visible through the iron forest, was of curious shape; a pointed ellipsoid, resting on a sixteen-sided polygon with slightly bowed edges. A wide frieze of Arabic calligraphy reminded you that "there is no god but Allah, and Muhammad is his prophet" above a contrasting geometric pattern, all glowing in fresh gold paint. The hexagonal blocks of green alabaster in the wall below added their own lustre.

Out in the courtyard, the door to the minaret stood ajar. The temptation was irresistible. "Thought's acrobat"? But I was no artist; the warning over the Sher Dor façade didn't aply to me. I waited for a moment when the yard was deserted to slip inside. Crouching to pass through the low doorway I shivered suddenly, for it was much colder there. Building dust and the feathers of innumerable birds strewed the lower part of the spiral stair. Much was in complete darkness, but here and there, as I climbed higher, shafts of light penetrated holes pierced for scaffolding rails.

The top gave an eagle's-eye view across Samarkand to the Registan; and a miserable close-up of the dome, with its ugly bird's-nest of poles. My eye travelled involuntarily beyond, to the spectacular mountain ridge far behind the town, outlier of the Pamirs and little more than a drift of white in the distance.

*

The old man was a professional mendicant. Dressed in a striped *khalat*, his face lined and leathery beneath the Uzbek skullcap, he held a heavy stick in one bony hand while stretching the other out to passers-by.

Beside him on the wall stood an elegant spouted jug, that would have looked equally at home on the coffee hearth of a Bedouin tent or brewing salt tea on the iron stove of a Kirghiz yurt. It contained water, which he used to perform his ritual ablutions as the call to prayer sounded from a minaret nearby. He prostrated himself with dignity, then rose again to stand with hands held out, palms upward, to receive the blessing of Allah as it dropped from heaven. His prayer finished, he returned to asking alms, his composure still impenetrable. Alms-giving, after all, is one of the Five Pillars of Islam, and he was granting the souls around him another step on the road to Paradise. Thus they would be twice blessed, for already they stood on some of the holiest ground in Samarkand.

Through the monumental doorway behind him, a flight of steps led upward. As I went up, I counted all thirty-six with especial care; for if I miscounted I must climb the entire stair a further thirty-six times or risk a curse. Through another portal at the top I caught a tantalising glimpse of dense blue tilework in the façades beyond.

This was the Shah-i-Zinda, the Tomb of the Living King, where Timur and his successors buried their favourite wives, their daughters, their honoured generals and one or two faithful retainers. The tombs and mortuary chapels here bear some of the finest decoration in Central Asia. They do not begin to approach the scale and grandeur of such as the Bibi Khanum Mosque; but are the more astonishing for the concentration of

74

their splendour into such little space, the explosion of pattern and form in the cramped corners of this Street of the Dead.

One wife is missing: Timur's eighth, who fled with her lover, pursued by five thousand horsemen. The shock of the betrayal was said to have hastened his death. Perhaps Timur's matrimonial problems made him all the more appreciative of his faithful wives. For whatever reason, it is on the Shadi-Mulk-Aka mausoleum, which houses one of his wives and her daughter, that the most striking tilework of all appears, its glorious blue and turquoise undimmed by the centuries.

Here, even the Arabic calligraphy is presented three-dimensionally in relief on the tiling. Three lines of stars run up each side of the door, alternating with Islamic prayers. Scrolled columns support the corners, their working like that of finely wrought iron in an elegant Victorian lamp-post. Leaves and tendrils twine over the arch, separated from the vaulted iwan above the door by contrastingly severe lines in white, turquoise and deep blue.

The sun was low, throwing long shadows down the narrow street, and the sanctuary at the far end was dim. This was already a long-standing place of pilgrimage when Timur began his necropolis here. Through the heavy wooden "Door of Paradise" is the shrine of Qasim ibn Abbas, the eponymous "Living King". Qasim, a relative of the prophet Mohammed, was credited with converting Sogdiana from the fire-worship of Zoroaster to the True Faith. A group of Zoroastrians, runs the legend, chopped off his head while he was at prayer. Qasim finished his prayer; then picked up his severed head and jumped into a nearby well. One day, he will emerge again and come to the defence of Islam.

As John Lawton drily remarks in his book *Samarkand and Bukhara*, "His failure to appear when the Communists seized Samarkand has... somewhat shaken his reputation."

*

Timur's empire outlived him by less than a century until it collapsed, torn apart by internal strife. Before the bloodbath, however, Samarkand enjoyed for half a century its period of

75

greatest flowering. Not, in fact, from trade; for the xenophobic Ming emperors closed the Chinese border in 1426, and with silk now in production in Europe, the Silk Road went into decline. Rather, the city acquired a reputation as an intellectual and cultural centre that brought the wise and learned from all corners of the eastern world.

Timur's son, Shah Rukh, moved his capital to Herat in present-day Afghanistan on his accession in 1404. Six years later he installed his son, Ulug Beg, as regent of Transoxiana.

Nature had designed Ulug Beg to be a scholar, not a ruler. Perhaps the best astronomer and mathematician of his day, he brought the Renaissance into the heart of Central Asia. Some of the finest minds of the time gathered at his madrasa to lecture and dispute, or visited his observatory to plot the course of the stars and measure the elevations of the sun.

Little remains of the observatory today. The light was going as I climbed the hill just outside the town, on the far side of Afrasiab, where Ulug Beg performed his life's work. The bricks of the little museum on its crown were turning pink in the last rays of the sun. Under a small hump nearby was what I'd come to see.

I ducked under the hump and leaned over the railing beneath, waiting until my eyes became accustomed to the gloom. As they did so, the cavern underneath began to take the form of a great subterranean groove, sweeping away into the depths beyond my sight. Ulug Beg's giant sextant - or what remains of it: a curving furrow, built to cradle the coulter of the colossal instrument, sweeping back and forth as its tip searched the heavens.

How on earth could fifteenth century engineers have made such a colossal, perfect arc? With its help, Ulug Beg and his assistants plotted the course of 1,018 stars, and produced the world's first chart of the night skies. He also calculated the length of the year to within less than a minute. His research had still not been superseded by the time it was unearthed two hundred years later in Oxford University's Bodleian Library.

At this hour few people were about. I waited until some footsteps behind me died away, then hopped over the grille and climbed down for a closer look. A damp stairway led into the bowels of the earth, and I could just make out the calibrations carved alongside the iron rails. From the bottom, the arc appeared even more enormous, the window of light at its top tiny and distant.

The original structure had extended into a hundred-foot observatory above. All had been levelled, though, by Moslem fanatics after Ulug Beg's death. The mullahs had opposed his scientific research; for how could they support a man who wished to take the universities out of the hands of the priests? Some went further, denouncing him as a heretic.

It was a convenient excuse for an upwardly-mobile son. Two years after Ulug Beg's accession to Shah Rukh's empire the ruthless Abd-el-Latif, who had already killed his brother, needed no religious pretext to murder his father also. Ulug Beg's favourite pupil saved much of his apparatus and fled with it to Constantinople.

Six months later Abd-el-Latif died at the hands of his cousin, who was deposed by another cousin, who was murdered by yet another cousin because he had killed his mother...

Meanwhile, Samarkand fell to another wave of desert nomads, Turks descended from Khan Uzbek of the Golden Horde. As for the Timurids, they were not quite finished. The last of them, Babur, fled from the invading Uzbek Turks to India... and founded the Moghul Dynasty.

V

There was no mistaking the descent of the lad sitting next to me on the bus. With his narrow eyes in a round, rather flat face, he might have ridden west only yesterday with the Mongol tribes who mingled their blood with that of so many others at this Central Asian crossroad. He wanted to chat to pass the time; but a sore throat left me literally speechless, my whisper inaudible above the clatter of the bus. So we sat in companionable silence throughout the seven hour journey to Bukhara.

Every community in every land tends to turn its back to the railway and its face to the road. So today gave me a much better view of village life in Uzbekistan.

In the immediate vicinity of Samarkand, the collective farms were unmistakeable. Formal layout of lookalike housing, big communal yards for animals and machinery, arched entrance bearing the kolkhoz' name and an inspiring slogan. Each had its own shop labelled, with the terseness of Soviet newspeak, *Khozmag*.

But the more rural villages gave little sign of their Soviet restructuring. The collective system here is still largely intact, but you would hardly associate these mud-brick houses, disorganised stabling and random collection of barns with an agricultural Great Leap Forward. In appearance at least, rural Uzbekistan can have changed little in the last century.

Every house owned its own small strip of garden, hoed ready for planting. Under the newly breaking almond buds the *divan*, a wooden platform spread with rugs, was placed to catch the March sun. The outdoor mud-brick oven, a large beehive with a hole off-centre, might have been the gigantic discarded chrysalis of some newly-hatched monstrous bug. While the bigger villages were Sovietised by the addition of a museum or library for the better education of the peasants, centre stage

78

always belonged to the *hammam*, or bath-house. The impression was overwhelmingly Turkish, the Uzbek swamping the Russian. The parent peoples of both Uzbek and Ottoman Turks may have divorced nearly a millennium ago, but, from my bus window at least, their descendants seemed more brothers than cousins.

In the barnyards were cows, sheep, chickens, the occasional turkey even. No pigs, though; for the underlying culture was firmly Islamic. Wheat and rice grew in the fields, along with whole areas devoted to pollarded willows. Brushwood was stacked high in farmyards and on roofs: kindling wood to fire the ovens.

Even this early in the year, irrigation was an unremitting chore. Dykes surrounded the field , and each planted row was separated from its neighbour by a groove, a potential water-channel. Kolkhozniks puddled in the mud like children on a beach building sand-pools. In fact they were skilfully at work, damming this sluice, opening that one, in a centuries old routine that allowed to each acre its proper ration of water at the proper time; while the steady, even passage of the stream to the furthest corner proved the spirit-level flatness of the land.

Here and there sudden mounds rose abruptly out of the flat earth. Near one of these a tall arch led from nowhere to nowhere, the gateway of some ancient mosque or madrasa. Were these old villages, once-thriving oasis settlements built up over the ages like high-rise flats? Or simply former burial mounds, like the many I'd seen from the train, but smooth from time and disuse?

Whatever the answer, they were to become familiar friends over the weeks lying ahead of me.

*

The Varahshah, booked of necessity through a local tour company so as to obtain my Uzbekistan visa, was my most expensive hotel yet, at a thumping fifty dollars a night. Still, I'd thought, it might be nice to see how the other half lived in Central Asia.

79

It wasn't long before I decided to stick to my own half. No hot water, no loo paper, no restaurant, everything dingy and grubby. At least, as the only guest, I got a warm welcome from the staff - and from the unexpected fire in my room. A lethal twist of red-hot wire about a central drum with no guard of any sort, it offered a choice of death by electrocution or by accidental ignition of the bedroom. Even so, it was a luxury I was deeply grateful for.

*

Everywhere else in the world, they say, the light descends from heaven to illuminate the earth, but from Bukhara the Holy it rises to light the heavens. Today it did neither. I set out to explore the city in a grey twilight, varied only by the occasional splatter of raindrops. It was weather that underlined the city's constantly recurring theme: water.

The Bola Khauz Mosque took its name from the *khauz*, or cistern, lying beside it. Once numbering over a hundred, these gracious, stepped reservoirs harboured all Bukhara's water - and all Bukhara's pestilence as well. The slimy water of the Bola Khauz looked as noxious as any I'd seen. But if you stepped around to the far side and looked into it at an angle, the greasy green surface gave way to a quivering reflection of the mosque's open veranda, where fretted paling and carved columns supported a ceiling radiantly painted in fresh bright colours to draw the eye towards heaven.

Half a mile further on I came to Chashma Ayyub - or Job's Spring - where Job struck water from bare rock. (How these Old Testament fellows did get around!) His subterranean shrine now held a water "museum". Describing one of the Soviet authorities' most necessary crusades, it told how the fight against water-borne sickness reduced infant mortality from 20% to 1/3%. "After 5,000 years of use," runs the accompanying commentary, "all but 3 of the 114 khauz were drained and filled in." So much for history and tradition.

They had a point, though. The primordial soup of Bukhara's reservoirs nurtured some of the vilest bugs known to man.

80

Bukhara Boil, the Blue Sickness, the Sartian Sickness... Worst of all was the loathsome Guinea Worm, recorded as early as 1558 by the English merchant Anthony Jenkinson, who came to Bukhara as the Ambassador of Queen Elizabeth I.

"The water thereof is most unholsome, for it breedeth... a worme of an ell long, which lieth commonly in the legge betwixt the flesh and the skinne, and is pluckt out about the ancle with great art and cunning; the Surgeons being much practised therein, and if shee breake in plucking out, the partie dieth, and every day she commeth out about an inche, which is rolled up, and so worketh till shee be all out."

Gustav Krist, an Austrian who travelled in Central Asia in the 1920s, gives a graphic description of the extraction process, which he himself carried out on one of his companions:

"I removed the rude poultice of sheep's dung that covered a ghastly sore which must have been causing him agony... Then I made an incision, and a thick stream of blood and pus gushed out over my hands. With my penknife I cut a splinter from one of the wooden posts of the verandah and made a narrow slit in it... a quarter of an inch of worm was exposed. I speedily inserted its head into the cleft of my small piece of wood. You must wind the beast out by very slow degrees so as not to break it off - if you do, the patient is done for..."

Within sight of Chashma Ayyub was another Bukhariot institution whose teeth the Russians drew. Hard against what was left of the old mud-brick city walls was the market, where once the Emir's subjects used to trade in slaves. The goods that change hands nowadays are more innocent. Among the usual cheap imports were more useful consumer goods; lengths of colourful flowered cotton, shoes and clothing; and the famous Bukhara carpets - made of course in Ashkhabad. Behind the pitches of the professional traders there were a few private stalls; odds and ends laid on a cloth spread on the ground and watched over by elderly Uzbeks in skullcaps and striped *khalats*. Round about, fast food men sold pancakes stuffed with meat and onions, and small boys weaved among the crowds with trays of tea.

At the far end, between high crumbling walls pockmarked by Bolshevik cannon, glowered the great west gate of Bukhara. The gatehouse was restored, but you couldn't mistake the age of the doors themselves, their heavy timbers bleached and buckled by the centuries.

On their inside, boys played football in an open space. I crossed quickly to the peace and quiet of Samani Park, searching among the maze of paths and under the trees for the Samani Mausoleum from which the park takes its name.

This tenth-century tomb of the Samanid rulers - successors to the Arab invaders - is one of the oldest features of Bukhara, having survived the Mongol destruction buried under a deep covering of blown sand. Considerably pre-dating the tilework that decorated the later and larger monuments of Uzbekistan, it is built of lattice-like brickwork of extraordinary delicacy. The heaviest part is the dome, bizarrely set with spikes and guarded by a mud beehive at each corner, looking too solid for such a fragile and insubstantial support.

On the floor inside lay an elderly lady, full-length. She sat up and unwrapped her face from its flowered scarf while I bought her permission to climb the gallery ladder, then resumed her torpor; but I noticed her open one eye from time to time to check that I was behaving myself.

At the top of the ladder and immediately below the dome was an ambulatory, crusted with pigeon droppings and blocked by a buttress in the middle of each wall. Tradition says that those who walk clockwise three times round the tomb have their wishes granted, a ritual perhaps derived from the obos of Mongolian invaders.

From Samani Park it was a short step to the centre of the old quarter. So much for the hors-d'oeuvre, the environs of Bukhara. What remained was its core, the heart of the city in which the notorious Emirs strutted their depraved stuff.

The eastern gate of the park gave on to a street leading straight to the Registan, the old market place. I shivered as I crossed it. Somewhere here, perhaps under my very feet, lay the bones of Stoddart and Conolly, those two unfortunates whose names are linked as tragically - and as heroically - with Bukhara as are those of Mallory and Irvine with Everest.

*

It was Conolly himself who coined the term "the Great Game" for the espionage Cold War carried on by Britain and Russia throughout the nineteenth century.

Both had their eye on the lucrative markets of Central Asia, then still a collection of Khanates: xenophobic city-states with suspicious, tyrannical leaders who lurked securely behind their enclosing deserts and their centuries-old regimes of absolute power.

But both sides tacitly recognised the potential for a bigger prize: that of control of India, the richest possession of the British Empire, towards which the Russians were slowly and inexorably advancing.

It was an obvious target for the expansionist Tsars, ever greedy to enlarge their territories. They had reconquered the lands lost to the Tatars, the Turco-Mongols of southern Russia, and then had reached out to swallow Siberia. They were contained on their western borders by Europe, whose power also blocked their periodic designs on Constantinople and Turkey; they were bounded to north and east only by the oceans. Their natural line of advance was south into Central Asia; and, maybe, onward. For had not Peter the Great reputedly said on his deathbed that the keys to world domination were Constantinople... and India?

So as the Russian frontiers crept south, the Khans quivered with apprehension; while the British played on their fears with overtures of peace and friendship, giving always the hint of better offers to come. It was on such a mission that Lt-Col. Charles Stoddart came to Bukhara at the end of 1838.

Stoddart wasn't the first Englishman to enter Bukhara that century. William Moorcroft, superintendent of the East India Company Stud, on hearing of the almost legendary superiority of the Turcoman horses, had come here twenty years before hoping to buy some. And in 1832 Alexander Burnes - "Bukhara

Burnes", as he was to become known - had suborned the Grand Vizier with charm and flattery, and succeeded in seeing much of the city. But Burnes didn't meet the reigning Emir.

"The dissolution of the times, yearly sinking into a deeper slough of vice, venality and superstition, was fitly expressed in the character and reign of... the infamous Nasrullah." Curzon's verdict was, if anything, understated. Nasrullah had murdered several brothers to secure the throne. It was the prelude to a reign fouled with atrocities.

Stoddart wasn't the most suitable emissary to such a man. Universally reckoned a courageous and resolute soldier, he lacked the supple imagination necessary for the minefields of Asian diplomacy. His message was threefold. Britain was preparing to respond to Russian manipulation in Afghanistan by toppling its ruler and replacing him with her own candidate; Stoddart was to reassure the Emir that this manoeuvre represented no threat to Bukhara. Secondly, he was to seek a trading treaty. Finally, he must try to persuade the Emir to cease trading in slaves - particularly Russian captives - an activity that presented Russia with the perfect excuse to invade.

He made a bad start. Riding into the city - a dignity permitted only to the Emir himself - in full dress uniform, he met Nasrullah in the Registan and saluted without dismounting. This may have been impeccable British military procedure, but it wasn't recommended in the Bukharan survival handbook. Soon after his first formal audience with the Emir, Stoddart was taken prisoner and thrown into the Emir's notorious bug pit, a twenty-foot shaft which Nasrullah kept stocked with parasites, vermin and all manner of creatures even more noxious than himself.

Meanwhile, the British Army took control of Kabul as planned, bringing Bukhara theoretically within reach of an expeditionary force. Nasrullah's confidence wobbled. Forced to embrace Islam, Stoddart was released and lodged with the fawning and duplicitous *Topshi-Bashi*, or Master of Artillery. He now became trapped in a game of cat and mouse, with periods of imprisonment alternating with house arrest or the

Akhal-Tekes race at the Ashkhabad Hippodrome

below
Katya and Natasha in the foothills of the Kopet Dagh

bottom
Moscow 1935: the end of the marathon ride from Ashkhabad
Photograph courtesy of Shokhrat

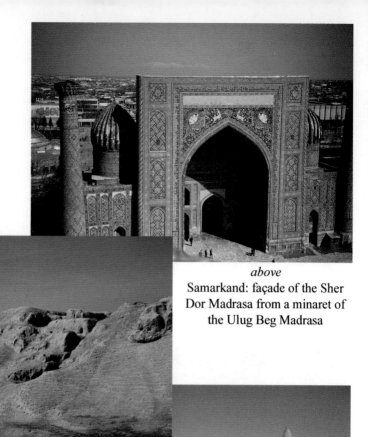

above
Samarkand: façade of the Sher
Dor Madrasa from a minaret of
the Ulug Beg Madrasa

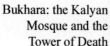

above
Karakul sheep graze beneath the
ramparts of ancient Maracanda

Bukhara: the Kalyan
Mosque and the
Tower of Death

top
Bukhara: a chai-khana
beside the Lyab-i-
Khauz

centre
Two of its regulars
exchange gossip

Khiva: approach
to the Islam
Khodja Minaret

Khiva: thousand-year-old pillars surround the Djuma Mausoleum

below
Kunya Urgench: the mausolea of Emperors Tekesh and Il-Arslan frame the tallest minaret in Central Asia

Parthian Nisa lies at the centre of the Akhal Oasis, mother of horses

relative freedom of the city, according to the ebb and flow of British fortunes in Afghanistan - or simply to Nasrullah's moods.

Stoddart had been captive for more than a year when Captain Arthur Conolly obtained permission to go to Bukhara and try to negotiate his release. Conolly was an adventurer who had already travelled briefly in Turkestan and written a book on his experiences there. He was also an idealist, and nurtured dreams of persuading the warring Central Asian states to unite in a federation for political stability, strength to resist Russia, and trading benefits; even, perhaps, of converting them to Christianity. And there may have been another, less rational, devil to drive Conolly to his death-or-glory expedition. For the woman he dearly loved had just turned him down.

He travelled first to the Khanates of Khiva and Kokand, and was well received. Both, however, had strained relations with Bukhara, and could do little to enhance Conolly's prospects with Nasrullah. But a letter from Stoddart reached him, promising a friendly reception in Bukhara - probably a trick of the devious Nasrullah.

All seemed well when Conolly arrived, but soon the Emir's mood turned ugly. Nasrullah had written to Queen Victoria, to whom he considered himself equal. He expected a personal reply. All he got, however, was a brusque note from the Foreign Office informing him that his letter "had been passed to Calcutta for attention". While he raged, the two Englishmen prayed for diplomatic intervention to soothe his wounded pride.

None came. It would have been a small concession to have sent a conciliatory word from London; but the mandarins of Whitehall thought it beneath British dignity to plead for the men's release. How Stoddart and Conolly must have despaired to be thus abandoned, surely only such as Brian Keenan and John McCarthy could imagine. Even the Governor-General in Calcutta, responsible for their mission, disowned them. Lord Auckland, writing at last to Nasrullah to urge their release, described the men as "private citizens"; to admit having sent soldiers to Central Asia could be a political embarrassment. But the denial was academic. It arrived too late.

For Britain's adventure in Afghanistan was over. The lavish lifestyle of the British garrison in Kabul, the attendant rising prices in the markets, the drinking and womanising of the soldiers, rapidly gave rise to disenchantment, then outright antagonism among their Afghan allies. They rose up on the "Night of the Long Knives" to murder Alexander Burnes and his household, and force the surrender of the garrison on humiliating terms.

No longer fearing reprisals, Nasrullah could now fully vent his spite on Stoddart and Conolly. He threw them back into the bug pit, where Conolly wrote a diary of his last days in the margin of his prayer book. Before long they were taken out for the last time and, having been made to dig their own graves in the Registan, publicly beheaded. Conolly, according to his Persian servant who lived to tell the tale, was offered his life at the last moment if he turned Moslem. "Stoddart was 'Moslem' for three years," he replied defiantly, "and that did not save him!"

Could anything have saved them? Few disagree that more could, and should, have been done. "The FO's lack of understanding of the Asiatic mind... was to cost Stoddart and Conolly their lives," concluded Philip Glazebrook in his 1992 book *Journey to Khiva*. It was a view generally shared. More than a hundred years earlier Sir Henry Rawlinson, a famous Oriental scholar, had gone further. He attributed far-reaching consequences, including the Indian Mutiny and the Afghan rebellion, to Britain's loss of prestige over the affair of Stoddart and Conolly. "Prestige may not be of paramount importance in Europe, but in the East, Sir, our whole position depends upon it!"

History had not quite finished with Stoddart and Conolly. Their grieving relatives, blaming the government for neglect, determined to find out whether the rumours of their death were true. A public subscription financed the visit to Bukhara of a spirited elderly clergyman, the Reverend Joseph Wolff, D.D. Dr. Wolff had travelled before in Central Asia, and understood how to impress, flatter - and grovel when necessary.

86

Arriving dressed in full canonical regalia, Bible under his arm, he presented himself at the citadel.

"His Majesty the Emir Nasir Ullah Bahadur was seated in the balcony of his palace, looking down upon us, and thousands of people in the distance. All eyes were bent on me to see if I would submit to the etiquette. When the Shekaul (Minister for Foreign Affairs) took hold of my shoulders, I not only submitted to his doing so to me three times, but I bowed repeatedly and exclaimed unceasingly, 'Peace to the King, Salamat Padishah', until His Majesty burst into a fit of laughter, and of course all the rest standing around us."

The Emir seems to have been both intrigued and irritated by Wolff. He lodged his eccentric guest with the Topshi-Bashi, and began a lengthy interrogation of him by messenger about the outside world. Wolff, he declared, was an extraordinary being - "a Star with a Tail". More ominous was his response when Wolff asked to take the bones of Stoddart and Conolly back to England. "I shall send them *your* bones!"

Beset with plots, threats and false promises, and constantly plagued for money by his venal host, Wolff saw his hopes for escape steadily eroded. All Bukhara, it appeared, speculated about his imminent death. The Emir's mullah was sent to ask him to convert to Islam. "Tell the King," Wolff answered, "NEVER! NEVER! NEVER!" and he prepared to meet his God. But a personal message to Nasrullah from the Shah of Persia secured a last-minute reprieve, and Wolff escaped from Bukhara with his life. He was luckier than the Topshi-Bashi whom, two years later, Nasrullah personally cut in half with an axe.

Nasrullah ruled until 1860. When he began to fail, he had his favourite wife executed before his eyes. He died in his bed.

*

Nowadays a city ring road slices through the Registan, and sterile paving has replaced the sand that once soaked up the blood of the executioners' victims. But the grim bulk of the *Ark*, citadel of the Emirs, still casts its shadow, and the gatehouse more than hints at the power and fear once concentrated behind it.

I bought my ticket halfway up the ramp at an office in one of the niches where once prisoners were chained. In another stood dejected waxwork figures of Stoddart and Conolly, in native dress. One of them had lost an arm which sagged, in its sleeve, to Neanderthal length. It made him look even more depressed.

Passing through a monumental doorway tiled in blue and flanked by stone lions, I entered the Emir's audience hall. A terrace ran round three sides, with little remaining of the wooden veranda which had once covered it. At the far end the Emir's marble dais stood inside a four-poster awning under an iwan. Once no doubt splendid, it was now little more than a decrepit bundle of matchwood on eroded marble columns. Opposite was a low wall where the Emir's departing suppliant, having crossed the length of the hall in reverse, face towards his lord, was at last able to turn his back behind the screen.

I sat on the dais, and tried to imagine Stoddart approaching with head high and all the authority of the British Empire in his bearing, while the hideous figure of the Emir gnashed its teeth and stored up fatal grudges. But the traffic buzzed and honked outside while tourist groups chattered in the passage, and the dusty old courtyard sulkily refused to yield up its ghosts.

The museum displayed a few artefacts dating back to the fifth century BC, when Bukhara was no more than a scattering of reed huts by the river Zerafshan. From its more recent past was the whip, symbol of power, which used to hang by the gate; its stock was four inches thick, and its lash, two. Here also was the Emir's gold and crimson throne, heavy with velvet and brocade. A mural compared the blessings of Communism with the hierarchical system of the past, depicting a pyramid with Tsar at the summit, Emir below, followed by layers of higher aristocrats, mullahs, merchants and kulaks down to a base where workers crawled on their knees, sweating under the weight of the rest.

It was all too clinical. Still vainly seeking goose-pimples, I went to look for the Zindan, the prison-house of Bukhara. I found it on a small mound in a grubby street behind the citadel, looking awfully small for a place of such terrifying repute. But then, comfortable living space was a low priority under the Bukharan penal system. "A hundred prisoners huddled together in a low room, and chained to each other by iron collars around their necks, wooden manacles on their hands and fetters on their feet, so that they could neither stand nor turn nor scarcely move." So a companion of Curzon's described it, having arrived unexpectedly and been let in by mistake.

The door was locked, for workmen were rebuilding the front entrance. I edged along to where a side gate closed off a rickety wall and sat innocently reading a book, while the builders ignored me and the locals having a tea-party by the house opposite eyed me with mild curiosity. I put my finger to my lips for silence, jerking my thumb at the workmen out of sight round the corner; then hopped over the wall. Was I, I wondered, the first person to break *into* the Emir's jail, rather than out?

It was hardly worth the effort. A couple of barred cells held a few more sad-looking waxworks, manacled hand and foot and covered in cobwebs - the most realistic thing about them. In the corner of one cell was a hole leading to a dungeon, a pale imitation of the famous bug pit in the Ark.

I climbed out again, the decaying wall swaying wildly below me. The workmen were still looking the other way.

*

Nasrullah had been cold for barely five years when the cities of Central Asia began to fall, one by one.

Russia had already annexed a few northern towns, in order, she said virtuously, to secure her southern boundaries against "undesirable neighbours". Now, though, one of her generals went in for a spot of private enterprise, capturing the important town of Tashkent supposedly against express orders from St. Petersburg. The fact that he was congratulated rather than cashiered was a measure of Russia's underlying foreign policy. "A glorious affair!" enthused the Tsar. To a background of much wind and little action from Whitehall, a Russian Governor-General of Turkestan was appointed.

General Konstantin Kaufmann had every intention of justifying his title, rather grandiose for a province that then consisted of just one major city. Three years later he got his chance, when Bukharan troops were reported to be massing at Samarkand to attack Tashkent.

Kaufmann advanced on Samarkand and the Bukhariot army fled - if it had ever existed. Leaving a garrison in Samarkand, Kaufmann pressed on towards Bukhara. Behind him, his garrison came under siege from a local warlord. Such resistance played into Kaufmann's hands. Quickly returning, he ejected the rebels, took reprisals on Samarkand and annexed it. The Emir of Bukhara, taking no chances, almost fell over himself to surrender in his turn, accepting harsh terms which included Russian control of Bukhara's water supplies, a practical and political strait-jacket. He became a vassal of the Tsar, his city officially a Protectorate. Now all of Transoxiana except Khiva belonged to the Russian Empire

History gave Bukhara one last chance to throw off its rulers. The Bolshevik Revolution of 1917 opened the door a crack, and the last Emir, Alim Khan, tried to jam his toe in it. He declared independence, and enjoyed it for three years. All too soon, with stability restored in Russia, the Red Army was knocking on his gates. As Bolshevik shells carved holes in his walls, Alim appealed to George V for £100,000, thirty guns and ten planes. His plea unanswered, "he fled", in the account of Fitzroy Maclean,* "headlong across the Oxus to Afghanistan, dropping favourite dancing boy after favourite dancing boy in his flight, in the hope of thus retarding the advance of the pursuing Red Army, who, however, were not to be distracted from their purpose by such stratagems." And so the Red Flag was hoisted on the Kalyan Minaret.

And so the Communists embarked on their seventy year crusade to convert the Uzbeks to the New Religion.

*

* See acknowledgement on p. 345

In the centre of Bukhara, half a mile from the Ark, the great monuments of the past, the mosques and madrasas, congregate around the old bazaars. At the height of the city's fame as a centre of Islamic theology, eighty madrasas accommodated thirty thousand students, who could worship at a different mosque every day of the year. By the time the Communist stranglehold was complete, just one madrasa and a few mosques remained open. "There is no God," said the cynics, "...and Lenin is his prophet."

The bazaars, too, were justly famous. In Krist's day they were intact. "If you climb up one of the many minarets of Bukhara, you see below an almost uniform mud roof, dotted with occasional large or smaller swellings... It is possible to walk from end to end of the city on the continuous roofs of houses and streets." His photograph bears this out, showing a moonscape of hills and craters fading almost imperceptibly into the mountain ridges behind. By the following decade this image had vanished for ever. When the great adventurer, diplomat and soldier Fitzroy Maclean visited Bukhara in 1938, he observed that little was left of what had once been the richest bazaar in Central Asia.

Until well into the twentieth century, these thoroughfares comprised the throbbing heart of the city, where people jostled to grab an inch to lay their prayer-mats, or to find the best bargain. Today, they were strangely lifeless. The monuments have been meticulously restored and rebuilt, the remaining bazaars tidied and sanitised, their once continuous skyline replaced by open, clean streets with sharp edges of new bricks, letting in the sunlight - and almost completely devoid of people.

The Kalyan Mosque, at least, made the hairs on the back of my neck prickle a little. The tilework at its gate, quadrangular arrangements of light and dark blue on plain brick, seemed subdued after the exuberance of Samarkand. Yet it was somehow the purer for it: built to praise God, not architect or craftsman. Inside, four bays of columned cloisters gave on to a wide courtyard, whose emptiness lent further sense of space to its considerable size. If I were a mediaeval pilgrim, I thought, I would come here, not to Samarkand.

Nearly eight centuries ago, these quiet cloisters had resounded to guttural shouts, rung with hoofbeats, as the Mongol army of Genghis Khan forced its way in here to stable their horses. Genghis himself, climbing into the pulpit, flung the Koran to the ground. "Mongols!" he shouted. "The corn is cut! Pasture your horses!" It was the sign for the slaughter to begin.

It took the Kalyan Minaret to stop Genghis in his tracks. He is said to have stood amazed before it, his finger in his mouth. For it was certainly the tallest building he had ever seen; probably, in fact, the tallest then in the world.

The minaret stands apart from the mosque, attached to it only by a sliver of a bridge. It is almost without colour, but for a blue stripe near the top; the remainder is baked brick... but not plain. It is patterned in bands, using some of the designs from the Samani Mausoleum, and without repetition. It tapers towards the top before swelling out in a final bulge, its underside vaulted like a convex iwan. For its size, the minaret appears almost delicate. It is hard to imagine it in its other guise: the Tower of Death. Throughout the centuries, condemned criminals have been hurled into eternity from its heights. The practice ceased only after 1920 - another feather in the Communist cap.

The streets around were disappointingly uniform, with deserted madrasa following near-empty chorsu. Towards the further end of the old quarter, though, before I could quite write Bukhara off as a ghost town, mortal life began to creep out of hiding. Here at last I caught a breath of olden times, sensed the faint fluttering of a pulse long past a vital throb. Here, too, was something left of Curzon's "wilderness of crooked alleys, winding irregularly between the blind walls of clay-built houses, which are without windows and have no apertures in their front but closely barred wooden doors. Trees line one of the principal streets and hang above the frequent tanks and pools..."

The trees are still here, and just one of the pools: the Lyab-i-Khauz, largest in Bukhara and lying between two of its many madrasas. One of these, the Nadir Diwan Begi, bears surely the most daring façade in Central Asia. Defying Islamic law it depicts a human face, with two flouncing peacocks, feathers a brilliant green, golden tails rippling down both sides of the arch.

The courtyard inside is a chai-khana, though in today's rain the divans were laid on their sides - the Uzbek equivalent of inverting café chairs on tables. Almond trees blossomed above rose bushes in the centre, and vendors lurked like predatory spiders in the bays around the edge, hoping to snare the few tourists.

But the chai-khana hard by the Lyab-i-Khauz itself did good business in any weather. For this was the "local" of Bukhara's old men, who collect at the poolside in the afternoons to drink green tea, set the world to rights and share the latest gossip. Their grey whiskers and gold teeth set off to perfection the striped khalats and Uzbek skullcaps. Some wore Russian fur hats against the cold, while others laid plastic sheets over their heads to keep the rain out.

They might have been sitting there since before the Bolsheviks arrived. Flattered by this background, even the green waters of the Lyab-i-Khauz turned clear and inviting.

*

Yes, there were fewer people now, said the young restaurateur, although still many visitors in summer.

Like most, he regretted the passing of the Soviet era. "The Communists ruled with a heavy hand," he said, clenching his own fist for emphasis. "But it made for equality. Then, if you took bribes, or assaulted someone, you got locked up for it. Now, you could buy your way out.

"Before, we could live happy. When I was ten years old, twenty years old, my life was good. Now, I get up, go to work, go to bed, get up, go to work... Though I'm lucky. I have a good job; I can manage. But a lot of people don't have enough."

"Inflation? Is that part of the problem?"

"Of course. Take bread, for instance. Before, it was twenty-five kopeks. Now, it's ten *sum*. Increase by forty times. Wages have increased by about ten. Don't write my name."

"So what's the answer? Is there an answer?"

He shrugged. "I'm not a politician. I don't know."

I had two burning questions. "The tourist attractions here are so good, unique. Why does the government make it so difficult for foreigners to get visas? Tourism could be Uzbekistan's biggest earner." If the system had not condemned me to a dump like the Varahshah, I thought, I would have stayed much longer, spent more money, come back again... How many potential visitors didn't come at all, because they couldn't face the hassle?

"In summer, the hotels are full. We have all we can take. That is, May through to October... Winter, the place is empty. Too cold. You can't blame the government for the weather."

"So then, how do you feel about closer ties with Turkey? Some sort of Turkic federation, even? After all, Turkey has already invested heavily in some parts of Central Asia."

"What can Turkey produce that is any use to us? Cotton, for instance: the cloth from Russia was good, very good. Turkey is far behind." Uzbekistan, one of the world's leading cotton growers, had in the days of the Soviet Union sent all its raw materials to Russian factories for processing. It saved the autonomous republic from building its own factories; more to the point, it meant one more tie of dependency on the Soviet Union.

" ...And chocolate," he continued. "British chocolate is good, Dutch is good; but Turkish is no good." Iranian, he added as an afterthought, was no *no* good. "Russia produced what we needed."

I had finished my meal, and was in a dilemma: to tip, or not to tip? The one was patronising, the other appallingly mean. I opted hesitantly for the former. The conversation abruptly ceased, and he went away, offended.

I saw him again the next morning, and gave him a cheerful hello; but he gave me only a sketchy wave, and turned his back. Perhaps he thought he had said too much.

*

I couldn't get the measure of Bukhara. It felt as if it had been built for many more people than actually lived there; but population density - or lack of it - was only part of my sense of dislocation.

It was a city of paradox, one almost of optical illusion. A city where a four-lane highway could fizzle out suddenly into a piece of wasteland; where the buses were crammed with people all going somewhere but the streets were empty; where the old part was pristine and hygienic and the new part grubby and decaying. The centre, it seemed, had been re-created as a living museum for tourists. Now, in March, its streets felt like echoing corridors in the school holidays. I had expected something like Cairo, like Damascus or Aleppo: busy, bustling, crammed with the atmosphere of past and present. What I had found seemed less than the sum of its parts. For the vitality of ancient cities is dependent on continuity. Communism had snuffed out the breath of life from Holy Bukhara, and it would take more than a spot of restoration to revive it. Now that the genie had been somehow stuffed back into the bottle, nothing on earth was going to tease him out again.

I wasn't exactly happy to leave, for I was thirsty for something Bukhara hadn't given me. But I felt also a sense of relief; for now my over-stretched imagination could give a long sigh and take a holiday, while my real senses took over once more.

VI

A few miles out of Bukhara, the Kyzyl Kum closed in. The River Zerafshan, which waters both the Samarkand and Bukhara oases, expires in the desert beyond the latter. It would be another two hundred miles before the road north-west towards Khiva converged with the lower reaches of the Oxus.

I spent them, at least while the light lasted, puzzling over the name of this desert. Why "Red" sands? Yellow would have been more logical; Grey, or Black perhaps - as across the Oxus back in Turkmenistan - plausible, from the colour of the scrubby, dark covering of saxaul bushes. Even Green; it had rained again heavily last night in Bukhara, and also for quite a long way north, judging by the dark wet patches and the occasional puddle. A faint green sheen was creeping over the earth, as this year's growth sprouted like designer stubble. But Red...? Maybe from all the blood that had been shed on it over the centuries.

Certainly the Khanate of Khiva gave the Russians more headaches, and for longer, than any other part of Central Asia. Capital since the sixteenth century of the oasis of Khoresmia in the Oxus delta, and shielded from the outside world by the impenetrable deserts of the Kara Kum and the Kyzyl Kum, Khiva is one of the most inaccessible places on earth. Yet as early as 1717 the Russian Tsar Peter the Great sent an expeditionary force to capture it. He had been told by Turcoman chiefs that the natural outlet of the Oxus was the Caspian, not the Aral Sea, and that it had been artificially diverted by dams. Glorious mirages of future trade swam before Peter's eyes; diverted back to the Caspian and thus linked to the Volga, the river might be navigated into the very heart of Central Asia. And did not everyone know that there was gold on the banks of the Oxus...?

96

He despatched Prince Alexander Bekovitch with a small army, and orders to take the town by force if his overtures of friendship were rejected. Bekovitch got an apparently friendly reception; his captains were divided among individual houses for "hospitality"... and slaughtered. Bekovitch's head was sent as a trophy to Bukhara, while his body was flayed, the skin stuffed with straw, and displayed over Khiva's main gate; and Russian slaves flooded the Khivan market.

It was a hundred years before anyone dared to repeat the experiment. This time it was a one-man expedition, in the best traditions of the Great Game. Captain Nikolai Muraviev travelled in disguise from the Caspian with a Turcoman caravan, passed off at one particularly hazardous moment as a prospective slave by his loyal companions. He offered the Khan gifts, friendship and a trading alliance; he received in return some useful military intelligence - and seven weeks as a guest of His Majesty, while it was debated whether or not he could be safely bumped off. The dice fell in his favour, and he was released from prison to return home with harrowing stories of Khiva's three thousand Russian slaves.

These slaves, rather than Russian expansionism, were piously cited as the reason for one of the biggest expeditions ever seen by Central Asia. In 1839 General Vasili Alexeevitch Perovsky set out to take Khiva with more than five thousand men and ten thousand camels. The fate of the Khanate appeared to be sealed; yet Perovsky never even reached it. He discovered, as Napoleon had before him and Hitler would later, that there are more lethal adversaries than man. For a fearful winter came to the aid of the Khan. The Russian army floundered in impassable snowdrifts and perished in freezing cold, losing a fifth of its men and most of its camels without a blow being struck. Khiva was to retain her independence for a few more decades, finally falling in 1873.

I had found it hard, from the comfort of an English armchair, to believe in such cold striking the deserts of Central Asia, where summer temperatures could reach more than 50°C; hard to imagine winters that froze the Oxus so that Turcoman slave dealers could ride their horses across to raid on the other side. Here and now, though, it was easy. With every mile further north the temperature dropped perceptibly, and before the halfway point my breath blew clouds of steam inside the bus. Outside, a vicious wind had swept every hillock smooth, and every bush, even the smallest pebble, trailed a wave of sand behind it. It was bitter when we got out for a brief loo-stop, squatting over a line of holes in a filthy hut with no partitions. Lorries crowded the pull-off, mostly Russian "Kamaz"; though a few brand-new Fiat trucks had found their way to this remotest corner of the globe. Their drivers cowered inside a shack, wrapping their chilled fingers about bowls of tea and stamping their feet.

Afterwards the night closed in, and the only thing to be seen was the vast power station, just before Urgench, that banished the darkness with mile upon mile of lights.

By the time I reached Khiva, all I could think about was getting warm, and getting to bed. I was freezing and feverish simultaneously. So when I caught my first glimpse, through the dark, of towers, domes and crenellated walls, I couldn't be sure if I was seeing truly or just hallucinating.

*

The Arkanchy Guest House was more dream than reality; but a dream tangible with warmth, food and comfort.

Leaving my shoes with the pile by the door (some stout boots there; evidently other westerners were in residence), I stepped into the blessed heat of what was the biggest family house I'd seen in these parts. A low table was laid in one corner; apart from this the room was uncluttered, its furnishings being mostly soft, rich Turcoman carpets and thick cushions. Despite the lateness of the hour the teenage members of the family were wide awake, lounging among the cushions and watching television. Within moments one of them had brought me a pot of steaming tea, and within a few more I was eating poached eggs and thawing by the minute.

Sabir Hassanov and his wife Nur Pasha had opened their guest house the year before, and offered the best service and hospitality east of Istanbul. The family were among the wealthier of Khiva. The daughters dressed extravagantly to leave the house, and the furniture was comfortable, colourful - and costly. There were even two colour televisions, politely switched on for the guests at mealtimes. That meant, three times a day. There was butter and honey for breakfast, at least two courses for main meals, and a table constantly groaning with fruit, nuts and bottled drinks in case you couldn't make it to the next meal. The Arkanchy was a glutton's paradise.

Best of all, after the spartan conditions of Intourist hotels, I found hot water, showers - and central heating on twenty-four hours a day.

It was the perfect place to be a vegetable for a bit. Although I'd at last got my voice back, encroaching virus had deprived me of several other faculties, including my legs. For the first day I lay on my bed, looking out across one plain dome to two glittering with sea-green tiles, beyond which the graceful finger of a minaret pointed to the sky. It was a view you couldn't tire of, nor could you if you lived here a hundred years.

*

Khiva's walls, even to the south-west where they were unrestored, were almost complete. Ancient graveyards thickened them, clinging to the base and creeping halfway up the sides. All the tombs were above ground, of the now-familiar designs: barrel-shaped, pointed, the occasional cube of a mausoleum. But all were of mud-brick, and not one had survived intact. They gaped open, violated, the bones long gone, or buried (if lucky) beneath debris fallen from the walls or from other graves higher up. I wondered what they were like, these not-so-old Khivans, who instead of being laid in earth for eternity were betrayed by changing times and fashions, so that their own mortal clay remained at the top of the heap to be scattered to the winds instead of lying under their own sons and daughters, their last resting places violated by loud, trampling tourists.

99

Up on the ramparts, I felt like a dissolute and lecherous Khan of Khiva leering over garden walls and into private houses to catch forbidden glimpses. They were pleasant walls for leering over. Prevented from spreading carelessly by the constriction of the city walls, Khiva's narrow streets were defined by houses of mud-brick, sides smoothly plastered, edges rounded and timbers protruding above carved wooden doors. Never a baked brick disrupted their harmony, much less a concrete block. Brushwood dried on the roofs, above small enclosed gardens freshly dug. A glorious skyline of tiled arches and blue-green domes framed every view. I was enchanted. I had expected here what I had in fact found in Bukhara: an echoing outdoor museum. Instead, I found bustling streets and a life little changed from the past. The very centre, true, was empty and a bit sterile; but the real, living Khiva enclosed it. Apart from the television aerials, you could have believed yourself back in the nineteenth century.

Restoration continues, but unobtrusively. And it is accepted that, as so often, the old ways are best. Mud brick remains the building material, with a thick layer of reed mat incorporated near ground level, as a sort of damp-course-*cum*-earthquake-cushion. I saw the same matting, almost disintegrated with age, drooping from fallen corners in very old buildings.

So solid were the city walls that I came down to earth only twice in the half-circuit to the East Gate. This was a huge, wide tower, bridging a dark tunnel some fifty yards long and heavily gated at each end. Niches along its length were once shop windows for displaying human merchandise. Nowadays, like Bukhara's slave market, they sell only innocent goods. Next door, in the 1835 Allakuli Khan Caravanserai, is what must surely be Central Asia's strangest department store, a supermarket clashing bizarrely with its old-fashioned setting.

Coming back full circle to the Arkanchy, I reached the West Gate - and, by it, the Ark. This, the Khan's residence as well as citadel, presented a series of confusing courtyards. But the Khan's audience chamber and the mosque were recognisable: spacious rooms with tiled verandas, supported on the columns which are Khiva's hallmark - elm from the oasis gardens, shaped and decorated with elaborate fretwork.

I came at last by a series of twisting passages and a wooden stair to the Ark's highest chamber, a small room with a lattice balcony. It commanded a view over the rest of the palace and much of the city beyond. I wondered if Captain James Abbott had sat here gazing over much the same skyline, while the Khan endlessly quizzed him about Britain and her Queen.

*

"Is your king really a woman? How can she rule, being *roo-posh* (concealed)?" The Khan had an insatiable appetite for news of the outside world, and spent many hours discussing cabbages and kings with the unexpected English stranger.

In 1839, news had reached British intelligence of the enormous army Perovsky was gathering to march on Khiva. Ever anxious to forestall the Russian advance south, the British could see only one way to pre-empt Perovsky's invasion: send an envoy to persuade the Khan to release his Russian slaves, thereby depriving the Tsar of the fig-leaf covering his colonial ambition.

Captain Abbott, having drawn the short straw, set off for Khiva in a state of deepest gloom. For he thought himself on a hiding to nothing. Well aware that Stoddart, sent on just such a mission, was at that very moment rotting in a Bukharan dungeon, he knew himself ill-prepared by those who had sent him. Lack of adequate gifts, money, language, the power to make any promises to the Khan... And the fear of being caught between a rock and a hard place, between the uncertainties of a secretive and little-known Asian despot and the tidal wave of the approaching Russian army that threatened to engulf the ancient Khanate. "My fame, as well as my life, was staked upon the venture."

He travelled from Herat to Merv then struck directly north across the Kara Kum, frantically learning Persian on the way, and daily having to scrape frost and snow off his firewood before he could cook food. In fact the snow, which he had not

101

seen since leaving England for India seventeen years before, delighted him, but "...the light breeze of night, blowing from the frozen wastes of Siberia, cut like the keenest sabre."

Arriving in Khiva, he was lodged in the palace in a dingy set of rooms, with an officer to spy on him. But he could still romanticise his situation.

"After dinner, I went out into the court. I gazed upon the stars, my companions in so many wanderings... Was I really at Khiva, that capital so famous, yet so little known, of which half the existing accounts are fabulous? Travellers presume upon its separation from the civilised world, to hang upon it their wildest marvels..."

Now Abbott could breathe again, for he was well received by the Khan, who was only too aware of his present need for friends. The description he gave later in the book of his travels showed less flattery than he would have used at the time.

"Ullah Koolie Khaun... is about 45 years of age... and rather under the middle height. His face is round, the features are high and regular; the expression is the most amiable possible; but there is an absence of vigour, for which, at the present crisis nothing can atone, unless it be the powerful interposition of some foreign power. His eyes are long, and not well opened. His beard is decent; his family having some mixture of Sart* blood. He is inclined to be stout... He shifted his posture from time to time. It was always ungraceful, and unkingly."

Abbott stayed for some time in Khiva, and had many audiences with the Khan. As well as the subject of the slaves, they discussed politics, religion, geography. (A world map in the Palace showed Italy north of Britain and Russia south of China.) The Khan asked Abbott about trains, the industrial revolution and telegraphs, and together they weighed the possibility of inventing submarines. Having assured himself of the Khan's goodwill, Abbott asked him to intervene with the Emir of Bukhara on Stoddart's behalf. "The Emir is mad,"

---

*   the name given by the pure Turks of the deserts to the city dwellers of mixed Turkic and Indo-European descent shrugged the Khan; nevertheless he wrote a letter that same night. "You have one English *Eelchie* (envoy)," came Nasrullah's reply. "What do you want with another? Do you grudge my having one?"

While the Khan was making up his mind what to do, Abbott explored Khiva. He was particularly struck with the city's favourite toys: "musical" kites, in which the transverse strut was bent like a bow and strung with cat-gut, so that it vibrated in the wind. "The effect is that of aerial music; monotonous, but full of melancholy interest."

At last the Khan made his decision: he would free the Russian slaves - if the Tsar called off the invasion. Abbott was sent on to St. Petersburg to convey the message. It proved the most perilous part of the mission; for he was wounded and captured by slave traders. When, however, they discovered that they had attacked the Khan's emissary, the Turcoman bandits were mortified. Abbott was released with a grovelling apology, and finished his journey safely.

By now, a second Englishman was on his way to Khiva. Lieutenant Richmond Shakespear, sent to find out what had happened to Abbott, was just in time to pick up the news of Perovsky's disaster - and the kudos for Abbott's efforts. For, if he had achieved nothing else, Perovsky had badly shaken the Khan's nerve. Although this invasion had failed, he decided that the Russian slaves were a liability, and should be got rid of forthwith. Diligently rounding up every one of the 416 Russians, including a beautiful child destined for the Khan's harem who had been accidentally "mislaid", Shakespear escorted them to St. Petersburg where the Tsar, already humiliated by the loss of his army, publicly thanked Shakespear and privately ground his teeth.

Abbott, too, must have been rather miffed. "All the sufferings fell to my lot, all the laurels to his," he wrote of Shakespear's part. "The former could not perhaps have fallen upon a spirit calmer under the burthen, the laurels never could rest upon a more deserving brow."

His ultimate praise fell elsewhere. In the poem that fronted his book, Abbott dedicated his mission to the young Queen

Victoria. Perhaps he might be excused, in his relief at coming home alive, a spot of vintage Victorian sentimentality:

> "Blessings on her whose very name,
> Breathed in the Scythian wild,
> The Scythian's stony heart could tame,
> And free sad slavery's child..."

*

They still fly kites, here. For Khiva's schoolboys it was as football to the English. They launched anything from a scrap of paper the size of an envelope to clever constructions of cloth and canes, half the height of a boy and trailing a long tail feathered with knotted fabric. More than one had yesterday's homework slung underneath.

And the fun wasn't just for Khiva's schoolboys. In the evenings the grown-ups joined in, competing with their children for the open space around the Khodja Minaret, that beautiful shining pillar which dominated every view from near and far. But, sadly, no musical kites.

I climbed the Khodja Minaret, starting the ascent from the outside by means of a rickety wooden ladder like the steps up to a helter-skelter. At the top was a narrow platform framed by arches, with metal grills to frustrate suicidal tendencies, nasty accidents - or Bukhara-style executions. Squinting through them, I could see that the town was larger than I'd thought, and retained quite big stretches of a second, outer wall half-a-mile beyond the inner one. Behind, to north and east, the oasis seemed infinite; while to the south-west, you could see where man's influence weakened, and the desert resumed its iron grip.

There were aspects, too, of the Old Town which you couldn't guess at from the ground. The way, for instance, that the *pishtak* or façade of a madrasa towers way above its quadrangle, looking false and two-dimensional like a film set; and is stepped at the back, perhaps to stop it blowing over in a gale. A pity that the bird's eye view showed up the unsympathetic roofing on some hastier restorations, like the corrugated iron on the caravanserai.

Some of the madrasas echoed that evening to the sound of chisels and hammers, as teenage boys learned the art of woodcarving from their elders. These were the new generation of artisans in an ancient tradition. Wooden columns made from Khiva's native elm appear everywhere: in the Ark, in the harem of the Tash-Khauli Palace. But the best place to see them is the Djuma Mosque, where a small, austerely white and plain mausoleum is enclosed in a dark hall densely filled with pillars.

Over two hundred of them; more than you would need to hold up the roof if it were solid marble. And some, they say, more than a thousand years old. Running my hands over their polished surfaces, some almost completely smooth, I could well believe it; for it would take many centuries to wear away the patterns chiselled deeply into the newer columns. Two gables let in light and air to thick, gnarled vines growing beneath. Sunlight passed diagonally between them, dust sparkling in its beams. The effect was hypnotic.

It was astonishing to find a site of such antiquity and complexity in one of the youngest of the Central Asian oasis capitals. But I'd forgotten that Khiva, while dominant for just a few centuries, had actually been around for a very long time before a wriggle of the Oxus' course helped to elevate its status. Tradition dates the city to around 1200 BC, when Noah's son Shem - another highly-mobile patriarch! - is said to have dug a well here.

The "Khei-Vakh" well flows still, though today the house that claimed it was locked and deserted. Wells were everywhere, one for nearly every house. So were bread ovens, like those I'd seen from the bus. Blackened from decades of use, they were flanked by ledges for working the dough, for stacking the loaves and, most of all, for sitting and supervising and generally passing the time of day.

For baking was a sociable affair. I joined a family where Granny rolled immaculate circles on a dough-board balanced on the mud ledge, then passed them to her daughter who stuck them inside the beehive until they swelled, bubbled and browned. Hand shielded in a thick glove, she removed them at a time perfectly judged, and added them to the growing pile. Three or four children stood and watched.

"Blessed is the visitor who arrives during baking," says an Uzbek proverb. Rightly so. "*Kushate!*" said the old woman. "Eat!" So I nibbled a delicious piece of steaming new bread. Too small. "Have some more!" she encouraged. But I was already staggering under the weight of an Arkanchy breakfast, and couldn't do it justice.

*

With the tourist season still some weeks away, Sabir's few guests at the Arkanchy were mostly foreign aid or development workers enjoying a couple of days off.

Michèal, from Dublin, and Jorgen, from Copenhagen, were the human face of an EU aid programme. Bruno, an Italian, represented TACIS, the organisation for Technical Assistance to the CIS. Their briefs ranged from specific technical help to the bread-and-butter work of setting up a computerised payment system for electricity bills to industry and collectives.

The latter must have been something of a shock after decades of free power. "Since market forces came into play," said Michèal, "demand has fallen by half."

From what I had seen so far of Soviet technology, I guessed that their work must have been a nightmare. But I was wrong, Michèal told me. They had found much to impress them, particularly in the less superficial, visible things.

"As in all the former USSR, the system of transmission of high voltage power is very good, but their local distribution is bad and their safety is awful: uninsulated wires everywhere, dangerous appliances and so on." Like the fire in my Bukhara hotel. "Do you know, there are no taps on the radiators - the government controls the heat! If you're too hot, you just open the window and waste it.

"But the engineers here are excellent. And they have the best maintenance manuals I've ever seen, with far more detail than our own. The same manual, of course, from Archangel to Vladivostok."

This didn't seem to add up. "So why do their buildings crumble, why is everything so poorly maintained, why do they mix the wrong concrete so that it falls down the moment it goes up?"

"Lack of money. Anyway, all their best engineers go into the army. Same with the pilots, by the way. Did you know that all the Aeroflot pilots are ex-jet-fighter? I've had some of the smoothest landings ever with Aeroflot pilots."

All agreed that Uzbekistan had no worries when it came to the power supply. "They have hydro-electric power in the Fergana valley, and generating plants all over. Did you see the big one on your way up here? This is why Uzbekistan is economically one of the strongest of the five republics. Turkmenistan, for instance, has masses of oil and gas, but they can't export it."

On the other hand, there were some major attitude problems. "It's difficult sending reports home, because e-mail doesn't work very well. Fax likewise. But you can't just send a written report, because it's likely to be censored. Because it contains information. Never mind that it's information freely given us by the government..."

"And they won't admit that they have anything to learn from us," added Bruno. "They have a lot of pride."

"So will they take your advice or not?"

"Some of it." Michèal shrugged with acquired Asiatic indifference. "But they don't really want to do the things we suggest. Most of all they want us because of the technology - computers, etc. - that come along with us in the package. Plus, of course, to bounce some of their ideas off." Technology, the great *deus ex machina* that will put everything right. I thought of Murad the kolkhoznik and his tractors.

Michèal's work had taken him to all corners of the former USSR: Central Asia, the Caucasus, the Baltic States.

"So which one would you bring your family back to for a holiday?"

"None of 'em! I'm sick and tired of visual pollution. Crumbing buildings, shoddy workmanship, wires everywhere..."

The list of things to admire was exhausted, forgotten. Everything industrial, all three agreed, was a mess. They summed it up briefly.

"Individual, good. Collective, bad."

*

Mary Carpenter was an International Relations Economist. Her work in the CIS for the last four years had brought her into contact with a number of ecological movements which had eventually sucked her in. Now a member of the American organisation "Ecologia", she was currently working in Nukus, near where the Oxus flows into the Aral Sea. Used to flow, that is.

There are many aid programmes operating in the blighted lands of Karakalpakstan, the autonomous Uzbek republic of the Oxus delta that embraces much of the old Khoresmia. A couple of weeks before I had met a representative of the American voluntary organisation Peace Corps, thankful to be placed in Samarkand while her friends were stuck in Nukus having their genes rearranged. And Save the Children had been heavily involved with the Karakalpaks for some years, supporting local health programmes aimed at children and young mothers. They were only two of the better-known among many such schemes. The Oxus delta is fertile ground for such work - if, or rather because, it is fertile for little else.

Mary was attached for now to "Perzent", an organisation for women's health and family planning. It was the first of its kind. Before, she said, "family planning" had meant a combination of abortion and coercion.

"It was as bad as China. When you were in hospital having your first child, it was routine to fit a coil while you were still under anaesthetic. Often you didn't even know it had been done. It was a common cause of infection; it could even lead to sterility."

"So your work now must be all the more appreciated?"

"Not really." Obviously, from the health point of view, women were delighted with the clinic, she explained. But the western concept of voluntarily limiting family size went down like a lead balloon.

"People here like having large families. Besides, they believe that the process of giving birth renews a woman's body - almost, that it confers a kind of cleansing." This, I was to see for myself, is one of the fundamental cultural differences between Turkic women and the Russians who have lived among them for so long.

"You should see the hospitals here," Mary continued. "They lack the most basic hygiene facilities. They've got no soap, no light bulbs, wooden floors which harbour bacteria. Yet if you ask them what they need most, they ask for technology! They think modern technology will solve all their problems."

"How do you feel about living somewhere like Nukus - about, maybe, putting your own health on the line?"

She was admirably laid-back about it. "When I went home after just three months, I had some checks done. They told me I had a high salt level. Now, I filter all my drinking water."

Salt is only one of the problems in Nukus. Here, in the Oxus delta, is the final dumping ground for the many chemicals that turn the wheels of intensive cultivation in both Turkmenistan and Uzbekistan. Fertiliser residues, pesticide residues, natural salt deposits washed out of the land and back into the water system; some of them even banned substances - DDT, the cotton defoliant Butifos, you name it... And the problem accelerates every year, now that the river no longer flushes this lethal cocktail off the land and into the Aral Sea.

So the people of the Aral littoral suffer probably the highest incidence in the world of pollution-induced illness. Among teenage women in Karakalpakstan, 20% have kidney problems, 23% thyroid dysfunction. Liver, kidney and oesophageal cancer ravage the population. The area has the highest infant mortality rate of the CIS, and even breast milk is contaminated.

Worst hit of all is Muynak, where a study* showed nearly three-quarters of the inhabitants have cancer or pre-cancerous cells. But then, Muynak always was in the front line of the developing catastrophe.

Forty years ago, it was a thriving fishing village on the Aral Sea. Now, it lies sixty miles inland, the only clue to its past being the rotting hulks of trawlers, high and dry in a desert white with salt and chemical residue. For it isn't only the people of the Aral who are dying; it is the sea itself.

The ever-increasing irrigation, the escalating voracity of successive five-year plans, have sucked the Oxus dry. One of the two main sources of water for the Aral - the other being the Jaxartes, or Syr Darya - it now doesn't even get there. Nor does the Syr Darya, nine years out of ten. The Aral is down to less than half its former size, and still shrinking.

The huge topographical change has a knock-on effect on the climate. Winter storms are more frequent and severe; and rip poisonous dust from newly-formed salt-flats to hurl it through the streets of Muynak and Nukus, adding the miseries of asthma, bronchitis and eye diseases to the agonies of cancer.

Perhaps the worst environmental disaster ever, the death of the Aral and the steady attrition of its people was wholly predictable. But the Soviet was complacent. After all, people had been saying for centuries that the Aral was drying up. There was the popular myth that an underground river drained it into the Caspian, two hundred and fifty feet lower. The American diplomat Eugene Schuyler had written of its imminent demise a hundred years ago. But it was still here, wasn't it? Anyway, what was a bit of water against cotton, the White Gold that would assure the prosperity of the nation?

Now, amid the I-told-you-so's, many heads are scratched but little is done. The most serious suggestion to refloat the Aral is the old chestnut that crops up for discussion every so often: to divert two of the great rivers of Siberia, the Ob and Irtysh, in a thousand-mile canal. The existence of djinns may be more credible, but the plan, on paper, looks Energetic and Visionary...

* Institute of Clinical and Environmental Medicine, Nukus

Meanwhile, the System continues to visit a plague of Biblical proportions on Muynak and Nukus. They are the modern Sodom and Gomorrah; their land buried in worse than brimstone, their people turning almost literally to pillars of salt.

*

The painted ceilings in the Tash Kauli Palace harem, said the guide book, are "best appreciated lying down". I could see what the writer meant; giving a fraction of the time due to just one of them made the tendons stand out on my neck.

A frenzy of blue tiling covered the courtyard's longer wall, which was broken by five bays. The vaulted wooden roof of each was brilliantly painted, in a mosaic of tiny detail. The Khivans of old believed in blending the most sophisticated culture with the most elemental pleasures.

Open balconies filled two of the other sides, supported on carved pillars. The upper rooms were again painted with bright colours but less sophistication. If the one was for the grown-ups, the other was for the children: patterns of flowers and circles on a plain base, fresh, cheap and cheerful.

A far door opposite led into a museum of social history, the artefacts including a Khivan cart, wheels high and narrow-rimmed. It scarcely belonged here, for its sisters, its cousins and its aunts still work the streets. But you could guess the age of its design from the deep ruts of similar wheels which had scarred the pavements outside.

The weapons room was filled with rifles, from flint-lock to modern. Had any come from the first, disastrous battle of the Russians against the Turcomans at Geok Tepe? Afterwards, Russian rifles had flooded the local markets, and the Khan of Khiva was said to have had so many that he didn't know what to do with them.

Outside the inner walls was one more interesting reminder of Khiva's history. Searching for the Post Office, I came on a former government office with the familiar veranda and carved elm pillars. The columns were plain; whatever the ceilings had once been, they were now a uniform blue. Further verandas led off to a splendid gateway, remnant of an old madrasa. Nearby stood the intact north gate of the outer wall.

From this building independence was proclaimed, briefly and for the last time, in 1920. The new Khoresmia was to last only four years before falling to the Bolsheviks, after which it was split between Uzbekistan and Turkmenistan.

Khiva had finally bowed to Russia in 1873. General Kaufmann, determined that this time there should be no mistake, had co-ordinated an advance on it from three directions simultaneously. As the pincers tightened the Khan fled, and the Russians entered the city without fighting.

The account generally given out was that this had been a bloodless coup. Far from it. The American journalist James MacGahan, embedded with Kaufmann's troops after an adventurous journey across the Kyzyl Kum, witnessed massacres of the Yomud Turcomans by Cossack troops in surrounding villages. It was hardly surprising, therefore, that the Khivans themselves were choking with fear as the Russians entered.

"We began to see small groups of men in the lateral streets, in dirty ragged tunics and long beards, with hats off, bowing timidly to us as we passed. These were the inhabitants, and they were not yet sure whether they would all be massacred or not. With what strange awe and dread they must have gazed upon us as we passed, dust-covered and grimy after our march of six hundred miles over the desert, which they had considered impassable."

The fugitive Khan was plucked from hiding, brought home on a leash and declared the "docile servant of the Emperor of all the Russias". From now on, said Russia, there would be "no foreign travellers in Central Asia". But they had reckoned without Captain Frederick Burnaby, one of the last of the Great Game generation.

Burnaby stood six feet four, weighed fifteen stone and was said to be able to carry a small pony under his arm. His more practical talents included fluency in seven languages. Possessed of a cheerful disregard for rules, he bluffed his way to Khiva with the same sort of impudence that Fitzroy Maclean was to employ half a century later.*

Burnaby had several audiences with the Khan, whom he found a "cheery sort of fellow", and was taken on an extensive tour of the city. The fact that he was genuinely a private traveller didn't inhibit his eye for military dispositions and political information. He stayed until his Commander-in-Chief, heavily leaned on by Russian diplomacy, ordered him home; and returned to write a best-selling book.

*

Back at the Arkanchy I found a group assembling for a wedding feast. Among the people arriving on foot or in taxis, a truck disgorged the contingent from a neighbouring village. All generations were present, from the baby passed carefully over the tailgate to the aged granny climbing down painfully, long after everyone else.

While the women disappeared decently inside, the men celebrated the feast on a large divan in the garden, dressed in styles ranging from extremely ancient to aggressively modern. Sabir was there, wearing the lower businessman's badge of a shell suit topped by the higher businessman's badge of a leather jacket; perhaps symbolising his rise in the world. It was a merry affair, and the talking and laughing and singing went on well into the evening.

It was my last picture of Khiva, for I left early the next morning. And an appropriate one; for I shall remember it always as a place of laden tables.

---

* Burnaby's later career included taking unofficial command of a Turkish brigade in the Balkans during the Turko-Russian wars, another similarity with Maclean, who fought with Tito's partisans in Yugoslavia.

VII

"Why do you not have a Turkmen exit stamp in your passport?" The policeman looked at me severely, and I wriggled like a schoolchild which had forgotten its homework.

"Um... No-one was interested in stamping it. There were no border formalities on the train." This was absolutely true. Nobody had given a monkey's whether I left Turkmenistan or not. Why should they? I hadn't given it a moment's thought. After all, I hadn't got an Uzbek exit stamp either. I had simply hopped on a bus in Khiva and arrived in Tashauz, Turkmenistan's northern metropolis, having crossed some invisible border in between. That was why I was at the Police Station now, trying obediently to get my papers in order.

It was an intimidating place, peopled by gangster types in trench coats and Homburg hats. I was grateful for Mohammed, the friendly Intourist man from the hotel, who had come to steer me through. I now stood back while he reasoned with the policeman. At last the message got through that I wasn't a heroin smuggler, just a rather dim tourist, and after heaving many sighs they grudgingly gave me the temporary visa which would see me back to Ashkhabad.

Mohammed was the only good thing about the Tashauz Hotel. At twenty-four dollars it cost more than a hundred times as much as the hostels I was to use later, and was at least a hundred times as vile. It didn't help that water was only turned on twice a day, and tasted sour and metallic. But they could have mended the loo, which I had to flush with glasses of water; or the window, where polythene flapped frantically in a wind straight off the desert. There was no point in the ostentatious fridge, which didn't work; nor did the bedside light; nor, of course, the lift. The first phrase I ever learnt in Russian was *lift ne rabotaet*, the lift is bust. It had always been the one feature

114

of Soviet hotels that could be relied upon from Vilnius to Vladivostok.

The waitress felt much the same about the place. "I work here all day, and see three people." Born in the mountains of Kirghizstan, she had come here to marry, and had lost her retreat when the old family home was sold on her mother's death. When I asked if Kirghizstan was a better place to be than Turkmenistan, she was silent. "We're not allowed to say anything bad about the country or the government, or they lock us up." It was a fear I heard expressed over and over again. Whether it was true or not, people believed it.

Outside, three rusting, life-sized dinosaurs prowled in the square. Nearby, a marble statue of President Niazov had replaced the earlier, silver, one of Lenin. I wondered if T-Rex was beginning to feel a little nervous that time was running out for his kind.

After this accidental touch of humour, Tashauz went downhill fast. It was a typical purpose-built Soviet town, and the only visible purpose was to depress. All was grey, all was covered in dust; part concrete dust that had fallen off the buildings, part salt dropped by the wind. I looked inside one of the shops, and found shelf after shelf full of bottled apricots; apart from one or two lonely tins, there was literally nothing else.

Yet the people here were the best: the kindest, the most hospitable, the most generous I had met so far. Like Mohammed had been; like the taxi driver who took me to the bus station and wouldn't let me pay him; like the man who insisted I take his seat on a packed bus.

Out in open country, the full impact of environmental disaster was apparent in the heavy white crust that covered everything. Even last autumn's winter wheat was thickly bearded; only fresh-turned earth was clean. The white frosting, the leafless willow hedges and dykes, the pale blue sky and gentle sunshine all combined to give the feel of an English winter day in the fens.

But the old man who passed in a side-car wore a telpek, its dreadlocks streaming behind him in the wind. The graveyards were filled with tin-roofed huts decorated with sticks and strips of cloth. The horses grazing in the fields were covered up to the neck in felt, tied underneath, Turcoman style. The impression faded. I was back in Turkmenistan, and on the road to Kunya Urgench.

*

Kunya ("Old") Urgench, formerly called Gurganj from the Turkic word for a fortress, was once the capital of Khoresmia, that most ancient of lands.

Khoresmia entered legend, like Samarkand, via Afrasiab, who assassinated its ruler (his own son-in-law Siavush); and history through the wars of Alexander, whose old enemy Spitamenes met his death at the hands of Khoresmia's Massagetae horsemen. Alternating between independent state and fiefdom of neighbouring empires, it reached its zenith at the end of the twelfth century with an empire of its own extending to the Indus and the Euphrates, and ruled from Gurganj.

The bus dropped me in the poorest of villages, with only a couple of mausolea and a madrasa hiding among the mud-brick houses to hint at its former glory. But the people here were even nicer than in Tashauz. The bus-drivers refused my fare; the sweetly smiling lady in the restaurant fed me wonderful goulash for a few pence, then allowed me to leave my baggage behind the counter; and a lorry driver stopped unasked to give me a lift half a mile out of town, as far as the first monument to Kunya Urgench's fleeting mediaeval glory.

In fact the Turabeg Khanum Mausoleum dated from a couple of centuries after the Empire, just before Timur delivered the *coup de grâce* to Gurganj. It looked from outside as if the dome had fallen in, but the inner ceiling was intact. Jagged patterns in blue and white tilework sliced the surface in bold straight lines like a child's drawing, carving it into 365 pieces: a symbolic calendar. Some vaulting had collapsed into the corners below, and pigeons had taken possession of the roof.

116

Their gentle calls echoed all around the dome, broken by the occasional beat of wings; and I nervously watched my head.

The mausoleum marked the entry to the biggest graveyard I'd ever seen. From half a mile away, the tallest minaret in Central Asia commanded the wide horizon. Beyond, two conical structures looked unlike anything I'd yet come across. In between was a landscape of utter desolation, punctuated with dusty hillocks and salt-filled hollows, ancient saxaul trees and funny little wooden huts. It took me a while to recognise the last as tombs, their rag-bound sticks betraying them.

The nearer I got to the minaret, the odder it looked. "Very sufficiently ugly" was the laconic comment of Abbott, who came this way on his long journey home. Its distorted lines suggested a succession of comparisons as I came closer; one minute a disintegrating factory chimney, the next a funnel with a nozzle at the top... something to launch a satellite from, or the prototype for the Iraqi Supergun?

Closer still, and I realised that the ugliness resulted from a later addition. Some way below the top the outline flared, like the top of the Kalyan minaret, above which the tip was mis-matched - and bent. ("Has suffered a very obvious declension from perpendicularity" says Abbott, never inclined to brevity.) Someone had been going for the Guinness Book of Records. Best to admire from a safe distance; it looked as if it might revert to the original height at any moment.

Beyond, the style of the tombs changed abruptly. Now there were earth burials rather than huts, but with a difference. Each grave had a ladder, six feet or more, sticking vertically out of it. There were more ways than one, it seemed, for the pious of Kunya Urgench to reach for the sky.

These graves were disconcerting, for they would give suddenly, and sink underfoot. Some were marked by holes in the ground. How deep were they? Carefully I picked my way between them, with the constant nightmare that I would put my foot down a hole and tread on a body. And at every step my foot crunched through a crust of salt. It lay thicker here than anywhere yet; the accumulated dried tears, according to legend, of the land's despairing people.

At the farthest end of this vast necropolis stood the mausoleum of Il-Arslan, the Khoresmian Shah who broke free from the Seljuk Empire and established an independent state. His tomb honours his achievement by its unique design: a cube, surmounted by a twelve-sided drum topped with a cone. Glazed tiles still cover the cone, zig-zagging round its circumference in a sea-blue frieze.

The mausoleum was open. Its ancient, carved wooden door squealed under my hand, the noise echoing through the bare, white chamber within. The tombstone itself was a plain lump of stone. Outside, the courtyard made a nice windbreak to sit and rest. A few brick tombs were scattered in one corner, borrowing holiness from the sanctity of their surroundings. Old snow still filled to the brim the well in the opposite side. Spring comes late to Kunya Urgench.

So much for the father; now for the son. Tekesh was the man who made Khoresmia great, reversing the rôles in one generation to take the rest of their empire from the Seljuks and rule a vast land spanning the very heart of the Silk Road. He died in 1200, little dreaming that the power he bequeathed to his son Mohammed would outlive him by so very short a time. He rests near his father under a conical dome with more of those ravishing blue tiles.

But the third member of this dynasty, the so-called Khoresmshahs, is missing.

Mohammed may have been born an Emperor, but he was not born a diplomat. Secure in his greatness, he treated with contempt an upstart nomad chieftain who had the impertinence to approach him with gifts and the proposal of trade and friendship. By this act he earned himself a pauper's grave, and incidentally changed the course of history.

For the nomad in question was Genghis Khan.

*

Not that it was yet, as it became, a name that rocked the world. The man who had been born, clutching a clot of blood in his clenched fist, as Temujin, had spent his first twenty years merely staying alive, and his second twenty uniting the squabbling tribes about him until all were collectively known by the name of his own, hitherto insignificant, clan: the Mongols.

By 1209, now already in his forties, Genghis Khan - the name Temujin took on his elevation to tribal leader - had radically restructured the Mongolian army into a decimal system, scrapping the old tribal units with their conflicting loyalties. Now he was strong enough to go to war. At first this meant only plundering the rich farmlands of neighbouring China, and sacking the odd city. But already the Uighurs, a Turkic people on his south-west borders, had foreseen the inevitable, for they voluntarily submitted to Genghis. Mongol expansion had begun.

Six years later, with the sack of Peking, the Mongol army came of age. For the first time these nomads-turned-regular-soldiers, bred only to local raids, carried out a sustained siege, for the first time they acquired the responsibility of a large number of subjugated people, the administration of conquered territory. And they learned voraciously from their new subjects. By the time of the Khoresmian campaign they were employing the most sophisticated Chinese techniques of investing and taking a city: siege engines, naphtha missiles, even explosives. They practised with these on the Kara-Kitai, neighbours of the Uighurs in Eastern Turkestan. Their conquest was almost a formality.

But these events took place thousands of miles from Gurganj, and it is likely that Mohammed was barely aware of Mongolia when in 1216 Genghis Khan sent him an embassy, a lump of gold said to be the size of a camel's hump, and the promise to regard him as "one of my most cherished sons" in return for a trade agreement.

What answer the Khoresmshah made isn't known. A Mongol caravan of several hundred merchants, arriving on his borders at Otrar two years later, clearly believed that trading relations existed. But Inalchik, the governor, denounced them as spies and had them put to death.

Outraged, Genghis Khan sent ambassadors to Mohammed for reparation. By his future standards, his demand was moderate: just Inalchik himself. Mohammed's reply was contemptuous. Executing one of the envoys, he sent the other two home with their beards burned - the ultimate Central Asian gesture of contempt. In so doing, he signed several million death warrants, including his own.

As many as two hundred thousand Mongols may have ridden to the Khoresmian war, divided into four armies. One besieged Otrar, two more were sent separately into Transoxiana. The fourth, led by Genghis himself, came down from the north and simply vanished into the Kyzyl Kum over the winter.

How such a host sustained itself and its horses in an empty land is beyond imagining; even for the Mongols, the toughest race on earth. Not for nothing did their enemies regard them as inhuman. "They were terrible to look at and indescribable," wrote an Armenian monk, Grigor of Akanc, "with large heads like a buffalo's, narrow eyes like a fledgeling's, a snub nose like a cat's, projecting snouts like a dog's, narrow loins like an ant's, short legs like a hog's, and by nature with no beards at all. With a lion's strength, they have voices more shrill than an eagle. They appear where least expected... They give birth to children like snakes, and eat like wolves. Death does not appear among them, for they survive for three hundred years..."

They survived for that winter, at least, emerging at last from the Red Sands to fall on Bukhara, baying for Mohammed's blood. But the Khoresmshah had fled, without even waiting for his army. In this last his judgement was for once accurate; for the Mongols caught up with the fleeing Turkish garrison and slaughtered every one. Entering Bukhara unopposed, they torched the city and enslaved its population. "They came, they uprooted, they burned, they slew, they despoiled, they departed," lamented a Bukhariot historian.

They departed in fact to Samarkand, driving before them a human shield of Bukhariot prisoners. The city fell after a three-day blockade, during which siege engines threw in pots of Greek Fire; the garrison again died to a man, the women were raped and enslaved, the artisans sent off to Mongolia, where the Emperor of the Felt Tents was planning to found a city.

Meanwhile Otrar had fallen, after a five-month siege. The city was rased, the citizens driven away; Inalchik himself was brought captive to the Khan, who ordered his execution by means of molten silver being poured into his ears.

Now the hunt was up for the Khoresmshah. A Mongol detachment went in pursuit, following a breast-high scent through Persia. Dressed as a beggar, Mohammed escaped in a fishing boat to an island in the Caspian, where fatal pleurisy removed him to the one place Genghis could not follow. His shroud was a torn shirt given by a servant.

*

Gurganj, seat of the Khoresmshah's power, came in for some of the harshest treatment. Capitulating after a seven-month siege, it lost its women and children to slavery and all other citizens except the artisans to the sword - twenty-four allocated to each Mongol soldier. The Mongols broke the dam, flooded the city and destroyed the precious irrigation system which gave it life.

Yet Gurganj rose from its own ashes, and by the time the Arab traveller Ibn Battuta came a hundred years later, he found "the largest, greatest, most beautiful and most important city of the Turks". This was praise indeed, while the Silk Road still thrived.

After Genghis Khan's death, his Empire had been divided between his four sons. To Chagatai, the second, went most of Turkestan - that is, roughly, Russian Central Asia and Eastern or Chinese Turkestan. But Chagatai was, and remained, a nomad at heart, unmoved by the prestige and power of the Silk Road cities. He lived on the steppe in his felt tent, while his patrimony fractured into a collection of city-states. By the time the silk trade collapsed a couple of hundred years later, the cities which had so often been partners under a great empire were once more isolated between deserts populated by warring nomads. Only Timur would knit them together again.

But Khoresmia, that distant land at the other end of the Oxus, opposed him. It took five separate campaigns by Timur

121

- and the final desertion of it by the ever-wandering Oxus - to reduce Gurganj to just a village with an over-large cemetery.

*

The village still reveals the odd living glimpse of its past. The "G" of the old name survives on the road name-plates. And the twin mausolea near its centre are deeply revered and carefully cherished.

Kunya Urgench, as so often happens in Asia, turned its back to the outside world, its face to inner, hidden courtyards. Solid walls lined the main street, with no windows to break their monotony. The soul of the village lay in the back roads of beaten earth, and in the many twisting alleys. Here, although the inevitable Soviet impedimenta of concrete and corrugated iron sometimes intruded, most was comfortable mud-brick. Children played in the street, and sheep bleated from behind the gates.

Dinner back at the restaurant brought an invitation.

"Come and stay with us!" said the friendly lady who had looked after my bag. Her younger, rakish-looking husband backed her up vigorously. So I waited, drinking tea, while they finished business and locked up, then strolled back through a glorious red sunset to their house. We passed the two mausolea, facing each other in black silhouette against the evening sky, their curves, bumps and square ends sharply outlined in bizarrely familiar shape: Thomas the Tank Engine and Friend.

Across the canal, village artery, was a quiet street of single-storey houses. "These were always private, even under the Communists," they said.

Khalbi Mohammedov and his wife Oghul-Gul Ashirwa were cheerleaders for the president. The times favoured them. They had taken over the restaurant, formerly government property, and now owned two houses and a car. "Niazov is great; we love him!" they said. "We have bread; we have land."

Earlier, all land had belonged to the kolkhoz. They outlined the gradual privatisation process: five years' free loan, followed by five years' repayment at a fixed twenty per cent. For Khalbi and Oghul-Gul, the system had worked. They now worked hard, but could bring up their four children in plenty and comfort.

Their second, "spare" house, the guest house, was luxuriously furnished with fine Turcoman rugs. Other furniture was sparse; the people of Central Asia don't fill their houses with clutter as we do in the West. As we stepped over the threshold we removed our shoes, Oghul-Gul lending me *dapochki* - soft slippers that wouldn't damage the rich carpets.

Her daughter Bacha brought water, towel and bowl, pouring from a graceful, curved jug for us to wash our hands. Bacha was the eldest daughter and, in the customary Turcoman hierarchy, the family châtelaine: she managed the house while her younger brothers and sister went to school and her parents to work. Laila, her sister, joined us at the table. Her clear and careful Russian made her the interpreter for the party, as I couldn't understand her father's dialect.

After supper - my second, for I had already eaten at the restaurant, but rose willingly to the occasion - came family prayers. These took the form of a brief thanksgiving with palms upraised, and ended with stroking the face: the drops of grace descending from above, to be caught in the hands and passed to the body. The rest of the family arrived, and a merry party began. As well as two kolkhoznik guests came a Tatar *babushka*, relative of Oghul-Gul's mother in Kazan. A tiny lady, she sparkled with fun, her lined old face beautiful under its blue wimple.

When at last it was time for bed two mattresses were laid in the big guest room. Bacha, observing the usual Turcoman courtesy, slept alongside me in case I should need anything in the night. Before going to sleep we compared our very different lives.

She asked me the questions I had become accustomed to: had I a husband, children? In return I asked if she planned to marry.

"With us, it is expected," she answered equably. "Meanwhile, I enjoy running this home. I am very happy, and the work is light."

I expressed admiration and envy for her contentment, she for my freedom.

"You are lucky," she said. "You can travel."

*

In the morning, Khalbi and I left early; he to open the restaurant and I to catch the bus. The last stage of the present journey was before me: due south, and straight through the middle of the Kara Kum, to Ashkhabad.

Kunya Urgench was coming busily to life. A rickety bus hobbled up to factory gates to disgorge a crowd of workers. From another direction, and another era, came an old man riding a donkey, short-stirrupped, as the Mongolians ride. His telpek had lost the wool off its crown, giving him the appearance of a wildly dishevelled monk.

Another ancient in Teke headgear bore features more Chinese than Turco-Mongol. His ancestors might have ridden west millennia before the Turks arrived. I watched them with fascination as they stopped to pass the time of day, symbol of the meeting of races over many Central Asian centuries. Grandfathers both; had their own grandfathers, I wondered, traded in slaves? The odds were for rather than against, for in the nineteenth century there could have been few Turcomans not in some way involved in what was then the national industry. Keeping livestock and hoeing the odd bit of land might keep body and soul together, but everyone wants to raise their standard of living. And the silver and cornelian that graced the Turcoman's best horses (and, occasionally, if they were lucky, his wives) didn't grow in the oases - except, perhaps, vicariously. Not for nothing did mothers hush their fractious children with the awful threat: "Quiet, or the Tekes will take you!"

Slave-trading was never a Turcoman monopoly. It was a habit common to all - including the Russians, who themselves outlawed their own participation only in 1861. All the more hypocrisy, then, in their pretext for moving against Khiva and Bukhara.

124

Besides, comparatively few Russians suffered such a fate. True, Muraviev, after his imprisonment in Khiva in 1819, had spoken of three thousand of them there; but, twenty years later, Abbott found only four hundred. Attacking the Russian settlements around the Caspian or on the northern fringes of Turkestan could be dangerous work. The really lucrative source, the easiest to plunder, was Persia.

Conolly, who on his first venture into Turkestan was nearly enslaved himself, described a typical assault on a Persian caravan.

"It is generally in the gray of the morning the Toorkmuns wait for the pilgrims, when half asleep, after a weary night's march, they have dispersed for prayers; then, with a Ho! Ho! they dart down among them, make haste to cut down a few of the least valuable persons, and do not find it very difficult to drive off the greater part of the rest... 'They come,' to use a Persian's own expression, 'like the whirlwind, and are only known by the traces of their devastation'."

There followed the weary trek across the desert, which cut off all hope of escape. Abbott met such a caravan on his way to Khiva.

"...their masters have no object in treating them harshly. At night they share with them their blankets and cloaks, and in the day time I often observe the women laughing with their captors. The children also, having plenty to eat and nothing to do, probably rather enjoy themselves. But the men are chained together by the throats at night, so that rest is scarcely possible, whilst the contact of the frozen iron with their skin must be torturous."

At least these victims could be grateful for the times, for the Scythians who once lived in these parts used to blind their slaves. Nevertheless, as mere Persians, they probably spent their entire lives in captivity. Not until 1886, nearly fifty years later, was slavery completely stamped out in Central Asia.

*

A small elderly gentleman, a Yomud Turcoman in a Russian fur hat, was deputed by my fellow passengers to look after me, for he was also going to Ashkhabad. He was an excellent guide, pointing out two fortresses on the way. The first, a large square in excellent condition, he named as that of Shabbas Khan; the second, smaller and reverting to nature, the palace of Shabbas' daughter.

Here, travelling south and more or less directly away from the Oxus, I could see for the first time the full extent of the irrigation. Not until a full hour into the journey did it loosen its grip on the desert. Now the main arteries were almost spent, though narrowing capillaries still broke away through the sand towards isolated pockets of cultivation. Whatever the consequences, such extension of the oasis was a mighty accomplishment. Maybe the Soviet engineers had mislaid half the Aral Sea in the process; but you had to admire the immensity of the concept, however flawed the execution.

The bus was bound for Ak Depe - the White Mound - Leninsk on my map, but now relieved of its Soviet name. My Yomud guide got out unexpectedly at a junction in the middle of nowhere, pulling me after him. I stood anxiously watching the bus continuing south, and hoped that he knew the form.

A huddle of men stood outside a police post, hunched over a fire fed by a pipe of the local gas. A leak close by hissed dangerously, but no-one took any notice. I had smelled several similar leaks in Kunya Urgench, also ignored. At least something, I thought, came cheap in Turkmenistan.

We joined the huddle, and waited. We waited and waited, while the wind played with the gas fumes, and piled half the Kara Kum into my nose and ears. A grinning sandy-haired dog rolled on her back before me in fawning self-abasement; little else moved. After a long time a lorry rolled through the sandy wastes and stopped beside us, engine idling. A man detached himself from the group and climbed in, and with a grunt of its ancient gearbox the lorry moved on. Now I understood. This was the Last Hitching Post Before the Desert, and we were the Queue.

One by one, the men found a lift and went; a few others trickled in and joined the group. A young policeman came out of the blockhouse to pass the time of day. Hours rolled by. One punter fed his boredom with gulps of brandy, becoming more and more noisy as the bottle emptied. At length he sent the young policeman off to make the rest of us some tea. With smiling good nature, the lad got up to put the kettle on. "You see how our Soviet Police serve us!" cried the drunkard in triumph, while the rest of us squirmed with embarrassment.

After three hours it dawned on me why, although we had long moved to the front of the queue, neither of us had yet got a lift. The old man, taking literally his instructions to see me to Ashkhabad, wouldn't consider trucks which already had two occupants, and room therefore for only one passenger. Since no-one would set out to cross the Kara Kum without a relief driver, we hadn't a hope in hell of travelling together.

When the next lorry came along, I waved it down and tried almost physically to push him on board. But the drivers refused him. "He's got too much baggage." He had little; two small bags to my big one. But I was a foreigner, and by definition more interesting. They would take me, they said, but not him.

Poor man; he might have been halfway to Ashkhabad by now but for his chivalry, and here I was sailing off and leaving him behind. But to refuse the lift would have helped neither of us; while now, relieved of me, he would get on the next truck. I prayed it would come for him soon.

Kemal and his sister Guljemala were a couple of professional truckers who lived their lives on the road, covering thousands of miles of Central Asia (and formerly most of the USSR), sleeping in the cab of their truck and reckoning themselves lucky if they got back to their home in Tashauz once a week. Both drove the great lorry with a skill that made it look deceptively easy, managing almost imperceptibly with the complete lack of a working clutch and passing improbably smoothly over a road which was more pothole than asphalt. "It gets worse," said Guljemala, as Kemal cheerfully negotiated what looked like a batch of shell-holes.

She was the more extrovert of the two, tolerant of my poor Russian and deeply inquisitive about every aspect of life in England.

"She's beautiful," she breathed, gazing at a picture of the Queen on a twenty pound note. "And how is Prince Charles, and Princess Anne, and Prince William, and John Major? And how many grandchildren has the Queen got now...?" Living in the cab of her truck and probably rarely reading even a newspaper, she was vastly better informed about Britain than I about Turkmenistan, despite all my preparatory research.

"And what is Margaret Thatcher doing now?"

"She's writing books, travelling and lecturing, making lots of money... and telling the Prime Minister how to run the country!"

She hooted with laughter and pressed a handful of sunflower seeds into my palm.

The pockmarked road stretched away before us for three hundred miles, snaking over and around rolling hillocks. The landscape was beautiful in parts, its golden sands erupting in foaming waves of dune covered in ripples, etched against a blue sky. Elsewhere it was just empty, but for spiky bushes of saxaul. But even here, there were people. Now and again a few sheep or goats betrayed the presence of human life somewhere over the next hill or dune, and once a plume of smoke drifted into the air half a mile from the road. As we went south, towards the spring, a faint green sheen began first to show and then to intensify.

In fact, the Black Sands were just like the Red... only were they just a little darker? In the hollows, more than a hint of alluvial mud lay in the yellow sand. Some hold that the whole Kara Kum is potentially fertile, enriched by former river deposits. Certainly the cliffs that ran to the right of our road for some miles had been formed by more than just wind erosion. Flash flood? Or regular spring meltwaters off the Pamirs and Hindu Kush? For they say that once the Oxus flowed this way.

Herodotus stated unequivocally that it flowed into the Caspian Sea. Surely he had confused the Caspian with the Aral? But, as so often, more recent study has agreed with him. Soviet

128

archaeologists believe that the Oxus reached the Aral Sea only around 2000 BC. Earlier, its water must have flowed somewhere else; and the Caspian, several hundred feet lower than the Aral, was the obvious destination.

But there is a paradox here, a contradiction in the dates; for records by mediaeval travellers also place the Oxus in the middle of Kara Kum. Perhaps when Turcomans told Peter the Great that the Oxus flowed into the Aral only because it had been deliberately diverted, they may have been expressing local beliefs, a memory transmitted through several generations. Conolly, musing on the same theme when he came upon "a large river bed a thousand yards wide", quotes Persian historians to show that the Oxus flowed *west*, separating "Khorassan (eastern Persia) from Karazm (Khoresmia)". He was told of a terrible earthquake five centuries before, causing serious flooding and greatly altering the face of the land. This takes us back to the time of Timur, about when the river deserted Gurganj.

So what about the four-thousand-year-old Aral delta of Soviet scholars? Conolly has the answer. There were once *two* branches of the Oxus, he argues, with separate outlets. This is a feasible proposition in such flat desert country, where rivers may split many times. And if indeed an earthquake choked the western branch around the fourteenth century, the increasing flow to the eastern might have been quite sufficient to shift the course of that also, leaving Gurganj high and dry.

Could this also explain the riddle of the Black and Red Sands? The colours find an echo in early Egypt, where once "black" described the fertile lands of the Nile Valley and "red" the desert. Perhaps such a concept was common in the ancient world; or perhaps the colour scheme came east with the Arabs? "Black" for the once-fertile Turkmenistan, "red" for the permanent deserts of Uzbekistan...?

Guljemala might have read my thoughts, for she reached behind her seat and brought out some cans of beer, an unexpected luxury. My first mouthful was turned to mud by the alluvial deposits on my own throat and tongue, but the rest was nectar.

129

Roughly halfway, we came into the settlement of Darvaza. Against a background of yellow valleys and roughly eroded sandstone tors stood a scattering of yurts, the round felt tent of the Turkic nomads.

They were small, shabby and - unlike those of the Kirghiz and Mongolians - wrapped in reed matting. Few Turcomans now live in their ancestral tents. Here at Darvaza, though, they made the basis of a large pit-stop. Guljemala pulled the lorry off the road several times, making a circuit of the yurts until she found one ready to serve tea and shashlik. It was a brief stop only, and after a bolted meal of tough chunks of meat we were back in the cab. Giving a master class in how to start a big engine without a clutch, Guljemala swung the vehicle back on to the road and resumed the slow journey south.

Darkness now came down rapidly, and a full moon rose. After endless hours Kemal, who was sporadically dozing in the well behind the seats, nudged my shoulder and pointed. A thin line of light smudged the horizon.

"Ashkhabad."

I hadn't remembered it as a lovely place; but after twelve hours in the Kara Kum it seemed like Shangri-La. As we entered the outskirts I looked on its crumbling buildings, its grubby yards, with something akin to affection.

Kemal and Guljemala were bound for, of all places, the Hippodrome, a regular truck-stop. They refused to drop me there, though, insisting against all my arguments on continuing nearer to the centre of town, where it would be safer for me to find a taxi late at night. Half a mile past the racecourse, the truck was waved down at a police checkpoint.

It was the second time in five minutes, but this time it was a lengthy halt while the police examined the big lorry minutely for any visible or invisible fault. "Does this happen often?" I asked Guljemala, as Kemal climbed resignedly back into the cab to fetch his documents.

"They demand money," she answered cynically. Then, "*Korruptsia*," she hissed, as a bitter afterthought.

I was appalled. If they hadn't been so kind to me, they would by now have been safely tucked up at the Hippodrome, and this wouldn't have happened. I hoped fervently that Kemal would let me stand the inevitable backhander, but knew even as I formed the thought that he wouldn't.

After a very long five minutes he climbed back wearily into the cab, contempt all over his face. "Do you know what they said? 'Your lorry is too dirty. Wash it!' "

"Any bribe?"

"No!" he laughed, and I breathed again. His documents, and the vehicle, had stood up to the scrutiny.

They dropped me near the old Peace Avenue, now renamed Turkmenbashi ("Everything now is named after Niazov," growled Kemal. "Even your toilet is named after Niazov!"), where the city life was still breathing despite the lateness of the night. Half an hour, two buses, and one taxi later, I staggered into the Hotel Jubliaynia, hopelessly dishevelled and leaking sand from every orifice.

Behind the reception desk sat Olga.

131

Part Three

In the Street of the Soviet Frontier Guards

VIII

Any other *administrator* of a respectable hotel would have had me out on the street at the double. And with extra good reason, since a block booking by a Turkish consortium had accounted for every single room.

But Olga was not just any other administrator. Olga, I was rapidly to learn, was special. Within a remarkably short time I was partially sanitised under the shower, fed, and tucked up in her own bed, while Olga moved out to a shake-down in a spare corner. When she came off duty the next morning, she took me home with her like a stray puppy.

Olga was blonde, plump, motherly and forty-five-ish. She lived near the hotel, in a flat in the magnificently named Street of the Soviet Frontier Guards, with her husband Sasha and teenage children Maxim and Katya. And, of course, Bim.

Bim was the family mutt, a dwarf something-or-other with bat ears, bulging eyes and chronic incontinence. On our first meeting he chewed my hand furiously while peeing on the floor in ecstasy. Such contradiction between opposing ends of his person was quite normal. He soon left me and attacked my baggage, allowing me to tiptoe away round the puddles - and gasp at the view from the kitchen window.

Winter was finally losing its grip on Ashkhabad. Whereas a fortnight ago the air had been damp and bleary, today it sparkled. Olga's second-floor flat was at the south-western tip of the city, close to the mountains. From her balcony there was a stupendous view out and up to their silver ridges, soaring literally and metaphorically far above the grime and litter where human insects crawled below.

For a long time I stood transfixed. Only exhaustion tore me away, to collapse on to Olga's sofa in blissful immobility until the family came home.

First to arrive was Katya, when school finished at lunchtime. Most thirteen-year-olds would have been rather miffed to come home and find a foreign stranger installed in their home without warning. Katya took it completely in her stride. She took me under her wing, and in the following days helped me through the complexities of Ashkhabad's awful phone system, found me spare carbon paper - and coloured, too - for my notes, and showed me in her teenage sophistication a hundred and one new ways of dressing my hair.

It was Katya who acted as my interpreter. Patiently, she steered me through the minefields of Russian conversation, repeating the others' questions for me slowly, and simplifying their vocabulary. Under her tutelage my Russian limped forward a little.

With Maxim, Olga's rather shy sixteen-year-old son, I returned the family compliment with some English practice. He had been taught entirely on paper, and it was slow work overcoming his reservations in spoken English. But when he saw me make a complete fool of myself in Russian a dozen times a day, he stopped worrying about his own slips and came on well.

For in reading and writing, his English was a mile ahead of my Russian. He showed me his school textbook, an old one dating from Soviet times. It gave no quarter to linguistic or ideological laggards. Among hymns to Soviet Heroes and Heroines, or comprehension texts on the All-Union-Lenin-Young-Communist-League, I read: "Why did the Manchester Working-men decide to send a delegation to Parliament?"

I hadn't the faintest idea, and turned over quickly before Maxim could ask me.

"Tell the class how the working people in Capitalist countries celebrate May Day, what slogans they carry in their demonstrations." I couldn't do these questions in English. What about the comprehension section? Surely I could manage that.

"Read the text and compare the situation in the USSR and Capitalist countries.

"To see the effect of pollution in rivers, look at the Thames... a hundred years ago you could catch eatable fish...

136

now factories are putting waste materials which are poisons into these rivers... (adapted from the British press)."

Adapted? Like hell! But my dented pride made it to its knees, for I could do this one. Hadn't I swum several times in the Thames, and survived to tell the tale? And after seeing the shockingly degraded Oxus near its delta, I was in an excellent position to compare. Better, at least, than an All-Union-Lenin-Young-Communist.

Maxim and Katya shared a room, which would be a surprising situation in the West. It was a big room, though, in a bigger-than-average flat. Olga's pay as a part-time receptionist was ten dollars a month, a fraction of what she had earned as a pharmacist before leaving work to start a family. But Sasha, a ground engineer at Ashkhabad airport, had a good, steady income. The result was extra space: three good rooms including a large living-room, separate bathroom and loo, a small ante-room to the kitchen, a conservatory *and* a veranda.

Life *chez* Olga was mostly carried out in the kitchen. Olga believed that everyone should eat as if about to set out across the Kara Kum by camel. After some weeks of travelling constantly and eating intermittently, I was strongly inclined to agree. The greatest luxury was access to kettle, teapot, and endless supplies of black tea. And when I discovered that I could buy tinned, condensed milk in the little market on the corner of the street, I was in heaven. The label read, "suitable for infants, convalescents or tourists". I wasn't sure what category I came under. But from then on, the incomparable Olga kept a tin constantly in her fridge. "Gill... *chai?*" became as constant a theme in the house as "Bim... *nelzya!* Stop it!" - or, for that matter, my own "*Russkii slovar...?*" as I scrabbled yet again for my dictionary.

I was propped at the kitchen table enjoying my twentieth cup of tea when the last member of the family arrived in the evening. Sasha was a sandy-haired man in his middle forties, with a long lean frame and a short fuse. A hint of the latter lay in the forbidding face; though not always so, for it could suddenly break from wintry reserve into a conspiratorial smile of rare charm, melting the ice-blue eyes.

137

He was not a family man, and strode about the flat with a restless energy that could only be satisfied out of doors. Born in another country, he might have been a Canadian wilderness guide, or an Australian stockman. He came and went at irregular hours from his shift work at the aerodrome. No sooner was he home than he would be out again, working at the plot on the city outskirts where he was building a *dacha*, or standing all night by the Kara Kum Canal, fishing.

On my second morning he came into the flat like a whirlwind, bearing a flush of triumph and a catfish two-thirds of his own considerable length.

"Only a small one," he said deprecatingly. "Until a few years ago we used to get them this big..." He held a hand level with the top of his head. And he was not the sort of man given to fisherman's tales.

The fish, still alive and writhing feebly, was put in a bath full of water. It stayed there for twenty-four hours, mournfully flapping its great gills, while Bim stood against the tub on his hind legs and dribbled over it, and Olga fretted that she couldn't have a bath. When I came home the next day it was gone, and the freezer was full. Olga produced deep-fried fish goujons for supper. They were delicious; but I could only think of the great sad, whiskery creature, captive for twenty-four hours while awaiting its inevitable end.

*

Down the phone wires, Sadiqmohammed Berdimohammedov's voice sounded rich and deep. I fleshed him out in my mind's eye: tall, solid, dependable, warm.

The figure that climbed out of the white Mercedes was unexpected. He was small and wiry, almost Italianate in appearance, with a slight air of arrogance. Under the courteous Central Asian welcome, a hint of boredom lurked in the corners of his otherwise blank eyes. I wondered if he thought it a waste of time to show his stable to a woman.

Sadiq was one of Turkmenistan's leading private breeders of Akhal-Teke horses. With the profits of a family business in wool and sheepskin, started under *perestroika* in 1985, he had bought and refurbished a former *Gosplemstantsia*, or Government breeding station, on the outskirts of Ashkhabad. Since 1991 he had built up a stud of thirty-five horses, with a further seventeen in training to race.

This was my first chance to find out about Turcoman horse -breeding at the sharp end. As we took the road west out of the city, Sadiq patiently bore my relentless interrogation. Like many, he wished to see more structure, more common purpose in the world of Akhal-Tekes. "We need to see breeders work together with the government to set up integrated breeding schemes. The old Soviet system had a different psychology. Now we, that is the breeders, need *power*!" Suddenly animated, he gesticulated passionately, both hands off the wheel. "Without power we can do nothing."

"Is the government too inflexible, too fixed to old ideas?"

This irritated him too. "Everyone criticises the government. Our system is better than any other. It gives help to those who need it. For example, the Central Bank gives low-interest, long-term loans..."

His stables were clean and well-kept, with conspicuous industry. Yet Sadiq, too, had his problems with feed. The stallions were all in fine condition, but his mares, housed loose in a large barn, felt the nationwide pinch.

"Terrible condition!" he shook his head in evident distress. "I brought that hay" - gesturing to a pile in the corner - "all the way from Tashauz: six hundred kilometres. It gave my horses colic. Twenty years I've been working with horses, and I've never seen such rubbish." Even private wealth couldn't conjure up feed where it simply didn't exist.

"Perhaps it's our own fault," he continued with disarming frankness. "Two years ago the government gave land to every horse owner - two hectares per horse. Perhaps we didn't make the right use of it."

But it wasn't that simple. "Water free, no tax for ten years. But nothing else. It takes time to improve it." Virgin desert, watered or not, wouldn't yield returns at once. And meanwhile, the cold winter, another late spring...

139

"All we need is five days at twenty-five degrees. Then the grass will grow."

"Everything is against you," I sympathised, and he nodded; then briskly changed the subject.

"Come on. I'll show you a real Akhal-Teke 'type'."

The big stallion was pale palomino, and Sadiq's pride and joy. Unbeaten on the racecourse, he now "had a leg"; but he would be fit, Sadiq asserted with confidence, for the big race in the autumn, the President's Cup.

"How will you treat the tendon?"

"There's a snake, a particular kind of snake. You dry it, grind it down, and feed it to the horse." I wondered if he was winding me up, but it got more credible. "Then there's a herb. You bandage the horse's leg with it, freshly each day, for a week. Afterwards, this leg won't break down again." He glared at me suspiciously, as if daring me to doubt him. "It's one of our traditional remedies. They used it on oxen in olden times."

On the way back to Ashkhabad, he unbent a little more. "You know," he said, "these horses are like a disease. There is no cure. Wherever I go, I ask, 'Have you got a hippodrome? Do you race horses there? Do you race *our* horses...?' "

*

Gasping, Olga pushed the heavy sofa into the corner.

" 'If you can't change your husband, change your furniture!'" She winked at me.

"Your turn next," I commented to Sasha. He scowled back.

Olga needed all the available space in the living room. The coming weekend, family and friends would arrive to celebrate Easter. Olga had joyfully converted, or reverted, to the Russian Orthodox faith after the ending of Communist restrictions. Among the works of Tolstoy and Pushkin on her well-stocked bookshelves was a two-volume Bible, published in Russia in 1991. A couple of posters of icons decorated her bedroom wall.

Easter, then, was special. Olga wouldn't go to the midnight service at the old church up the road, for she feared walking home alone late at night. But the Russian TV channel would carry the service from Moscow, complete with the fine unaccompanied choirs of the Orthodox Church.

Food was traditional: home-made yeast bread with currants, baked in a tall cylindrical tin and topped with icing; rich, sticky flans packed with dates and oozing syrup; *pelmeni*, or meat-filled dumplings; and, of course, eggs, hard-boiled and hand-painted in all the colours of the rainbow plus a few more for luck.

No work of any kind - not even taking a bath - was allowed on the day. So for two days beforehand Olga and the two children scrubbed the house spotless, and mixed and boiled and baked until the table sagged with food, ready for the guests. Unfortunately, the first hot weather of the year had arrived. With the oven on and the windows closed for the bread to rise, the temperature in the kitchen climbed steadily. Sweat poured, tempers frayed, voices were raised. Sasha retreated to the dacha, working until his back creaked in agony. Bim got under everyone's feet, now and again shrieking like a whoopee cushion as someone trod on him. Shut away at last on the veranda, he retaliated by methodically stripping the paper off the wall. For this misdemeanour he was locked in the loo, where he whimpered dismally until someone came to put it to proper use and accidentally released him.

The mountains, imitating Sasha, retreated glowering into cloud. "That means rain," said Olga. Then, as an afterthought, "or a dust storm." The dust storms that descend suddenly on Turkmenistan are infamous. But Easter Day dawned fine.

I spent the morning at the Hippodrome. The Akhal-Teke cognoscenti would be at the races. Increasingly convinced that I would have to hustle for myself in finding a horse, I wanted to make their acquaintance.

The "in" crowd of owners and trainers collected under the judges' box opposite the finish; on the rails, and in front of the barrier of armed police. To my good fortune Sadiq arrived just after me, driving directly up to the rails in the white Merc, and exchanged a familiar wave with me in front of the *militsianer* who was preventing the *hoi polloi* from polluting the course. I claimed an appointment, slid past before Authority had time to object, and joined the bigwigs.

Sadiq had a runner in the fourth race. It went to post looking a million dollars and broke like a greyhound, but after leading down the far straight it went backwards fast and finished last. The winning owners were a syndicate from a kolkhoz. They went beserk with delight, jumping up and down and thumping each other on the back. The jockey was hoisted shoulder high, a fistful of manats thrust into his hand. After a brief round of honour the horse was led away, a silk scarf fluttering from its neck.

And now my luck was in, for the country's leading private breeder arrived. I was anxious to meet Geldy Kyarizov, both for the reputed excellence of his stud, which I hoped to visit, and because he, more than anyone else, might be in a position to solve my transport problem.

Geldy was a tall man, with mild, almost lazy-looking eyes belied by a decisive expression and manner. Brazenly, I went up and introduced myself - no help here from the inscrutable Sadiq - and asked if I might come and see his bloodstock.

He was genuinely welcoming, giving me his undivided attention for a few moments. By the time he excused himself to watch his runner in the next race, he had made me feel that my impending visit might actually be a pleasure rather than a chore. His horse, like Sadiq's, looked stunning; and also came last. I hoped I wasn't putting a jinx on them.

The stables might be good for a spot of networking. After the last race I crossed to the far side of the course, where four barns the size of aircraft hangars accommodated the horses in training. Their lads lived in yurts or old railway carriages nearby.

There wasn't an owner in sight. But the walk wasn't wasted, for the trainers were friendly and informative. One of them took me to see his stable.

Khaliq was a real old pro, with a passion for Akhal-Teke horses and a pronounced limp. I didn't like to ask whether the first had been responsible for the second. With almost urgent enthusiasm he carried me off into the dark interior of the barn to show me a horse of the definitive "type", running over its important points and enjoying my interest. "We must preserve the 'type'," he declared emphatically, "...the type that generated the English Thoroughbred." Until recently, I would have disagreed with this last remark; for didn't everybody know that the world's fastest horse was descended from three Arab stallions? Now, I had learned enough to keep silent, while Khaliq went on to display an impressive knowledge of the English and American turf.

Like everyone else, he despaired of the current situation in which international competition and trade were impossible. "Only Ashkhabad Hippodrome to race on; no transport across Kazakhstan, war in the Caucasus..." Pyatigorsk, the nearest centre in Russia for racing, exhibiting and selling to international dealers but the far side of Chechnya, might as well now be on another planet. "When we could sell in Moscow, Kiev, Pyatigorsk, our horses made five thousand dollars, average. Now we're lucky to get two."

Outside, a dilapidated bus pulled up. A chattering crowd spilled out, kolkhozniks come to visit their horse. Half-past one; high time for me to be getting back for Olga's celebration meal at two. I couldn't find a taxi for love nor money. At five to two my nerve broke and I jumped on a bus. At five past I ditched it for a taxi. When at quarter past two I staggered up the stairs to the flat, the sweat was running off me from anxiety as well as haste, for I would no more willingly have dishonoured Olga's Easter pelmeni by keeping them waiting than I would have dared to offend my own mother's Christmas dinner. Maxim opened the door and I fell in, gibbering my apologies, waiting for wrath to descend.

There was no wrath. The family, too, had been delayed, and had only just now walked through the door. I was barred from helping, dispatched for a rapid wash; and actually got my bottom on to a chair thirty seconds before Olga did the same.

*

In referring to the "type" that generated the English Thoroughbred, Khaliq was speaking of a theory given little

143

house-room in the West, whose text-books attribute its ancestry almost exclusively to Arab horses.

More than three centuries ago the obsession of King Charles II with horse-racing gave a massive injection of interest to the sport. In a drive to improve English bloodstock, enthusiasts imported a number of oriental horses to inject lightness and speed into the heavier native breeds. The direct male lines of only three stallions survives: the Darley Arabian, the Godolphin Barb and the Byerley Turk.

Why "Turk" for the last one? At first glance this isn't so very significant. Ever since the Crusades, "Arab" and "Turk" had been used almost interchangeably. Often "Turk" meant "Moslem"; as for instance in the seventeenth-century Book of Common Prayer. This lack of clear definition carried over into the horse world, where any animal from the East, was thought sure to be some sort of Arab - or, "equivalently", Turk.

Was the Byerley Turk, then, so named through linguistic vagueness, or for a better reason? The answer may lie in its history.

The stallion was captured by Captain Byerley at the siege of Vienna by the Ottoman Turks in 1683 (the very last thrust of Central Asian peoples against the West). It is well documented that the Ottomans preferred Turcoman horses to Arabs as warhorses, although their Empire encompassed the breeding lands of both; and the Imperial Guard at Constantinople was exclusively mounted on Turcomans. So was Captain Byerley's "Turk" an Arab that had borrowed the name from its former Turkish owner, or was it really a Turcoman horse? Paintings of the stallion strongly indicate the latter.

And if so, how many others were there? The record books are full of "Turks". It is reasonable to suppose that their names reflected their origins more often than not.

Supporters of the Turcoman horse certainly argue thus. More, they contend that untold numbers of Turcoman mares were captured in successive wars, many finding their way to England. Concerned mainly with their stallions, the English often neglected to record the breeding and origins of their mares. But it has long been held in Turkmenistan that the Turcoman horse had far more influence over development of the English Thoroughbred than has ever been credited; more, indeed, than the Arab.

Romantic theory? No, because in recent years, it has been substantiated in the laboratory.

DNA analysis carried out by Dr. Gus Cothran, of the University of Kentucky, with the help of Iranian breeder Louise Firouz, indicates that the Turcoman horse may be the dominant ancestor of the Thoroughbred. More; that the Turcoman is the ancestor of most breeds of oriental horse, including the Arab itself.

This is incendiary stuff, threatening to overturn centuries of received wisdom. Analysis continues, but the hot money lies on the Turcoman horse emerging near the head of the family tree.

*

The flat was still full of Easter guests, and Sasha had cabin fever.

"Come on. I'll show you the dacha."

I needed no persuading. Having begged for Katya to come too ("Papa doesn't usually take us; he says we hassle him"), I set off with them in the family Moskvich.

Sasha had bought the car a couple of years ago, shortly after acquiring his plot of land very cheaply on a Niazov privatisation initiative. With 300,000 miles on the clock, it cost about thirty pounds. Now it would be ten times as much. "*Inflatsia*," he said resignedly.

The two were excellent city guides. "That's the Iranian shop... there's the American Embassy... that's the Philharmonia Hall" - a pretentious-looking building, now closed down - "where Katya used to take part in dancing exhibitions... See that installation? An Argentinian firm is digging for oil there."

Sasha took the Meshed road that leads directly through the mountains to Iran. Just before it curved uphill he turned off on to a broad carriageway of shiny, brand-new tarmac. A row of ostentatious hotels were in various stages of construction, their styles ranging from angular and plastic to the mock-up of a mosque. The first bore the alluring name "Candybil" in neon. A night in one of these, commented Sasha, would set you back several hundred dollars.

"Whoever has that sort of money?" Here, at any rate, I meant.

"Mafia, *narcoz*..." he said cynically.

"Drugs? From Iran, Afghanistan, I suppose?"

"And home produced." Not entirely a cotton monoculture, then.

First we would see a friend's dacha. He pulled on to a rough track leading up into the hills. "It's a toothache, this track! You see where it's green, with the grass coming? It'll be yellow in a couple of months. It reached 47° in Ashkhabad last summer."

Rais had built his own dacha in three years, singlehanded, on a plot given free to him as a war veteran. Afghanistan again? No, he had been lucky, doing his Army service in Russia. His wife Tatiana showed us round the house with pride. Sasha, who had been here many times, wanted a closer look at the construction; Katya and I, after a quick look round each room, hurried to the window and admired the view: this side, back over the city, the other, straight up to the mountains. From every ceiling dangled inert light fittings, or neatly bundled loose wires. So when did they expect electricity to be connected? "Oh, whenever!" answered Tatiana cynically.

No dacha is complete without its garden. Theirs was huge, and already producing onions and carrots under the fruit trees. All the beds were set several inches deep, ready for irrigation later in the year.

An excavated hole brought one side to an abrupt edge. "Lemons and orangery," explained Tatiana, and my thoughts of a swimming pool abruptly vaporised. "The sheds are for chickens - and down there we'll keep the pigs." Pigs? Yes, it seems there are a few in Central Asia, Moslem taboos notwithstanding. But only for private use. When Turkmenistan turned to Iran for trading relations, the Ayatollahs laid the law down. The result was a compromise: keep your pigs, but don't sell the meat or we don't want to know you.

The mountains were retreating into the dusk when we reached Sasha and Olga's own dacha - or, rather, would-be dacha, one of many half-constructed future homes on this stretch of land. Forget the wooden country *izba* of Chekhov's depiction, sitting romantically in an assart hewn from Siberian pine-forest. These were gaunt, concrete cubes, huddling behind coils of barbed wire on an open hillside of reclaimed desert. By definition, a dacha is a home beyond the confines of the city, with a large, productive garden. Above all, a self-sufficient garden. In these times of tight belts, many people who had never sown a seed or pulled a carrot were urgently hearing the call of the soil. The result was a heavy crop of dachas, springing from formerly barren land with that same frenzy of growth intended for their gardens.

Sasha's was so far less than a storey high. But it was all his own work, and he hid his evident pride under a dismissive modesty. "By the time it's finished, the kids will have grown up and left home, and it'll be just me and Olga living here!" But the garden, like Rais's, was already nursing infant vegetables and fruit trees, and Katya picked a spray of fragrant blossom which we sniffed in turns all the way home.

*

Geldy Kyarizov's yard, "Akhal-Yurt", lay in the Shor district, where Ashkhabad's northern suburbs fade into the desert. On the way there we passed a huge new mosque, in the final stages of construction. It isn't only the Russians in Turkmenistan who are rediscovering the faith of their fathers.

We turned off the main road past a circular arena with a high wooden fence. "That's where Geldy holds his dog-fights," said Yusup. This seemed a strange pursuit for a man who passionately loved horses; though it wasn't for sport, I reminded myself. I knew that the Turcomans deliberately train their great, brown-and-white "Ovcharka" shepherd dogs to fight off wolves, although I hadn't realised until now what such training would mean.

Contradiction sat lightly on Geldy. His immaculate dark suit and expensive loafers were made for city use, but he wore

147

them in his stables as comfortably as if they were jeans and boots. His heavy-lidded eyes looked lazy and inert, but flashed and glittered when he spoke of his horses, and after half an hour of warming to his theme they burned like black coals. "Akhal-Teke horses are his religion", Jonathan Maslow had observed. It was no exaggeration.

One by one he presented his best stallions, drawing the distinctions between three types: *sukhoi*, "lean" or, literally, "dry" (the latter word most appropriate, for it is the horses of this type which are most efficient in the heat of the desert); massive; and a third somewhere in the middle.

"You remember Absent?" - this was the horse that won Olympic gold for the USSR in dressage - "He was *massivnoi*; long, powerful movements." Geldy's stallion Yanardag[*] - "Volcano" - was an example of the "dry" type. The horse was golden dun with a metallic sheen, the classic Akhal-Teke colour, with the long back and lean frame typical of the breed.

Geldy clipped a lungeing rein to the headcollar and led the horse outside to the sand paddock. Handing Yanardag to a lad, he stepped back and pointed out the Akhal-Teke characteristics.

"The face should be long and dry" - that word again! - "...tapering both in width and breadth to the nostril. It shouldn't have a wide forehead, nor one that bulges, like an Arab. It should run straight, then back just a little, to the ears." He drew in the sand with a stick, to illustrate his point. "The shape of a ram's forehead. The eye should be bright, like a bird; the cheeks dry, little muscle; the ears should be clean inside, no long hairs, and they must not" - he shook his head emphatically - "they *must* not be short, like an Arab's, but long. Here is the proof that this horse is *kulturnoi* - not a horse of the herd, but one which has developed over a long time to have a close relationship with people.

"The classic Akhal-Teke," he continued, "appears to have a long back, but in fact it's quite short; the shoulder should slope right back..." - this accounted for the enormously long wither -

[*] Yanardag was subsequently gifted to President Niazov, and became a national symbol of Turkmenistan

Buzkashi

right
Vlad playing
chicken with a
cobra

below and bottom right
Geldy Kyarizov's champion stallion
Yanardag lives up to his name (Volcano)

Sasha and the catfish, with Bim in attendance

Olga prepares a feast (*photo by Maxim Briusov*)

Rep with Gerakle in the tamarisk grove

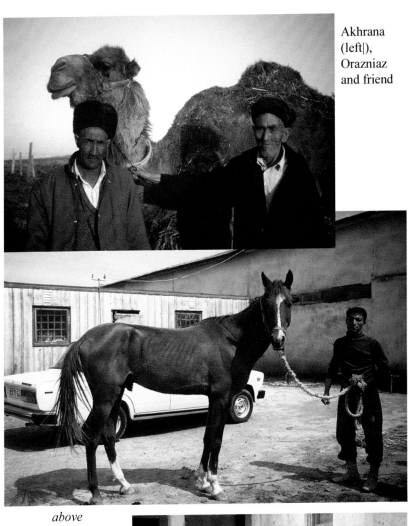

Akhrana (left|), Orazniaz and friend

above
First sight of Atamekan: Kako introduces us at the Hippodrome

Yalya (2nd left), Tokhtamurad (second left crouching), Rustam (with Kaan), and family

Aina's daughter Gulseren displays the silver and cormelian jewellery of a Turcoman bride

below
Aina aged sixteen
photo courtesy of Ainabat Annadurdieva

right
Younger daughter Sarai
photo taken in 2002

"...and the hip should be well forward. There is good bone; more, in fact, than the English Thoroughbred, though it doesn't appear to be so because the surrounding membrane is thinner. See the tail: it's thin. So, too, is the mane - another peculiarity of the breed." The description was fluent, practised, as one which had been given many times before. If so, familiarity would never dim its fervour.

Head up, the stallion danced with delight at escaping the confines of his stable, and even in the growing dusk the golden lights of his coat shone. Geldy compared him with the English Thoroughbred.

"In the first volume of the English Stud Book, you'll find this colour, this golden dun. Now, there's no colour like it; it's bred out.

"Of course, when you English were no longer interested purely in a warhorse, and started to breed for racing, to develop in fact a racing machine, you threw out every characteristic except..." he paused for emphasis, then finished softly, "speed.

"The Turcomans wanted speed, but they wanted also good movement, smoothness of pace, an elegant form..." As he spoke, the stallion, exulting in space and freedom, reared up on his hind legs until nearly vertical, raking the sky with his front feet. After a long minute of perfect balance he came to earth, then exploded again in a series of leaps.

"He's an athlete," I breathed in admiration.

"No." Geldy corrected me. "Your English Thoroughbred is an athlete. This horse..." he almost whispered "...This horse is a *dancer*!" The stallion moved across the heavy sand like thistledown, then rose again, higher than before.

"This type of movement allows the horse to cope with hot, dry conditions. The conformation allows him to move very lightly, allows economy of effort." Strength-to-weight ratio, in fact, the attribute so dear to climbers and long-distance runners.

The horse had now led his lad at speed to the far end of the paddock. Geldy gestured after him. "This is the pure, lean, 'type'. Look at the musculature, look at the fine legs." He spoke with the ardour of an Old Testament prophet.

"This isn't just a horse. This is is a work of art, an antiquity. And no museum piece. You can't just keep it in a glass case and look at it. It may die tomorrow or live for years. It's ever-changing..."

*

If it hadn't been for enthusiasts such as Geldy, the Akhal-Teke, possessor of some of the world's oldest equine genes, might have survived for several thousand years only to die out in the last century.

Finally defeated by the Russians at Geok Tepe, the Turcomans turned from slave trading to farming, and their horses became an anachronism. An idle luxury, almost; for, stripped of their usefulness, they were now kept only for racing. Yusup had described to me how, at a Turcoman wedding, the main attraction was the race between the bride's and groom's *a'uls* - villages - often tens of miles apart.

But outsiders, too, could appreciate the uniqueness of these horses. The preservation of the breed in the early years of Russian rule owed much, said Yusup, to the Mazan family, Cossacks who established the first stud at Ashkhabad. Rather than impose their own methods, the Mazans took pains to study the horsemastership of the local people.

The breed looked tolerably secure; but then the blow fell. Enter Lenin, with his decree on the breeding of livestock. Thou shalt not own thine own horse; all animals henceforth the property of the State, to be removed from the age-old expertise of local families and concentrated in collective farms or State studs. Scores of Turcomans voted with their feet, fleeing with their precious horses across the border to Iran. The Ashkhabad stud became the property of the Komsomol, the *Kommunisticheskii Soyuz Molodezhi* or Young Communists' League.

Worse was to follow, for the person of the State became vested in Marshal Budyonny of the Soviet Cavalry. He had his own ideas about the perfect cavalry horse, and the Akhal-Teke did not conform. He began to tamper with the breed, introducing other, heavier bloodlines, until by the 1930s few pure-breds remained. In a desperate attempt to prove the quality of their animals, the Turcomans staged their famous, 4,300 km ride from Ashkhabad to Moscow. Its effect was galvanic. For the first time the Russians properly recognised the extraordinary abilities of the Akhal-Teke, and began once again to breed pure.

But only temporarily. For now horses in general were rapidly becoming obsolete. Stalin, in his post-war drive to mechanise agriculture, wrote off horse-breeding entirely. From now on, horses were to be seen purely as fodder for sausage and glue factories. The Komsomol Stud was allocated its quota for horseflesh.

Such a fate for their horses was insupportable to the Turcomans. Many a horse was spirited from the breeding stations into the desert and released, to take its chance in the land that had given it birth so long before. Even today there are feral horses in the Kara Kum, many generations on from that most perilous of times.

But a few individuals were beginning to make their mark as sporthorses. Such was Arab*, showjumping champion in the USSR and Puissance record-holder. Such, also, as Arab's son Absent, the most prolific winner ever of Olympic Dressage medals.

Meanwhile Vladimir Petrovitch Shamborant, former *Direktor* of the Komsomol Stud and a champion of the Akhal-Teke, had established a breeding programme in Dagestan. His extraordinary knowledge of the breed now began to be sought.

In Turkmenistan, some of the feral horses were recaptured and breeding recommenced. From these fragile roots, the breed once again grew and prospered. By Shamborant's death in 1996 Akhal-Tekes were being bred throughout the former USSR, and significant numbers had reached the West. Their future was beginning to look secure.

*

* his name, not his breed!

I had a thousand questions, but Geldy was short of time. Before he hurried away, I begged a moment to outline my chief purpose here: to ride an Akhal-Teke horse along the ancient route from Nisa to Merv.

"Yusup has already told me your intention. In him, you have the best man to help you. There should be no problem."

"Yusup is very busy, and has not managed to find me a horse so far," I answered as diplomatically as possible, for Yusup was standing right next to me. "You have many contacts; might you know someone who could help?" If I could get this man interested in the project, I felt instinctively, doors would open.

Geldy's reply was courteous, but non-committal: he would be at the Hippodrome for the next race meeting, and would try to arrange some introductions then.

By then I would have returned from a brief excursion to western Turkmenistan. As I climbed the stairs to Olga's flat that night, I permitted myself a breath of cautious optimism.

Maybe, just maybe, the plan was going to work.

IX

After the submission of Khiva and the subsequent annexation of Kokand , only the Turcomans stood between Russia and her goal: total control of Western Turkestan. A few miles east of Ashkhabad the two sides met in the bloodiest battle so far.

It should have been a formality; an exercise by a modern army to mop up a few half-nomad savages armed only with scimitars and carbines. Perhaps General Lomakin was over-confident when in 1879 he attacked the concentrated power of the Teke Turcomans at their fort of Geok Tepe in the Akhal Oasis. The Tekes inflicted defeat on a scale Russia had not known in Central Asia since Peter the Great's attempt on Khiva nearly two centuries before, and would not know again until her ill-fated adventure in Afghanistan a century later.

Such a setback, such loss of prestige, couldn't be countenanced. When Russia again moved against Geok Tepe two years later, she was better prepared.

The walls of the old fortress were still clearly visible, despite time and Russian artillery. From the vantage point of the railway bridge I looked down on their perfect square, nearly a mile wide. In the nearest corner stood a gleaming new mosque, its turquoise dome and four slender minarets throwing back the sunlight. Memorial to the dead of Geok Tepe and the loss of Turcoman independence, it was a celebration, too, of the new freedom. Its surrounding wall was coincident with the line and height of the old mud brick, complete with parapet. All about, where once the yurts of the assembled Tekes had stood, vines now grew. Herds of sheep and goats browsed among them.

It was a scene of absolute tranquillity. It was as if the place had forgotten that, not so very long ago, some twenty thousand Turcomans had fought and died there.

*

153

In attacking the Turcomans, Russia had more in mind than just control of a few thousand square miles of desert.

She gave the pretext which had served her well before: the Turcomans must be "pacified", so as to put an end to their barbaric habits of raiding and slave-trading. It was convenient to forget that Russia herself had finally outlawed slavery less than twenty years before.

The real aim, though, was to complete the subjugation of Central Asia; moreover - in the minds of many, if not in admitted foreign policy - to create a springboard from which to threaten India. From a foothold on the eastern Caspian shore, Russia had begun construction of a railway, the future Trans-Caspian Railway. If this could be pushed across southern Central Asia to link up with Tashkent, the fearsome deserts which had hitherto provided the British with a buffer would now be an irrelevance, for troops could be brought straight up to the borders of Afghanistan. Already General Kaufmann, sitting polishing his bayonet in Tashkent, had prepared an invasion plan to send thirty thousand troops to India should Britain and Russia - who were just now glowering at each other across Constantinople - declare war. In the event they did not; but should a future opportunity arise, Kaufmann intended to be ready to take it. But first the Turcoman problem must be addressed.

The man sent to dispatch them was one of the best soldiers in Russian history. Newly arrived in Central Asia after victories in the Turkish wars, General Mikhail Skobelev was an ardent supporter of the "forward" school of military thought, which saw Turkestan as but a stepping-stone to India. "Otherwise," he said, "the hide is not worth the tanning, and all the money sunk in Turkestan is lost."

A larger-than-life figure who scented his beard and set off his habitual white uniform with a diamond-hilted sword and a white horse, Skobelev was known to his men as *Ak Pasha*, the White Lord. To the Turcomans he was "Old Bloody Eyes". His views on subduing restless natives were uncompromising: "The harder you hit them, the longer they stay quiet afterwards."

Outstripping the railway, which hadn't yet reached Kyzyl Arvat, Skobelev brought up eleven thousand men and heavy artillery in readiness for the return match at Geok Tepe. Swiftly taking position on a nearby hill, he settled down to lob a steady stream of shells, some of them petrol-filled, on to the town's main fortress, into which the Tekes had withdrawn along with their families.

For three weeks the Tekes resisted the bombardment, making one or two sorties and capturing a couple of guns and some prisoners. They even found the time to beat off a raid on a nearby Teke village, launched by an opportunist Kurdish Khan who reckoned, to his misfortune and the death of all his men, that the Tekes already had their hands full. But they couldn't fight off the Russian guns for ever. Nor, when Skobelev began to mine their walls, could they guess what was happening. The infidels, they scoffed, were rooting into the ground with their snouts, like pigs.

The end came on 24th January 1881, when the Russians blew a great hole at the south-east gate and streamed into the fort. Watching the ensuing massacre was a young Irishman, who had spent the last three weeks sitting on a nearby mountain, field glasses in hand. Edmond O'Donovan was a correspondent for the London Daily News, and afterwards described the rout in his classic book *The Merv Oasis*.

"A crowd of horsemen began to ride in confusion from the other side of the town, and spread in flight over the plain. Immediately afterwards, a mass of fugitives of every class showed that the town was being abandoned by its inhabitants. The Turkoman fortress had fallen, and all was over with the Akhal-Tekkes."

The slaughter inside the walls and over the surrounding desert resulted in an estimated twenty thousand dead. Enthusiastically joining in what might today be described as a turkey shoot were Yomud Turcomans, old tribal enemies of the Tekes; also vengeful Kurds, "abroad," said O'Donovan, " like flocks of seagulls in troubled waters, seeking what they could pick up".

Even by the standards of the day the bloodshed was excessive. That was the official account of why Skobelev was relieved of his command; although there were those who reckoned that it was because he nursed dangerous political ambitions. For whatever reason, his next posting was to a military backwater. He died eighteen months later from a heart-attack in a brothel. Always reputed to pursue danger and women with equal ardour, he hadn't perhaps expected to flirt with both at the same time.

As for O'Donovan, his greatest adventure was yet to come.

*

The breach is gone now, its place filled by the courtyard walls of the new mosque. For a century the only memorial here was to the 268 Russian dead. A few years ago, someone smashed it to rubble.

Olga, fretting that I was setting off to my ultimate destination of Kyzyl Arvat with no accommodation, had sent me off doubly well equipped: with an Olga-sized lunch of four large meatballs and half a loaf which kept me going for the next twenty-four hours; and a priceless piece of advice. "If you need information, or help of any sort, ask at the *Hakimlik*. Every town, every village has its *Hakim*." - or, roughly, mayor. It was advice which stood me in good stead over the next few days, and even more so the next few weeks.

Strolling through the vineyards, I ate my lunch sitting on the far walls. They were almost perfectly preserved here, furthest from the present-day town, rising to their full height of twelve feet and complete with battlements and ditch. Could the potential of mud brick to survive be in inverse proportion to its nearness and accessibility to small boys? The odd strand of sagging barbed wire was enough to deter grazing animals from climbing all over it. Outside the wall three carefully tended mausolea, each just a small cube topped by a dome, honoured the memory of Teke leaders. Inside, close to the north-west corner, rose the ancient city-mound called Denzil Tepe, the original site of settlement.

I looked past the new mosque to the mountains behind. Impossible to believe, on this peaceful day with the first butterfly of spring drinking from a few early flowers among the vines, such Beau Geste scenes of confusion and carnage, to imagine the thunder of the guns and the screams of terror, the reek of blood and cordite. Yet only just over there, Skobelev's men had poured through the broken wall to deliver death and conquest, while all around where I sat now fighting men, women, children, the old, the animals, all fled in panic or died in flight. For many, their last sight would have been these mountains, serene and beautiful with their snow-capped peaks, looking down on them as indifferently as they now looked on me.

*

Back across the railway bridge I jumped on the first bus travelling west out of Geok Tepe, a rattling old charabanc going only as far as Bacharden. I would have done better to wait, for after five minutes it was overtaken by a sleek coach - the last through bus to Kyzyl Arvat.

Every few hundred yards along the road were patriotic slogans on billboards, spattered with exclamation marks. Most bore the name of Niazov; those with fresh paint were signed Sapurmurat Turkmenbashi, in the new style rendering the person of the president inseparable from his office.

West of Geok Tepe, the natural resources of the Akhal Oasis began to outstrip those of irrigation. A succession of streams, boiling with thick, brown water, carved deep chasms through the sandy waste to feed a large reservoir north of the road. On the verges, patches of grass were at last beginning to grow. I hadn't long to find a horse. The shortage of animal feed meant that I would be heavily dependent on natural grazing; and when spring finally arrived, it wouldn't stay long in Turkmenistan before the fierce summer sun burned off all that grew. This urgency, more than my desire to see western Turkmenistan, was the main reason for my trip to Kyzyl Arvat. Here was the territory of the Yomud Turcomans. One or two breeding farms

157

hereabouts housed what was left of the Yomud strain of the Turcoman horse. If I couldn't get hold of an Akhal-Teke, it might be possible to hire or even buy a Yomud.

The rattling bus dropped its passengers at Bacharden and went off to expire somewhere private. No more buses would leave that day, said the stallholder already packing up at the small rinok; but there would be a train to Kyzyl Arvat in three hours, he added soothingly. So I waited with the slowly-growing crowd by an old station building dating back to the early days of the Trans-Caspian Railway, until the Tashauz - Krasnovodsk express arrived.

West of Bacharden, the farmland receded and the desert gradually closed in. Lack of water wasn't the cause, for deep pools lay on the surface, and the stretch of ground by the track, deeply cracked like crazy paving, glistened with wet mud. A goods train of some thirty wagons passed, heading east. Each truck was full of sand. Some smart dealer, who could sell sand from one end of the Kara Kum to the other.

Above, the last blue skies of a cloudless afternoon gradually faded. Out to the south the mountains, in a separate climate, bore their own personal wreaths of mist. The express limped with agonising slowness into a pink sunset which rapidly outpaced it to the west. When the last light faded, the sky filled with brilliant stars.

We crawled into Kyzyl Arvat at ten. I remember little save the length of the train as it pulled past me out of the station, and the pot-holes of streets even worse than usual. Perhaps it wasn't wise to ask the taxi-driver for the cheapest hotel, for I ended up in a truckers' hostel behind the bus-station. The kindly caretaker gave me tea, and found me a bed in an empty dormitory.

It was an iron bedstead with a single blanket, and one sheet which had obviously been used many times before. As I went to sleep on it fully clothed, the dust of Geok Tepe and the dirt of the train still on me, I had no cause to worry about hygiene. My successor would get the worst of the bargain.

*

158

The Hakimlik stood in a garden graced by a marble bust of the president, and more so by the full flush of spring. Fresh new leaves, a generous burst of blossom and rich growth underneath; momentarily I yearned for home and an English spring, as my eyes devoured the unaccustomed greenery.

A huge Turcoman carpet hung on the wall behind the Hakim, Niazov's face woven into it. A slogan on his desk exhorted the people to Work Together For Ten Years' Prosperity. The owner of these talismans was anxious to get rid of me, and palmed me off on to a subordinate.

Atashka was friendly and helpful. Yes, he knew where to find the government stud breeding Yomud horses. Better, he could fix me up with a jeep, driver and escort. Full marks once again to Olga, I thought, as we set off for the village of Purnuar in the Kopet Dagh foothills.

Plunging into the hills, the road cut through a cleft coarsely driven into rock. To one side the mountain ridge seemed softened by time, its bare bones covered with scree and even grass; but to the other it rose and fell harshly in great pleats, just as it had been forced up and out of the crust of the earth only a few thousand years ago - a geological nanosecond. The valleys that creased it were filled with silt scraped off by time and weather; silt through which the river courses bit deep as they raced down to water and fertilise the plain below.

The Yomud herd was quartered in a big square yard, with covered barns down two sides. Of the eighty horses some thirty were kept here, while the rest grazed out on the mountain. They were bony, though not so painfully thin as many I'd seen.

Could these horses possibly be related to the Akhal-Teke? Much smaller, they lacked the charisma of their cousins. Heavy heads, thick necks, straight shoulders, more growth of mane and tail, ears shortish... nothing eye-catching. Yet Conolly, travelling through the lands of the Yomud and Göklen Turcomans in the 1830s, gave a glowing description of their horses, similar to those of the Tekes except for coarser heads. Perhaps these Yomuds, the poor relations among Turcoman horses, had been allowed to become degraded through careless breeding, through absence of any selection for "type". If the

159

attitude here was anything to go by, that was certainly what had happened.

"What are the typical Yomud characteristics?" Ahmed, my escort, put the question in Turcoman, but everyone shrugged.

"So how do you plan your breeding programme?"

"There is no selective breeding here."

"Does the farm pay its way?" This was my chance to slip in the question I had wanted to ask: how much are these horses sold for? Though it was academic. The Yomuds were too small for my purpose. They might be able to carry me for a bit, but not the saddlebags as well.

The farm didn't pay, Ahmed translated. At local prices, the horses were worth only an average 500,000 manats, about £125. Now if the stud could be partially privatised, injecting a bit of enthusiasm, there was scope for improvement - and the necessary selective breeding.

As we left, we had an invitation from a man who had joined the group in the yard. Would we like to see a Yomud racehorse?

He took us up to the village, half a mile away under a rough granite ridge. Disappearing into an orchard, he came back riding bareback on a Yomud stallion bigger and stronger than any at the government farm. Dun verging on bay, with the suggestion of a dorsal stripe, the horse stood over fifteen hands. Although it was only from on top that I realised he was bigger than he looked, because he, too, was thin. At the owner's invitation I rode him briefly through the orchards, and found his paces long and comfortable - except for the thin backbone, which dug in like a knife. He was surefooted, too; after I had dismounted he hopped away quickly despite both forelegs being tightly hobbled.

Quite soon, April 28th, was the National Day of the Horse, said his owner. There would be races here, and his stallion would be running. But not over short distances, as the Akhal-Teke. The Yomuds raced over nine, ten kilometres.

It would take enormous stamina to race over such a distance. One Turcoman characteristic, it seemed, had survived in the otherwise degenerate Yomud.

*

160

Mrs. Atashka was a supervisor at one of Kyzyl Arvat's two carpet factories, and took me along next morning for a visit.

The factory consisted of several large rooms, bare except for the looms. What might have been a Dickensian scene of near slave labour was brightened by the rainbow costumes and animated chatter of the girls. They sat cross-legged on the carpet itself, shoulder to shoulder in a tight-packed row, tying threads to a complicated pattern at dazzling speed. One or two kept an exercise book before them with a diagram of colours and shapes, but most worked from memory. Under their fingers a seemingly random jumble of colours transformed itself into an intricate pattern on the rug slowly growing behind them. Every few rows they dropped the wool, picked up heavy wooden combs and beat to a simultaneous rhythm, packing the threads tight; then trimmed the pile with long scissors before resuming their synchronised threading.

Sometimes the loom was vertically strung before a window, giving the workers the double advantage of good light and a more comfortable posture. Even then, the most experienced team managed only an inch or two a day, so that a carpet five metres by four takes eight girls three months to complete - around four thousand working hours.

In the last room, teenage beginners worked on small rugs. Unlike the other ladies, who tightened their headscarves primly when I took photographs, these kids whipped theirs off altogether, running their fingers hurriedly through their loose hair for the camera.

Time to go, for the jeep driver was coming at two to take me to Iskender, a village well out on the Krasnovodsk road where some kolkhozniks kept a private string of Yomud racehorses.

There was no sign of the jeep. Ahmed and Atashka finally ran it to earth at the home of the driver, who emerged from under a raised bonnet with a spanner in each hand and no sense of urgency. It was decision time, for the last bus back to Bacharden left at three. I took a chance on the jeep, not so much for the lure of the horses as the tingle factor in the name of their village. Iskender is the Arabic form of Alexander. How long ago, I wondered, did somebody stamp his name on a place where he had probably never been?

The jeep left at ten past three, made it to Iskender, and irrevocably broke down. Fortunately we were within two hundred yards of the kolkhoz, and Ahmed and I went visiting while the driver sighed and picked up his spanners again.

The kolkhoz possessed a number of racehorses, both Yomud and Akhal-Teke, in training for the races on the National Day of the Horse. They were in excellent shape, the best-kept horses I'd seen outside the Ashkhabad Hippodrome.

They were tethered under cover in a wide lean-to. The day was warm, yet they wore the thick rugs that the Turcomans have used on their horses since time immemorial. First came a felt saddle pad, then the rug itself, also of felt with a jute outer and a tongue completely covering the neck. Just so stood the early Turcoman horses picketed outside their owners' yurts, well wrapped against the bitter winter winds that come straight from Siberia across the Kazakh steppe.

Their descendants shared this yard with outsized combine harvesters, drums of fuel, piles of firewood and all the bits and pieces of a working farm. But the horses obviously came first, and half the kolkhoz turned out to join us.

In fact the farm was no longer *kollektivnoi*, or a state-owned collective, but *kooperativnoi*, still a shared venture but in private ownership. Such an arrangement was becoming increasingly common under the new system, where state loans on easy terms allowed workers to buy their own land. Often, people joined together to buy as a syndicate, combining long-term experience of co-operation with the benefits of ownership. It was a process that seemed to work well, providing a manageable stepping-stone to individual private enterprise. Certainly it appeared to have been good for this kolkhoz; for some smart new houses were going up, solidly block-built and with ornate shiny roofing that made me think of Victorian public lavatories.

Behind Iskender the mountains rose immediately, breaking in the pass to Iran which, the villagers told me, was the reason for Alexander Makedonskii coming this way. One declared that he had stayed here; another denied it. It is likely that he never came within a hundred miles of the place, but the name was a further proof of how widely he was esteemed in these parts, how his memory lingered.

The jeep was still quite dead. Somebody gave us a tow back to the main road, where we joined a small group of people waiting to hitch a lift to Kyzyl Arvat. The only other vehicle in sight was a stationary lorry. Our driver wandered over to check it out, but came back shaking his head. After five minutes another lorry appeared and towed the first one away. There was something in the water of Iskender, apparently, that the internal combustion engine just couldn't swallow.

It was a familiar situation. This was by no means the first time I had sat beside a defunct vehicle on a road in Central Asia, waiting for something to happen. We were a mixed group; the rather despondent driver, a couple of ancients in Teke hats and long beards, and a few hangers-on. With all the time-wasting over the jeep, the hour was now late and traffic was thin. So we sat and sat, becalmed in this lonely spot under the mountains where Alexander the Great once passed by. Or probably didn't.

We got a lift at last, and at seven I was sitting by the road out of Kyzyl Arvat hoping for another one to Bacharden. But the roads were now almost empty, and the few vehicles that passed didn't stop. To wait or not to wait? I would give myself a definite term, I decided; on the dot of seven-thirty I would head back into town for the night.

With time running out, a solitary lorry appeared after a long gap. With little hope I again stuck out my thumb. To my amazement the driver slowed down and began to pull over.

As I ran for the cab I glanced at my watch. There were just fifteen seconds to go.

*

Rechem and his brother Kurban were on their way to a wedding in Ashkhabad. "My *bratishka*, my little brother, is getting married," said Rechem.

As he turned the big lorry back on to the road, the light was fading. A glorious sunset unrolled itself behind us, and the hills

163

slowly sank into a pink haze. A jackal slunk furtively across the road on the way to its nocturnal hunting grounds; its high shoulder and hunched rear end made it look like an oversized flea.

How was life in England? they wanted to know. The questions were the ones I had learned to expect. How much was a kilogram of bread? Of meat? Did I know that the average month's wage here was equivalent to three kilograms of meat?

"What would this lorry be worth in England?" asked Rechem. I had no idea, but told him I had paid about four thousand dollars for my little Bedford van when it was three years old.

"You know, in Ashkhabad they sell vans like that - second hand - for five or six thousand dollars." He turned to me with a curiously patient smile. "How can we possibly afford something like that on our wages?"

Abruptly, he veered off the rather dismal subject. "Can you drive?... but I bet you've never driven a left-hand-drive!" "Oh, yes, I have!"

"Come on, then!"

And the next thing I knew, I was making my way along the eastward road behind the wheel of a ten-ton truck.

At Bacharden, Rechem gallantly refused to dump me in a lay-by, insisting on driving me into town to find the hotel. First, however, after a quick exchange in Turcoman, he dropped Kurban off by the roadside "for a smoke", he explained innocently. It was the first warning that Rechem had decided to try his luck.

Unerringly guiding the monstrous vehicle one-handed through tiny streets, he tried to pull me to him with an arm round my shoulders.

Turcoman weddings are earthy affairs. Rechem's thoughts were running ahead of time. "What's a girl like you travelling alone for?" he whispered in his most seductive voice, the question already answered in his own mind.

"I prefer horses to men!" I assured him with a laugh. "I find them more reliable!" He was running out of time, for directions to the hotel were now coming thick and fast, and he accepted defeat with a good grace.

I knew he wouldn't take money for the lift. But he had gone out of his way to look after me, at least partly out of altruism, and had given me an entertaining ride. I wanted to pay my way, and worked out how I might do so without offending him.

"For the wedding," I insisted as he refused the notes I tried to put into his hand. "Get your bratishka a present from me!" He couldn't turn them down on someone else's behalf and accepted without embarrassment, tossing the notes into the glove compartment without looking at them. I hoped that he would be pleased rather than offended when he discovered that they were dollars, not manats; and felt most uncomfortable that so few of them, no more than a taxi fare to me, were to him a fortnight's wage.

*

The night caretaker at Bacharden's hotel looked like the archetypal fierce Russian matron. Underneath she was a pussycat. Tenderly she fed me bread and a hard-boiled egg (for Easter, she said, though Easter was a week past), and found me some sugar for my tea.

The *Mikhmankhana* was, like the hotel at Kyzyl Arvat, more of a truckers' hostel, though with separate rooms instead of dormitories. It wasn't the most comfortable bed or the quietest of mornings, but fourteen hours horizontal wasn't to be accepted without gratitude. When I finally emerged at a very late hour, I found my friend of last night replaced by an even sweeter person.

Tamara Feodorovna Ovezova was a gentle and cultured lady, small and birdlike, a Sybil Thorndike in dapochki. She would not let me leave without breakfast, feeding me excellent bread she had baked herself - "You can't buy decent bread here. It's rubbish, so I make my own" - and then kindly walked me all the way to the bus station.

Tamara Feodorovna had been around. Born in Tomsk, she had met her first husband, a Turcoman, in Armenia. When she came home with him, she found herself the only Russian in a village of Turcomans.

"It made no difference. They made me completely welcome. They're good people here, such good people."

She had a step-daughter by her first marriage, and a daughter by her second, this time to a Russian. She had lost both husbands, and now her step-daughter pressed her to go and live with her family in Ukraine.

"But I prefer it here, because of the people. They're good people, so it's a good land."

We said goodbye at the cheap and cheerful bazaar, where I got apples and directions. A bus-ride and a lift later I was at my destination.

*

Bacharden is famous for the subterranean lake nearby, where hot sulphur springs feed a natural reservoir deep under the foothills of the Kopet Dagh. For a few manats you can descend by iron steps far into the roots of the mountain, and swim. But today the cave entrance was closed, the gate padlocked.

A group of young men, lounging and smoking on a divan under some trees, spoke to me in English. They were Russian engineers, with two days to spare after finishing a job, and spending one of them here.

"The lake's closed," they told me. "No lights. They've shut off the electricity in the village."

A whole day wasted. I let fly with a violent expletive.

"Exactly - shit," one of them agreed tolerantly, and I reddened. I had several more weeks in Turkmenistan; they, one day.

But the afternoon sunshine was glorious, the mountains seductively beautiful. Behind the cave entrance was a long, sweeping ridge. No, I decided; too far, and too high. I would settle for the small hill immediately above the cave.

Its top was a perfect arête, where you reached up to a sharp spine to look directly down the other side. The whole was a long rib protruding from the main ridge and linked to it by a couple

166

of switchback passes. It was very tempting, and who knew how long the light repairs would take...

Meanwhile, the walk was a delight, with red tulips flowering thickly underfoot, and white puffy clouds floating through a blue sky. As I gained height the further mountains slowly opened out before me like flowers in the sun; line upon line of crinkled ridges stretching up and away to the snowline, and Iran.

There was only one drawback. "Don't forget," Sasha had said as I left for Kyzyl Arvat, "the snakes will just be waking up." He wasn't the only one. "Look out for snakes," said both the other walkers I passed on the way. Instead of admiring the scenery I nailed my gaze to the ground ahead, on any possible cover, on cracks in the rocks, telling myself fiercely to concentrate... always, always careful where you put your hands and feet. Cobras lived in these mountains, I knew, and the knowledge made for excellent concentration.

But when I did finally come face to face with a living creature, it was only - in this high, dry place - a frog. Later, I found a very small snake, curled into a bulls-eye spiral and blissfully asleep. I stepped over carefully, and it didn't even know I'd been there.

There was plenty of bird life up here, though: ravens, black and white wheatears, rock martens and pipits. A couple of hoopoes postured on the rocks ahead, and a cuckoo sang almost in my ear. Further up, a steppe eagle slowly quartered the hillside. Perhaps that was what kept the cobras at home.

From the pass, where I'd intended to turn back, the main ridge was irresistibly close. Just here was a reminder of how these mountains are constantly heaving under pressure from below. A wide crack ran along the exact centre of the ridge, visible in retrospect right back up the arête to the local peak I'd just left. At the lowest point it was a broad trench, filled in with sand and loose rubble. Would this be two separate mountains in a millennium or ten?

The top was a pleasant stroll over a rounded summit speckled with tulips. The highest hill hereabouts, it gave a wonderful vantage point. To the left, rolling, rugged peaks led the eye gently up to the high snows; to the right, but for the rib I had just ascended... nothing. A landscape without feature, almost without colour, on which dim green patches ran out into even dimmer yellow desert, which in turn ran out into a colourless haze. Over in the distance the Geok Tepe reservoir winked blearily.

An iron tetrapod marked the peak. Rusty, like all Turkmenistan's iron, it seemed almost an insult. I wouldn't even grow my runner beans up it, I thought as I regarded it with disgust. Yet even this eyesore had scraps of cloth tied to the legs, making into a sort of symbolic obo. It was a reminder that these mountains divided the Turks of desert and steppe from the Indo-European peoples of the settled lands.

There could be no hanging about on the way down. I'd been much slower than I'd intended, and it was now nearly six. I was afraid the lad at the till, who was looking after my bag, would pack up and go home.

The downward slope was soft earth, dotted with chamomile and punctured by thousands of evil-looking holes, about the diameter of a snake. My feet sank three inches into the ground at every step. My scalp prickled, and I was thankful to find a slab of solid rock leading to the bottom.

I came round the corner of the hill peering anxiously ahead. The gate to the cave was open.

*

The stairway led deep into the belly of the mountain. The descent felt like the start of a caving expedition, but for two things: the steamy warmth drifting up from below, and the choking smell of sulphur.

From high in the ceiling of the cave came the throbbing noise of pigeons, a troglodyte colony nesting in the rock crevices. At first they were the only noise I could hear; but as I went deeper and the passage narrowed, distant voices began to echo from the chamber at the bottom. Quite a relief; lights or no, it would be rather daunting to swim on my own.

168

I counted 263 steps. At the bottom a concrete landing stage ended in stairs down to the pool, which stretched away from dim electric lighting into total darkness. Very strange, having walked right over this mountain, to be now right underneath it.

The water embraced me with warmth and welcome. It wasn't, as I'd expected, a chilling underground lake with unimaginable slimy demons, but a comfortable warm bath which stroked your fears away. My hesitation gone, I swam to the edge of the light and round the corner of the cave into darkness, then trod water and looked back.

The rocky wall was gently defined against the low light. On the water surface below, beams flickered like phosphorescence on the faint ripples sent out by the other two bathers, diffused by a ghostly blanket of steam. It was a scene from the Creation; the smoke of life-giving substances arising from the primordial soup.

There were two more pools, said the other two swimmers, and water all the way to Iran. I would have given my eye teeth for a caving lamp, and a stronger nerve.

But when I had finally limped back up all those stairs, on rubber legs, to the entrance, I couldn't suppress the caver's delight at returning from the dark up to light and air.

*

Sitting by the road hoping for a lift, I noticed how the grass was really beginning to grow. Sadiq had been right; it was astonishing what a difference four days of warm weather had made. The wheat was shooting up, and the grass was already in flower. Suddenly, the landscape was turning green; and my eyes, starved for so long of vegetation, greedily ate up every blade of grass, every new leaf.

More to the point, there was now enough growth by the roadside to feed a horse at least partially, so that I would not be totally dependent on scanty and unpredictable feed supplies. I began to think that, whatever Aleksandr might say, the ride to Merv should be possible.

169

When I got back to the flat, it was like coming home. Maxim opened the door with a broad smile; Olga, beaming at my exclamations of hunger, rushed into the kitchen to prepare a laden table; and Bim peed on the floor in welcome.

X

Sunday, and race day; the day I was to meet Geldy Kyarizov. I went to the Hippodrome brimming with hopeful expectations. Geldy wasn't there.

There was nothing for it but to try again for Yusup's help. I met him in the Florida Cafe, a new neon-light-and-plastic-counter affair in down-town Ashkhabad modelled on MacDonald's, with the girls at the counter dressed in green baseball caps and the food served in plastic trays.

I suborned Yusup with a couple of chocolate eclairs oozing fake cream, then asked him bluntly whether he could find me a horse or not. It was time to abandon polite, oblique negotiations, Central Asian style, for some good western straight talking. I said exactly what sort of horse I wanted, for how long, and what I could pay. As an extra incentive I threw in my saddle; for, guessing at a shortage of tack in Turkmenistan, I'd brought my own. Here, even racehorses were sometimes ridden in no more than a felt pad. A good saddle was rare, a powerful bargaining chip.

Yusup assured me that he would find me a horse. I'd heard that before; but today he spoke positively. Perhaps my appeal to Geldy, in front of Yusup himself, had galvanised him. He wrote some notes and promised to ring round his friends right away.

It couldn't be soon enough. I had meant to be on the road by now.

*

When he rang the following morning it was about something quite different.

"I need you urgently. Meet me at the Foreign Office."

Yusup had discovered that, as well as registering with the authorities twice, once at Tashauz and again on my return to Ashkhabad, I should have registered yet again - this time with the police in Ashkhabad. Of course, no-one had mentioned this on either previous occasion. Now, I was about to be highly unpopular with Officialdom.

With typical Turkmen treacle-bureaucracy, the matter took four days to sort out.

Day 1: Go to the Police Station, wait for hours, get a form, go to the bank (two blocks away), queue interminably, pay a fee, get a stamp on the form, come back to find the Police Station closed all afternoon.

Day 2: Return to the Police Station, get wrists slapped, receive a fine - mercifully very small, with Yusup exercising all his charm ("the man on duty was a Teke, like me") - take paperwork to a different bank, also two blocks away, queue interminably, pay fine, get a stamp on the form, come back to find Police Station closed for lunch, return afternoon, get further form to complete in duplicate, don't come back today.

Day 3: Police Station closed all day.

Day 4: Return, get final stamp, breathe huge sigh of relief and suppose (wrongly) that correct documentation has now been given in full.

As if it wasn't enough to fine me for the negligence of the previous authorities I'd registered with, they also had the brass to fine Yusup for contamination through knowing me. (A fine which of course I paid.) He had kindly, through the Akhal-Teke Association of Turkmenistan, underwritten my application for a visa; for without a formal "invitation" from a local organisation, visitors may only stay in the country for three days. I noticed it was Yusup's name, not mine, on the official receipt. I only hoped I hadn't got the poor chap a criminal record.

The good news, he announced almost casually the second morning, was that he had found me a horse. For some reason I couldn't see it yet, but it cheered up a dreary morning sitting outside Ashkhabad nick.

For one of the complications of this crazy pantomime was that suppliants weren't allowed actually to enter the Police

172

Station. You simply announced that your attendance was required inside, then joined a dismal crowd of others kicking their heels for, often, the best part of a day, until summoned to the Presence. As I sat on the pavement on the second afternoon, wondering if I would get to ride this horse before being thrown out of the country for Conduct Unbecoming, a pompous policeman approached.

"Get up! Go away! You can't wait there!" You're not allowed to wait inside; you're not allowed to wait outside; but you're not allowed *not* to wait somewhere, or you get collared for lack of the fruits of all this waiting: the Bureaucratic Stamp.

I came home to the flat in a foul and voluble mood. Maxim was sympathetic, but surprised that I was surprised. He shrugged his shoulders.

"But what do you expect? This is Turkmenistan!"

I sounded off instead to Olga in a litany that was by now becoming habitual. "Look at the opportunities for tourism here! The government could make a fortune from foreigners. Instead it fends off people with a bargepole!"

Olga was equally exasperated. "Take Krasnovodsk, for instance. It's got the sea, the mountains, a wonderful climate... Yet when you go there, there are absolutely no facilities for visitors, nothing but factories and refineries. You can't even buy an ice-cream!"

It was the old Soviet maxim: don't encourage people to move around, or they might get to like the idea. It was profoundly depressing to find the view so firmly planted that it still flourished in the post-Communist era.

So the only industries which thrive are those whose purse-strings the government can best keep under tight control: cotton, gas, oil - all intended for export, all bringing in precious foreign dollars through official channels, which can be more or less discreetly tapped.

And although the first of these was still the mainstay of the economy, it was on the latter two that the government moguls pinned the best hopes for their old age.

*

Turkmenistan has been in the oil business longer than most. The thirteenth century geographer Muhammed ibn Najib Bekran mentioned oil being extracted in leather bags from shallow wells in the Nebit Dagh area just east of the Caspian Sea. But already the lands bordering the Caspian had been known for their oil for nearly two millennia.

The first deep well here was sunk in 1876, when a shaft brought a gusher from forty metres below the surface. But it is the cast of the country that nurses Turkmenistan's potential crock of gold; for the Amu Darya fields alone are believed to comprise the world's third largest hydrocarbon deposits.

Estimates of Turkmenistan's gas reserves vary from 2.66 x 10^{12} m^3 - that is, 2.66 trillion cubic metres - to ten times that amount; oil from 6 x 10^8 to 2 x 10^9 barrels - 600 million to 2 billion. This would make Turkmenistan one of the leading players in the world of hydrocarbon exports - if she could freely export.

In the years following Independence, existing refinery and pipeline infrastructure allowed Turkmenistan to continue exporting to Russia and the CIS; but her customers, going through their own economic upheavals, couldn't pay well. Plans for a pipeline across the Caspian to Turkey were frustrated by the inability to agree of the five countries bordering the sea. In desperation the Turkmens turned to Afghanistan's Taliban government, securing their backing for a route across Afghanistan to Pakistan and India. Necessarily shelved for years, this plan is currently being revived with the support of the Asian Development Bank. But her preferred partner, in the best traditions of the last two thousand years, was China, and gas is now beginning to flow through a 2,000 km pipeline to feed the world's fastest-growing economy.

Meanwhile, oil - crude, or refined at Krasnovodsk - continues to follow the old tanker route across the Caspian. Further plans for a pipeline across Afghanistan have been quietly dropped; even so, Turkmenistan has managed to double her oil exports in the last ten years.

"Turkmenistan: Another Kuwait!" One of the Thoughts of Niazov that just might come true. But it depends on another slogan: "Positive Neutrality". The country is desperate to avoid the civil unrest and even war that has broken out in three of the other "Stans". Towards this end, the newly independent Turkmenistan was quickly declared a neutral country, only the third in the world after Switzerland and Ireland. No external enemies, friendly relations with all neighbours, no territorial claims...

...and secure pension plans for the ruling élite.

*

Spring was coming to Ashkhabad at last. Slowly and cautiously, leaves were creeping out of their buds. The verges began to sprout with fresh grass, which housewives tore up in handfuls to feed to the chickens in their back yards. Now there was lilac blossom on sale in the *Russkii Bazaar*, the big covered central market open to the weather at one end and uplifted by a Gordian Knot of Soviet concrete sculpture at the other. The brightly-scarved ladies had discarded their heavy, quilted jackets. New stalls had appeared, their owners fenced in by tightly-packed sacks brimming with tiny grains. Spices, narcotics? On a closer look, they were sacks of seeds. You just bring your own container to be filled, then head for the dacha.

"Babushka's coming to stay!" announced Katya one day. Olga's mother was green-fingered to the elbows, the family horticultural whizz. It was unthinkable that the dacha garden should be planted without her to oversee the work.

Babushka came from Mari by plane, for Sasha's work provided concessionary tickets. It was hard to recognise her as parent of the comfortable, motherly Olga, for she was elfin in stature, with the bright eyes of a robin in a face burned brown as a nut by a lifetime of Central Asian summers. Ever-active despite her seventy years, she rarely kept still even indoors, moving busily about the flat with an idiosyncratic, flat-stepping walk that reminded me of a small boy playing trains, or Mrs. Thatcher.

For there was no time to waste. Spring here is fierce, and short. When it's time to plant, it's time to plant everything, all at once. For two days Olga, Sasha and Babushka worked flat out, travelling to the other side of Ashkhabad each day laden with the seedlings that Olga had nursed on her balcony for weeks, and returning hot, exhausted, and sunburned.

Life began to spill from the confinement of the flats into the street. Olga's flat, like most round here, had a pleasant, sociable outlook on to spacious back yards, where people worked in their gardens, fed chickens and rabbits, or just sat and chatted. "We call that one the zoo!" said Katya, pointing from the balcony down to a garden opposite that was more densely packed with livestock than most.

The skies were filling, too. The first swifts had arrived a week ago, and now sliced through the sky in screaming gangs like exuberant teenagers. On the edge of the city the swallows were coming in. Blackbirds began to sing, staking out their pitch behind the cover of the new leaves, and pigeons hooted softly in the eaves above the balcony. Down the road the first pear blossom was coming out.

Babushka went home, and a few days later another visitor arrived. Olga's brother Kolya was a mechanic, and had been called for an emergency. Sasha's elderly car was critically ill, and more family expertise was needed. For a couple of days the two men sweated in the garage, coming in only at dusk to shower and eat, until the car was restored to health. The following two evenings they went off to the dacha to dig, sow and mix concrete. With them went various plants which Olga had found in the bazaar; and five fine, young fruit trees which had started life in Uzbekistan. When Kolya left to return to work in Mari, he must have felt as though he was going for a holiday.

"Come and visit us when you ride through Mari," he said as he left. "My mother is expecting you."

*

I found work of a different sort going on in Ashkhabad's Mir suburb, when I visited a three-man Aid organisation.

176

The Mir was a modern quarter, where Ashkhabad had spilled over its south-eastern boundary on to virgin land in an explosion of new building. Brand-new apartment blocks looked straight on to empty desert, and wide highways gave uninterrupted views to the Kopet Dagh foothills not a mile away. I doubt whether I could have slept easy in these high-rise buildings, some of them ten storeys, in an earthquake zone where not fifty years ago the entire city had been levelled. But David, Radik and Byoung Sou were made of sterner stuff than me.

Operation Mercy was just two months old. David, Canadian-born and US-bred, had first come here six months before, equipped only with his own skills - and his ideals. "I wanted to come to the neediest place on the planet." Via various Aid organisations he had made contact with Radik, a Turkmen Tatar. Byoung Sou was their first recruit, a Korean who hadn't been put off by his lack of a common language with the other two.

Still seeking a well-defined rôle, they meant to concentrate at first on health and, especially, education.

"As Communism and the Russian way of life are on the way out, so Capitalism and the Western way of life are on the way in," said David. "Therefore English becomes important in the structure of government, the legal system, and so on." So for now he taught English in the University, meanwhile getting the feel of the country and assessing its needs, learning the language - and deciding how to give help without treading on toes.

"We have to walk a fine line," he said. "Turkmenistan wants to be part of the modern world. It's also a proud country. It's very poor, but it doesn't feel poor. The government strives for control and stability, and the last thing it wants is to be seen as a country in crisis. So it wants a slow change into a modern state.

"They want to have help, but without losing face," he summed up. "We want to give help, but tactfully."

Turkmenistan, he said, was suspicious of NGOs - Non-Governmental Organisations.

"Take Peace Corps. Local people simply don't know what to make of them, because they give all and take nothing." Peace Corps, whom I had already met in the person of the American girl in Samarkand, had much the same aims as those of David and Radik: mostly, to teach English, and provide health care where possible.

"So how do you plan to set things up?"

"We want to provide a structure by which all kinds of Aid can come in. Human resources, financial resources, material resources. For example, we want to set up a reading centre." English language books, he explained, could be obtained very cheaply from standard sources which could be tapped by Aid organisations.

"And how will you recruit people?"

"A lot of organisations involved in this part of the world disseminate information to potential volunteers. People who join us may get funding from an organisation, or find individual sponsorship." David himself was sponsored by his friends and his local church.

"So do you see yourself ultimately as boss of a large office channelling Aid?"

"I see myself as a starter. I'd like to get the thing established, and once it's up and running, go off somewhere else - Iran, or Afghanistan..."

The first task was to register here as a company. But there could be awkward implications of thus formalising their set-up. One, the matter of bribery. "It was expected under the USSR. But people here are learning that Western countries work by the book."

There could be painful moral dilemmas here, the Scylla and Charybdis of Fall versus Failure. "Would you ever compromise your principles to grease the odd palm - say, if it were the only way to achieve something important?"

"We hope it won't come to that. Not compromising would be a blessing for the country. We may not get all the things we want, but sticking to our principles would be an example, a

178

testimony." He shrugged. "Maybe that's a long shot, maybe I'm just the crazy guy, but..."

There was something about David and Radik that was familiar. The sensitive beginnings, the idealism, the slow, patient approach of "learning the language, assessing the needs, getting the feel". This, I remembered, was exactly what I'd found among the American missionaries I'd met two years before in Mongolia.

"Are you really missionaries? Is evangelism part of the plan?"

"I'm a Christian," David answered. "It would be very hard for me not to share my faith."

"But it'll be a part of the way you live, rather than a specific purpose of Operation Mercy?"

"Yeah, I guess that's how it'll be."

Faith plus Works: the ultimate example, and a more powerful teaching tool than a thousand sermons. These two, I guessed, would make their fair share of converts.

*

Friday, and I still hadn't seen the promised horse.

Bureaucracy had finally settled back into its cave. I now had the Police permit. I'd also discovered via forensic double- and triple-checking of my other documents that officials had "forgotten" to include Mari *Oblast* (Province) on my visa, which I'd now remedied - for a consideration. In theory, I could now ride off into the sunset (or, rather, sunrise). In practice, just now, I'd be lucky to be riding a bicycle.

Yusup was serenely unconcerned. The horse's owner, he told me, had "gone away to the mountains", and couldn't be contacted; but he would be in touch tonight. This was what I'd heard for the last three nights. My hopes sank through the floor. Was I meant to be steered back to Aleksandr, to spend the rest of my dollars with him?

At Yusup's flat, where I had left my saddlebags and tack, I sorted through my gear, ostentatiously spreading on the floor stove, knife, veterinary goods, sleeping bag and all necessities for long-distance travel. It drew further flights of fancy from Yusup: he and I would travel together to Mari, hire horses when we got there; together we would ride through the desert, visit his friends in a Turcoman *a'ul*, explore the ruins of ancient Merv...

His face alight with enthusiasm, he switched on the video player to show me for the twentieth time breathtaking film of Akhal-Teke horses, their riders clothed in telpeks and striped khalats, galloping through the desert on celluloid.

Still the horse didn't materialise; not that day, nor the next.

There was more bad news at the Ministry for Nature Conservation.

"No, I'm afraid you can't visit Badkhiz," said its leading academic, Professor Atamuradov.

Badkhiz *Zapovednik*, or Nature Reserve, was the best and the most famous in the land. Occupying the extreme south, where Turkmenistan, Afghanistan and Iran meet in a point, it embraces a more diverse topography - mountain, desert and steppe, rivers and salt lakes - and a wider variety of animal life than anywhere else in Turkmenistan. I'd hoped to ride among its giant fennel and pistachio groves; to watch the bird-life teeming on its salt-marshes, swelled by spring migrants; above all, to see *kulan*, the Asiatic wild "half-ass", cousin of the onagers that pulled the first war-chariots in ancient Mesopotamia.

Gently, and with great sympathy, Professor Atamuradov dashed my hopes. There was trouble on the borders: drug-smuggling, shooting, extortion... The innocent Nature Reserve had become a sink of iniquity. Only last month a man had been shot dead by drug smugglers. Badkhiz, the Professor asserted with finality, was off my agenda.

As far as kulan were concerned, though, I'd struck oil here. Professor Atamuradov was a world specialist on kulan. He corrected my misapprehension that I could only see them at Badkhiz. Far from being endangered, the kulan were thriving; so much so that his staff had distributed herds throughout

Turkmenistan. They had been re-introduced to zapovedniks at Kara Kala, near Kyzyl Arvat, and in the north near Tashauz. Better still, there was a population near Anau, and another near Tedzhen - both right in the path of my route to Merv.

"Look for them here... and here... " The map he spread on his desk wasn't available to tourists. It carried far more detail then either of mine, and while he spoke I looked it over carefully. My Tactical Pilotage Chart, on to which I now sketched the areas he indicated, was great if you wanted to avoid flying into a mountain; but not for navigating on the ground, and some of its roads and even towns were hopelessly misplaced. While I had map and pencil ready I copied another detail of the Professor's map which set my pulse racing, and which I hoped to look for later.

Before I left, Professor Atamuradov presented me with a signed copy of his book on Badkhiz. His friendliness was as refreshing, after all the official hassles of the week, as standing under a cool shower after sweating over a hot stove.

*

At the weekend, I prised out of Yusup the name and address of his friend with the horse, and set out to track him down myself.

He turned out to be the deputy boss of the Komsomol/ Niazov Stud. Far from being incommunicado, Obbly-Guli had been at his home by the Hippodrome or predictably at work all week. He was bemused by my urgency. Yusup had told him that I wanted a horse, but had not told him when. He seemed to think that next month would do very nicely.

Since Yusup had insisted that he be present at any discussion, we all three met at his flat. Here Obbly-Guli described the horse he had in mind for me, a Yomud stallion.

"You hear that, Gill? A stallion!" exclaimed Yusup, as if he had personally arranged a unicorn for me. (In fact, since horses aren't castrated here, half the horses in Turkmenistan are stallions.) My own enthusiasm was minimal. Having seen a number of Yomuds, I had already dismissed them as too small.

On the other hand, by this stage I would probably have been grateful to set off on a Shetland pony. Well, we would see.

*

There was still Geldy Kyarizov. I would have one last try to see if he could help.

Moving about Ashkhabad had become very complicated during the last week. Yusup's flat in the Street of the Astronauts was cut off by road repairs. This being Turkmenistan the road was closed in both directions, including the underpass which was the sole railway crossing for miles. The only way to cross was to take a very rough, potholed road to a spot where it was possible to bump straight across the tracks, then weave through a maze of back streets to arrive, after about three miles, a hundred yards from where you started - but on the other side of the railway. Most taxi drivers, very reasonably, refused any passenger wanting to go this way.

By the time I had found a taxi and reached Geldy's yard in the Shor district, it was late. But Geldy still wasn't home, and wasn't expected tonight. I accepted defeat, and headed for home.

It was beginning to get dark. I footslogged it to the main road and settled down to hitch. Eventually a bright red jeep stopped to pick me up, driven by a jolly Armenian. He was friendly and chatty, and the drive from the dark suburb back to the bright city lights passed in moments.

My friend was a third-generation Turkmen whose family had been deported here in one of Stalin's mass movements of population. Now, he had relations all over the country; his brothers and sisters alone amounted to nine (or twelve, if you counted those who had died in infancy); all his roots were here, and he had no inclination to return to the land of his fathers.

"Don't go out of your way!" I begged, as he searched for the best route round the roadworks and straight to Olga's door.

"No trouble," he answered kindly. "I will take you anywhere you want. It's the first time I've met an English writer."

"But I'm not much of a writer." Had I been peddling inflated ideas of my station? "I'm only..." Red-faced, I desperately

182

trawled my meagre Russian vocabulary for a word worthy of my inconsequence. "...only a very... *small*... writer!" I finished lamely.

"I know." He winked at me. "If you were a... *big*... writer, you wouldn't be walking!"

*

Obbly-Guli picked me up on the dot next morning. Such punctuality in Turkmenistan was rare, and promising. Under a thunderous black sky with rain tipping down, we took the road west to where the Komsomol Stud lay in the foothills of the mountains.

A massive bronze statue of an Akhal-Teke horse marked the start of the huge complex. There was time only for a brief glimpse inside at a few pitifully thin youngstock wandering in an earth paddock, while Obbly-Guli exchanged words with a stable lad; then it was about turn, and back the way we had come. The horse, it seemed, was grazing loose in the hills with others from the Stud.

At the head of a dirt track stood a policeman on guard duty. The reason for this was clear: ahead stretched a barbed wire fence, the only well-maintained fence I ever saw in Turkmenistan, with watchtowers at intervals. We were approaching the border area.

The fence ran away into the distance up and down the adjoining hills. A neat, double line enclosing a strip of turned earth in the middle, it looked as innocent as a trainer's gallops. I wondered if the dirt strip was mined.

This was only the edge of the frontier zone. Nevertheless I, as a foreigner without credentials, could go no further, and must stay behind while Obbly-Guli went on to find the horse.

The guard, hunched miserably in an inadequate raincoat with a rifle slung at his back, slouched over to speak to him as he set off towards a herd of some fifty mares and foals. Meanwhile, a very young soldier came up to look me over. He bore a Russian fur hat, dashingly complemented by a Soviet star on his battledress, a wicked-looking Commando knife, and a pronounced limp. He knew Obbly-Guli well, for the latter's work brought him regularly to oversee the herds here, and he chatted desultorily about the horses before limping away.

Obbly-Guli came back after a long time; but hadn't found the horse. He would send someone to bring it down to the Hippodrome later, and I could see it there.

"I suppose you know," he said casually as he turned the car round, "that was the KGB* checking you out."

*

My horse was shelved for another day, for Ashkhabad had bigger fish to fry. The Day of the Horse had arrived, and half the city was converging on the Hippodrome to spend the first day of a major Bank Holiday celebrating Turkmenistan's national symbol.

On the lawns behind the stands iron yurt-frames began to come to life. Layers of thick Turcoman rugs transformed them from sad skeletons into festive booths, where businessmen entertained their chums or sold luxury goods. Around them a vast market suddenly mushroomed in the space of an hour or two. Bored-looking youths with white telpeks and striped Turcoman khalats, carelessly worn over cheap western tracksuits, sold cakes stacked in pyramids and crusted with multi-coloured sugar.

On the steps under President Niazov's portrait, Turcoman culture was exhibited by troupes of dancing girls, their long plaits escaping from jewelled head-dresses to fall waist-length over brilliant silk robes. Poetry readings from the pages of Makhtum Kuli filled the interval.

A massive police and army presence guarded the racing. Most of the stands were shut off to all but VIPs, and spectators, like unruly schoolchildren, were made to sit down and behave themselves. The course rails were heavily defended. The result was a real exhibition of Turkmen military might. It felt more

---

* now under a different name, but still universally referred to as the KGB

like a parade in Red Square than an afternoon's racing; you half expected to see tanks rolling down the finishing straight.

In the milling crowds, I bumped into Aleksandr.

"How did you enjoy Uzbekistan?" he asked. "Are you still planning to ride to Mari?" And, the crucial question, "Will you be coming back to Firyuza, to do a longer ride from my stables?"

"If I don't find a horse to travel with," I promised him with barely suppressed irony, "I probably will."

*

Back at Olga's flat, I made my final preparations to leave. I hoped that this time they were for real. It wasn't the first time this week that I'd said goodbye. If Obbly-Guli's horse didn't materialise, or wasn't suitable, I might be turning up here again like the proverbial bad penny.

My head buzzed with last-minute advice. Olga: Remember, if you need any help - with finding accommodation, for instance - ask at the Hakimlik. Yusup: Don't let your horse drink out of irrigation ditches - they might be contaminated with chemicals. And don't worry about poisonous plants; he will know what's poisonous and what isn't. Obbly-Guli: Never pass up the chance of any grazing. Olga again: The headman of a kolkhoz is called the *Bashlik*, not Hakim. And don't forget to let us know when you reach Mari. We'll be worrying about you!

Sasha volunteered to drive me to the Hippodrome himself. He probably wanted to be sure they really were rid of me at last. Before I left, Olga made us all sit quietly for a minute or two.

"It's an old Russian custom. A chance to ask God to bless your journey; a moment to collect your thoughts and make sure you haven't forgotten anything."

Then, with a quick hug and a "Goodbye, good luck and God bless" from Olga and the children, I was off.

Sasha had his own advice, which he delivered with fierce intensity as he drove through the busy streets.

"Whatever you do, don't camp anywhere near the canal. The mosquitoes are frightful. You won't rest, the horse won't rest...

"Most of all, if you must camp at all, be sure to put your tent up somewhere where you can't be seen, somewhere at least two kilometres from the road."

He turned to face me, and his blue eyes were glacial, his voice harsh with the urgency of his warning. "Never forget: the Turcomans are a wild people, an uncivilised people."

I thought of Tamara Feodorovna. "They're good people, such good people."

In the coming weeks, I would find out which of them was right.

Part Four

Old Road to Merv

XI

The good news was that the horse had arrived. The bad, that he was in a pitiable state.

He was a little grey Yomud stallion, barely more than a pony. He stood huddled in the box, head down and covered in sweat. He was as thin as a rake. A great raw wound showed red on the ridge of his spine and another, yellow with septicaemia, dripped pus down the inside of one leg. Ticks, obscenely bloated with his blood, hung like vampires from his belly.

I was appalled. This horse had been ridden here, in this state, on my behalf. Shaking with guilt, I literally wept for him. Should I cancel the whole project, get on the next plane and go home? There could not, must not, be a repetition of this.

At least there was no argument. Obbly-Guli agreed that the horse could not possibly do my journey; any journey. He went off to think again, while I set out to make amends to the little horse.

Borrowing a headcollar, I took him to the best patch of grass on the Hippodrome. While he ate as if he had never seen such grass before - which he probably hadn't - I brushed off the sweat and then tackled the wounds.

Antibiotic spray for the back, and the half-dozen minor wounds, until he was covered with blue blotches. Animalintex - a sort of instant poultice - for the septic leg; I borrowed a kettle from Obbly-Guli's wife to sterilise it, and strapped it on with a thin cotton dressing which would fall off by itself in a day or two. Finally I burned off the ticks with matches, afraid of leaving the heads in. Before very long I was to become rather more blasé about ticks.

When the little horse was patched up, I put him back in the stable with a large pile of hay filched from the racehorses, and went out to find Obbly-Guli looking for me with Horse Number Two.

She was a tiny grey filly, dwarfed by the child that sat on her back. She was even thinner than the Yomud, her hips like hatracks, her back an inverted V. I slipped a thumb into her mouth and lifted her upper lip. A set of milk teeth grinned back at me, complete except for the central pair. Three years old. I was agreeably surprised, for she looked about half that.

"Are you serious?"

"Yusup told me to find you a small, quiet horse," he replied.

I was seething. What I needed was a big, strong horse - and one with some guts about it. Yusup knew that; he'd discussed my plans, had seen the size of my saddlebags, filled for several weeks' self-sufficiency. The message was obvious: no way would I cross Turkmenistan on horseback. They would find me something to play with for a few days before I gave up and came back, tail between my legs, pipedreams in tatters.

Now Obbly-Guli put the knife in.

"You don't think," he asked me contemptuously, "that someone's going to lend you an Akhal-Teke?"

It was meant to soften me up, and it succeeded. When he played his third and final card, it was perfectly clear that this was the best he could offer.

This was a black stallion of indeterminate breed, and the ugliest horse I'd ever seen. His enormous, convex head was attached by a ludicrously short neck to a skinny body that tapered towards the back, so that seen from the side he looked more like a buffalo than a horse. He had badly capped hocks, and his heels were so contracted that the frog - the foot's shock-absorber - stood a good three inches off the ground. He had evidently lain repeatedly in cow-muck, which caked his ragged coat in tear-drop globules an inch long. And he was thin. Not as thin as the tiny filly, nor even so much as the Yomud, but thin.

Obbly-Guli dismissed this last objection. "We don't have enough feed," he said angrily. "You won't find a fatter horse here, not in Turkmenistan in the spring!" The horse was, he swore, up to the job.

overleaf:

Map 2

Central Turkmenistan

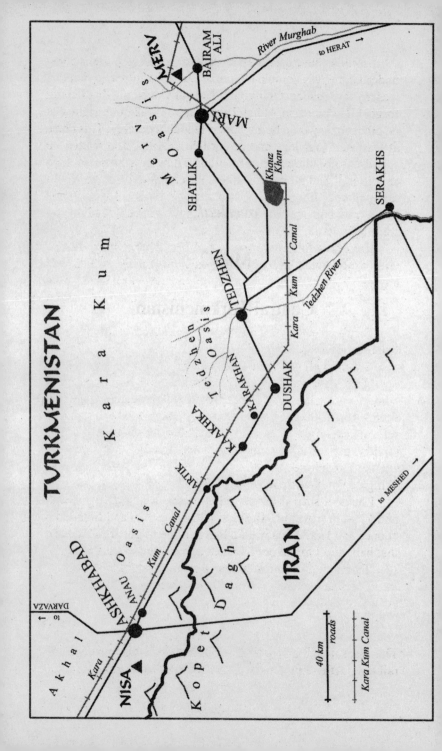

I couldn't have disagreed more. For one thing, besides being underfed, he was completely unfit. But it was obvious that this was my last chance. Obbly-Guli had convinced me that I could forget all hope of an Akhal-Teke. And he was quite right that no other horse would be any fatter. I thought quickly. This horse at least had four legs and no terrible wounds, and trotted up sound. As for the ethics of setting out with a horse in such condition, I had no worries; there was no doubt that he would fare better with me than he had with his owner. I would give him a trial, and see how he shaped up with decent feeding and some light work.

There now followed some very difficult bargaining. Obbly-Guli exaggerated my original tender to Yusup, which had anyway applied to a decent horse and an extra week, now wasted. Finally we reached a compromise, though it pleased neither of us.

Then came the next problem. I proposed to pay half up front, half at the end.

"I want it all now!" he snapped.

"That's not usual," I answered with as much patience as I could. "For instance, what happens if the horse goes lame?" It wasn't said with any foresight; it was just that, of the hundred things that might go wrong with this travesty of a horse, I couldn't put the other ninety-nine into Russian.

He looked me straight in the eye. "In that case," he said, "I'll give you your money back."

I made a snap decision. After all, he was Yusup's friend, and I had to trust him. Besides, if the horse indeed foundered at once and I had already paid him half, he might argue to keep that half, and I might not have enough money to start again.

"Fair enough." I gave him an equally straight look back.

It was an exchange I would later remember cynically.

*

The black horse and I left Ashkhabad by a track beside the railway. After a mile or two, grubby wasteland gave way to

193

fields, and I could ride among low fruit trees that provided a little shade from the sun.

Setting out from the eastern suburbs around the Hippodrome, rather than from Nisa itself, was a necessary compromise. The latter would mean to cross, or by-pass, Ashkhabad. Riding through a capital city on a strange horse wasn't an option; immediately south were the mountains with their forbidden border zone, while to the north the Kara Kum lapped directly at the city. I had already ridden an Akhal-Teke horse to Nisa. I was satisfied with that.

Mid-day was hardly the best time to launch myself on such a journey. Spring had spent itself in a brief flush that had lasted precisely the week I was stuck in Ashkhabad, and summer was hard on its heels. The sun burned down, the irrigation ditches flowed urgently, and everything within their compass was in full growth.

The horse stepped out willingly enough. He trotted on for a bit and popped over a drainage ditch with no hesitation. A spot of cautious optimism stirred in me.

I unsaddled in an orchard to let him graze for an hour, on thick grass dotted with blue flowers; and picked the first tick off the back of my neck. As he grazed, I went on scratching at the cow-dung. He was looking a great deal better without it. It was a pity that, while my back was turned, Obbly-Guli had pulled out most of his tail in great handfuls, his notion of tidiness. It was the last straw for, with only a ridiculous whisk at the back to balance his top-heavy head, the poor little horse looked more bizarre than ever.

Half a mile further, and the irrigation stopped abruptly at the barrier of higher ground. The power of water, the fullest sense of an oasis, was graphically illustrated here. It was like the edge of the Nile Valley: one step took you from lush farmland straight into the Kara Kum.

The dunes nudged the railway, leaning over it in places to spill sand on to the track. I left it to pick a path among the low scrub of saxaul. There were times when, passing through hollows, I could see nothing around me but desert, and revelled in exotic fantasies: I was Lawrence in the Nefudh, Thesiger crossing the Empty Quarter, Chang Ch'ien braving the Taklamakan... Then a telegraph pole would appear, hung with rusty wires; or a break in the dunes revealed the railway, and beyond it the approaching village of Anau, with all its ugly symbols of twentieth century urban sprawl; and the daydreams vanished like water into the sand.

It was time to cross the railway, for I hoped to find lodging at a kolkhoz in Anau. There was no alternative to riding straight across the five sets of tracks. Halfway across I saw an approaching train in the distance, and the horse's stride had never seemed shorter, or its pace slower. Safely over, I crossed a final dune and stopped where the last saxaul of the desert shaded the first grass of civilisation. The horse was beginning to tire visibly, and needed a good rest. I untacked, tethered him with a length of rope, and sat under the tree contemplating past and future.

Should I have taken this horse? Could I have found something else if I had waited a bit longer? But this was the fruition of fifteen months of promises from Yusup; there would be no more help there. I had drawn a blank with Geldy Kyarizov. And Obbly-Guli insisted that I would not get hold of a thoroughbred.

Ashkhabad, I decided, hadn't got a horse for me. There was no alternative for now but to press on with the black horse. I would find stabling somewhere round about Anau and stay for a week, riding out every day, exploring the Kopet Dagh foothills, and getting a feel for the country. With decent feeding and gentle, steady work, the old nag might shape up better than he promised. If not... well, it was only a day's ride back to Ashkhabad.

And meanwhile, I just might find something else, a kolkhoznik with a spare horse and pocket room for a few dollars. Haggling with Obbly-Guli, I had withheld my saddle from the final bargain. I wasn't letting go of my ace until it had rested for a few weeks on a rounder back than the black horse's.

Though if he went on eating like he was now, I thought as I lay back and watched him with pleasure, the back in question would fill out fast. What was I going to call him? Obbly-Guli said his name was Racer, which might be all very well in Turcoman but sounded in English like a bad joke. Rosinante would be more appropriate.

That he was a stallion there could be no doubt, the measure of his facilities being the only impressive thing about him. But I had to admit that, from the front, his frame foreshortened and his mangled tail hidden, he didn't look so ugly. In fact, the white star on his forehead was almost pretty. It reminded me of another horse I'd known, and so he became Tom.

It seemed that Tom and I would never reach Anau's kolkhoz. We set off down the main street, spooking a pair of camels that took one look at my strange mount and freaked out. Everyone I asked for directions said "*Priamo!* Straight on!" as if the kolkhoz were just down the end of the road. But at the end of every road there was another road to go just down the end of, while poor Tom's stride got shorter and shorter and his head drooped.

The trouble was, I still hadn't grasped what a "kolkhoz" really was. Until now I'd seen only parts, imagining them to be the whole. I expected a big farm, a cosy single unit on the edge of Anau. But a Turcoman kolkhoz, I was to find out, is a large, self-contained village, existing in isolation from other towns. Kolkhoz Makhtum Kuli was several miles out from Anau, and nearly a mile across. And when we finally reached it, the Bashlik was out.

A tribe of small boys escorted us to and fro in fruitless search. By now Tom was exhausted and footsore, and I was walking. Something urgent had to be done. I did the unthinkable, and found a militsianer.

I was lucky, for he was human. Better even; he was positively charming. He assumed the obligatory scowl to inspect my documents; but once we'd got that ritual over, he turned into a knight-errant.

Yes, he knew just the place for Tom and me to stay. He pointed down the arrow-straight road to where a pair of gateposts stood well beyond the kolkhoz. "Do you see those posts? Well, head for those, and keep going. I'll meet you there."

The flat landscape, and the heat-haze, made distance deceptive. As I trudged up the road beside Tom, the gateposts first seemed to recede before me, then grew monstrously into a pair of water towers, ten times the height of my first estimate. Halfway there a man fell into step beside us. He was a disreputable figure, his fierce, piratical-looking face framed by a shaggy hat above and a thick growth of stubble below. His conversation took the form of an interrogation - where was I from, what was I doing, where did I get the horse...? He spat out his words in a hoarse bellow, such as Captain Ahab might have used across the decks of the Pequod in a gale; and punctuated them by spitting gobs of phlegm, mercifully away from me and downwind.

In other circumstances, it would have been a glorious evening. The sun was dropping low now, sharply delineating the pleated foothills of the Kopet Dagh just a mile ahead. In the tamarisk bushes overhanging the roadside stream a flock of rose-coloured starlings chattered; when we passed there was a sudden hush followed by the clap of wingbeats as they rose together.

At last a low, white building detached itself from the shimmering horizon and began to grow noticeably bigger with each step. My companion turned up the track towards it. At the gate the militsianer was waiting for us.

*

The yard belonged to Captain Ahab, alias Akhrana, who bred camels there. A tractor had just arrived with a load of fresh-cut grass for them and I begged a pile for Tom, who was now installed in one of the stables. Mice exploded in all directions as I threw it into the tin manger.

My tent caused much interest. Many hands made light work, and it was up in moments. Meanwhile Akhrana disappeared. He returned followed by a horse, who cantered athletically up to his call on tightly hobbled front feet. It was small, but unmistakable in form.

"She is an Akhal-Teke," said Akhrana proudly. "Her name is Aina. We use her - and that one" (he pointed to a stallion grazing nearby) "for herding the camels."

Akhrana was fascinated by my saddlery, which he examined as I brewed tea for us both. Covetously he fingered the supple leather of the well-oiled bridle, and exclaimed at the strength and lightness of the synthetic saddle. "Give it to me! Give it to me!" he begged. "We've got nothing like this in Turkmenistan. Give it to me!"

"I can't," I protested laughing. "I can't ride to Merv bareback!"

"Then when you go home, *give it to me!*"

Two Akhal-Tekes, and desperate for my saddle. As I fell asleep to the roars and gurgles of the camels, I was in a considerably better frame of mind. The situation had definite possibilities.

*

There was another horse at the stables, a chestnut pony whose owner had tethered it to a lump of concrete and then gone away, for how long no-one knew. The *ménage* was completed by a little brown donkey with a broken leg. Apparently untroubled by its disability, it hopped about like a rabbit on three legs while the fourth dangled uselessly. Its bray was hoarser than Akhrana's voice, a parrot copy of a dying camel.

Every day the camels were taken out to graze in the hills, watched by Akhrana's chief camelherd. Orazniaz was elderly, with a goblin face and a button mouth in which one pointed tooth clung precariously to the upper jaw. He was a kindly old man, and lent me a bucket to draw water for Tom, from the well in the corner of the orchard where my tent stood.

The first day, he had a visitor. The vet, Uraz, had come to check the camels.

"Do you want to see the racehorses at the kolkhoz?" he asked me. I jumped at the chance.

His jeep was a box-like machine with no bonnet, like a truncated diesel locomotive. But it rolled like a tank over the rough tracks and through deep ditches and fords. Uraz drove round two sides of a huge farmyard, a hundred yards square, fenced with eight-foot prefabricated concrete blocks in a style that was to become familiar. Like all things ex-Soviet, the fabric was crumbling; cavernous holes yawned in the concrete and lengths of rusty iron framework poked out, awkwardly exposed and faintly indecent, like suspenders under a lifted skirt.

Defying the dilapidation, flowers rioted in the fields around. Red poppies, pink poppies and brilliant buttercups grew in a carpet so thick that no room was left for grass. In the distance, something white carved a path through the deep pile, its outline vibrating and insubstantial in the hot air. As its path converged with the jeep, it gradually took the form of a horse, its rider hunched in jockey-length stirrups. It came to a halt outside a long shed, and disappeared inside just as the jeep pulled up.

Makhtum, the trainer, was delighted to show off his stable. "This is my best horse. He won at the Hippodrome two days ago. And this one was third - he won the President's Cup last year... This is the main stud stallion... This mare is about to foal..."

Surely, somewhere here was a spare horse. But he shook his head doubtfully. "I'll ask the Bashlik. But I don't think so."

Barley was a different matter. He led me into a stall where a great pile remained from the racing season, now nearly ended. Waving my money aside, he seized a sack and shovelled generously until I could hardly lift it. I couldn't wait to take it back to Tom.

Now, Orazniaz' tin bucket came into its own. Barley is indigestible, and feeding the raw grain wastes much of its feed value. To squeeze out every last calorie and swell Tom's skinny frame, it needed to be boiled... for several hours. I could hardly do this in billycans, and on a camping stove. But twenty minutes on my powerful little petrol stove brought a bucketful to a rolling boil, whereupon I covered it and buried it in the muckheap. Here it would retain its heat for hours, at the end of which the hard grain would be soft and digestible. By the end of his day's rest, Tom would have had three corn feeds, one of them boiled.

He was going to get some flesh on those ribs, and in double-quick time. By the Nine Gods I swore it.

*

As I was wrapping a pan of part-boiled rice in my sleeping-bag - sauce for the goose, I thought, but didn't quite fancy the muck-heap - Uraz came back.

"Come to our party! Today is our major festival. Every year we kill a sheep."

Uraz lived in one of many almost identical houses in an unmade side road of the kolkhoz. A group of women sprawled on a wooden divan in the spacious yard. Children and babies spilled out of the door, followed by the hum of many voices. This year, it was Uraz' turn to entertain his large family.

He led me through an anteroom and introduced me to his wife and daughters; some of the women drew their scarves across their faces as I took their hands. In the next room was the male gathering, and Uraz saw me comfortably installed here before hurrying off to do the duties of host elsewhere. Today, it seemed, I was an honorary man.

The room was spacious, empty of furniture but for a chest or two and a television. A cornice was cleverly painted on to the walls, and from it hung painted curtains so real that I wanted to stroke their virtual folds. On the floor a wide cloth did duty as a table, bearing the focal point of the room - the most enormous pile of food, a kurgan of pilau almost two feet high, which all present were busily reducing.

Someone brought me a cushion. I followed my companions' example by doubling it under one elbow to recline awkwardly on the floor. It needs practice to be a Turcoman at a feast. Practice and a hard head; for now came the toasts, and you were expected to sink your glass of vodka in one, every time. As a foreigner I was let off this hook, and got by with a sip followed by a gulp of camel milk.

At last everyone had eaten and drunk to capacity. Uraz said grace, passing his hands over his face in the ritual Moslem gesture of cleansing. Conversation died to a murmur. Some of

200

the older men rolled over and slept. Others sat back to watch the television, which showed scenes of festival across Turkmenistan. The cameras ranged over signs of plenty - boxes of melons, baskets of tomatoes, well-irrigated lines of monster cabbages. It was a well-massaged picture of reality, for the feast this year was squeezed by the country's financial straits, and with rice at a record price Uraz' "pilau" for some forty or fifty people was made from shredded bread. And he was one of the officers, the elite of the kolkhoz.

Each kolkhoz had its *zooteknik*, or para-vet, explained his father, justifiably proud of Uraz' scholarship. It was his job to monitor the kolkhoz livestock for any disease harmful to people. The old man was also proud of his medals, on display today for the party. He had twenty-four decorations in all. "This was for the Great Patriotic War" - World War II - "I took part in the liberation of Berlin."

When it was time to leave, Uraz insisted on scooping a bagful of food from the remaining heap and giving it to me. Neither Tom nor I, it seemed, would starve at Kolkhoz Makhtum Kuli.

*

Beyond Akhrana's yard the hills gathered then drew back to reveal a gorge, its pink jagged rock rising sheer to meet a deep blue sky. Through this ran a stream, its banks bearded with tamarisk. Rose-coloured starlings flitted between the bushes, and the strident call of nightingales came from deep inside. On the higher branches sat rollers, striking birds in kingfisher colours of blue and amber.

A day's rest and plenty of food had transformed Tom. He hopped lightly over a deep ditch which would have stopped many a horse, and set off at a smart canter. Encouraged, I tried him up a gear, and he rollocked along with enthusiasm in a headlong unbalanced gallop. For the first time it was actually necessary to apply the brakes, rather than just easing the accelerator, in order to stop him.

201

I jogged through the canyon at a leisurely pace, passing on the way one or two gypsy camps where a few goats or sheep huddled in an enclosure beside a caravan or canvas tent. As the rock walls began to widen, a green valley opened out on the far side. I came round a corner, and saw a herd of Akhal-Teke horses coming straight towards me.

Ten, twenty, thirty mares and foals emerged from the bushes and walked purposefully down the track. They parted as we met, passing by on either side without a glance and closing again behind, as if Tom and I didn't exist. It was a surreal experience: was it they or ourselves who were a figment of my imagination? It was as if we came from a different time and space, and had met through some hiccup of the celestial clock.

In a few moments they had vanished back among the tamarisk, the only signs of their reality being a rustling among the bushes, the occasional call of a mare to her foal. The figure that followed them was no ordinary horseherd. For a start, she was the only Turcoman girl I ever saw handling horses. For another, she was dressed in jeans and a shirt, with her head bare. I stopped to pass the time of day, and she answered me in English.

Jamilia, I discovered, was training to be a jockey. She came from the kolkhoz and worked at a stud farm near Kalininskii, the village beyond the gorge. As we spoke, a palomino foal came racing out of the tamarisk, skidded to a halt beside Tom in a cloud of dust, then turned about and vanished at speed. A worried mare came trotting in pursuit, and Jamilia said a hurried goodbye and went to sort them out.

Vineyards surrounded the village, their edges thick with grass. I stopped to graze Tom for a time before returning the way I'd come. As I passed the grazing herd, the little palomino foal was still high-tailing it in circles; there, I thought, was a future winner on the Ashkhabad Hippodrome. I couldn't see Jamilia, who was somewhere deep in the tamarisk. Instead, we had a different sort of meeting. A grey stallion, scenting Tom, appeared from nowhere and squared up to him, every hormone thinking him a rival. No sense in waiting for the stallion to discover his mistake. I kicked on and retreated quickly, thankful that Tom still had some juice in the battery.

He had done better today than I could have dared to hope. Akhrana's horses slipped to the back of my mind as I considered the possibility that this ugly little horse, with his skinny ribs and lack of fitness, might after all make it to Merv. I was beginning to think that he made up in guts what he lacked in physique.

If so, there was no doubt it would be a hell of a journey; not least because his straight shoulder and short stride made him horribly uncomfortable to ride. And he was already a bit footsore. Tomorrow I must have a word with Makhtum and see if I could find a farrier.

There was something quixotic about the idea of transforming this clapped-out nag into a fit horse capable of an epic journey. It wasn't quite what I'd planned, but it had a certain romantic appeal. Well, we would see.

Give us, oh Lord, the grace to accept the things we cannot change, the courage to change the things we cannot accept...

...And the wisdom to know the difference.

*

Wisdom was dished up the next day.

It started promisingly - after a fashion. Having taken Tom to the stream to drink, I climbed on his back to save myself the return walk. He promptly set off at a full gallop back to the stables. I wrapped my fingers in his mane, bouncing in agony on his knife-edge of a backbone. To my relief he stopped when he got home. As I slid weakly off his back, I couldn't help thinking that there was more to this horse than met the eye.

The constant coming and going of the camels was in full swing. The three corrals were emptied, in rotation, of their occupants, Orazniaz or one of the younger men riding out with them to keep watch while they grazed in the hills. Akhrana's two horses, essential for this work, were well cared for. No-one, though, took the slightest notice of the chestnut pony.

I watered him when I saw to Tom, and pinched an armful of feed for him whenever possible. As the circle round the

203

concrete post turned to a dust bath with his increasingly frantic pacing, I kept untying him and moving him to a patch of good grass, only to find every time that someone else moved him back again. The little three-legged donkey had taken a shine to the pony; the fellow-feeling, perhaps, of companions in misfortune. He followed all these migrations, braying loudly in his hoarse, cracked voice.

Who would look after the pony when I'd gone, I wondered? "It's not my problem," was the universal attitude. "He doesn't belong to me, so I don't care if he's starving or has a raging thirst. Let someone else do it!" It was an attitude, I thought angrily as I moved him for the tenth time, that seemed to be a metaphor for so many of the problems in Turkmenistan.

It was as Katya had said. No-one was personally responsible for an animal, or a piece of land, or a stretch of road. So nobody bothered if things went from bad to worse. After nearly a century of Communism, nobody knew how to equate pride in ownership with duty of care.

Of course, that pride was a two-edged sword. On the one hand it could lead to envy and greed, just what the idealistic Marxist wanted to abolish. But there were other sorts of pride; the opposite manifestation, self-respect, was the baby thrown out with the bathwater. Add that to the Central Asian sense of *laissez-faire*, and the result was a shambles: a thousand starving, thirsty animals; a thousand plots festooned with weeds and rusty, broken wire; a thousand streets full of pot-holes, uncovered manholes and other hazards.

As I saddled up Tom for the day's ride, I was still busily putting Turkmenistan to rights in my head. But not for long, as I soon had something else to think about.

He was hopping lame.

*

It was time to find Akhrana and lay my cards on the table. Perhaps he had his own views on Tom, for he wasn't entirely surprised when I asked if I could ride one of his horses to Merv.

He chewed his lip thoughtfully. "It would be a very difficult journey." But he hadn't refused out of hand. He still badly wanted the saddle, which was part of my bid.

His mare grazed nearby. She was small, no taller than Tom, and lighter than Akhrana's other horse, a bay stallion. But she was the fitter of the two, for every day she carried a man's weight into the hills to herd the camels, whereas the stallion had only just come into work.

I put out a hand to stroke her neck while I deliberated. At once she turned, pirouetting like a ballerina on her hobbled front legs, and dropped me a crack on the leg with both barrels of her small, hard feet. Mercifully she was unshod.

Once a bitch, always a bitch. If I came to terms with Akhrana, I would ask for the stallion.

I might have to, for Makhtum arrived with bad news. The kolkhoz President had turned down my request to hire a horse. But Makhtum had another suggestion.

"Have you tried Rep?" he asked. Rep was the owner of Jamilia's herd. He lived in the kolkhoz... here. Makhtum sketched me a map.

Meanwhile, Akhrana was weakening. Yes, he would let me have a horse... but on condition that he came with me as a guide.

Much as I was getting to like the old pirate, this didn't fill me with enthusiasm. I wasn't too sure what Akhrana's concept of a guide's duties included, but I had an idea it might run to a bit more than finding the way. Besides, two horses would be harder than one to accommodate, particularly in view of the feed situation.

It was just about now that my problems moved up a gear. For on checking my kit, I discovered the latest crunching blow.

Someone had stolen my stove.

With all my comings and goings, I feared constantly for my baggage. I'd buried the saddlebags, with the bulk of my gear, in a thick pile of brushwood by the camel corrals. For the most important things, I'd tried a bit harder. With what I'd thought to be inspiration, I'd hidden them in the cab of a bulldozer that lived, slowly dying of rust, round the back of the stables. They

205

would have been safer with the rest of the stuff. For someone had found the hiding place, and the stove was gone.

The implications for my journey - if I ever got hold of a horse - were calamitous. If I couldn't cook, my light food supplies of such things as rice and pasta were useless; anything ready-to-eat, if available at all, would be much heavier. Far worse, if I couldn't boil water, I couldn't drink. Already the clear water from Akhrana's well had given me colliwobbles. On the road, my water was far more likely to come directly or indirectly out of the Kara Kum Canal. And I couldn't travel all day in burning heat and not drink.

The moon was full that night. The mountains glowed vibrantly at dusk, the shimmer of the day's heat stilled. Every fold of the foothills stood out sharp as a knife, and on the main ridge the threads of snow lying in the north-facing gullies threw back the moonlight brilliantly. It was as beautiful an evening as I have seen anywhere on Earth.

If Turkmenistan was trying to cheer me up, it failed dismally.

*

Saddam Hussein's *doppelgänger* chewed his pencil and glowered at me across the grubby table.

"Your papers are not in order. You only have a stamp for Ashkhabad city, not oblast, and are therefore in Anau illegally. And you have a business visa instead of a tourist one."

There were eight of us in the room altogether. Six on his side, including the obligatory KGB officer; while mine was a team of two, the other half being a Turco-British businessman who had kindly stepped in to interpret. Captaining the opposition was a policeman of large girth, whose pasty, depressed-looking face, half hidden by an ill-pruned moustache, made him a dead ringer for the Iraqi dictator.

He shifted in his seat, and rearranged his stomach more comfortably against the desk as he began to warm up.

"You will be fined. You will be deported from Turkmenistan tomorrow, and not permitted to return for a year."

"I want to leave at once and not come back, ever." Fortunately I didn't say it out loud. Anyway, my friend Dr. Tekin didn't look unduly concerned when he translated my fate. He knew where all this was leading. I had a good idea, too.

The fat policeman licked his lips. He was in the finishing straight. "As far as your stove is concerned: we can register it as 'stolen', in which case we will have to go and look for it. Or we can register it as 'lost', in which case we simply put it on a list, and return it to you if it is found."

It made no difference to me. There wasn't a cat-in-hell's chance of recovering the stove, and I knew it as well as he did. I had only come to report the theft because the stove was worth a hundred pounds, and I needed a police report to claim the insurance. "Fine. Put it down as 'lost'."

He relaxed, and smiled at me: a ghastly rictus that bared an uneven row of gold teeth. Saddam Hussein disappeared, to be replaced by Terry-Thomas. He seemed to have forgotten about deporting me.

Preparing the insurance report was a leisurely affair. He trailed off into general conversation, returning to the matter in hand with a desultory question every ten minutes or so. All but one of his team drifted off, leaving both sides evenly matched. During a longer interval in the proceedings than ever, I asked him to show me what marked out my visa as "business", "so that," I asked innocently, "I can avoid a similar error in future." He couldn't answer.

Three hours after first entering the police station, I was presented with a copy of the report. "Thank you so much," I said, with exaggerated formality. "Not at all," he replied graciously, with another pronounced leer. For poor Dr. Tekin, my thanks were sincere and profound; his whole morning had been wasted.

I looked at the precious report before stowing it safely in my moneybelt. It was almost illegibly written in Cyrillic longhand. The few words I could decipher told me it was in Turcoman. The paper was unheaded, torn off a cheap writing pad, and without so much as an official stamp to prove its

207

credentials. And how many insurance clerks, I wondered, could read Cyrillic and understand Turcoman?

I could have given the police a miss, and forged the bloody thing myself.

*

Hitching back to Akhrana's for the umpteenth time, I got more than just a lift from a couple of young men in army fatigues, driving a squat, workmanlike jeep like Uraz'. Vlad and Yaz ran the Serpentaria at Kalininskii, where snakes were milked of their venom for antidotes.

"Do you want to have a look? We're about to feed them."

The Serpentaria was deep in the foothills of the Kopet Dagh. Beyond the plain of Kalininskii the valley narrowed again, the hills tightly squeezing the road. Vlad parked the jeep behind a long, low building, and led the way inside. A frowsty smell came from the heated room, where a block of cages lined the wall.

Vlad opened a cage with such apparent lack of concern that I stepped close to look. At once he pushed me back.

"Careful!" He poked in a hooked stick and withdrew it with a writhing snake wrapped round it. "This is a viper. *Vipera Lebetina*."

Vipera Lebetina writhed on the floor, looking thoroughly cheesed off at being woken up and hissing at us sourly. Vlad picked it up with dexterity and flipped it back into the cage.

Next to it was a tiny, thin, silvery snake with beautiful markings. It struck irritably at Yaz as he scooped it out. "Oi, that's enough!" he ticked it off fondly. It began to coil round his arm.

"It's OK; it's not poisonous," he said as I looked on, aghast. "But it still bites!" he added, replacing it with care.

Now came the cobra, the most deadly snake in Central Asia. Vlad handled it with bare hands and all the aplomb of a child playing with a pet hamster. He teased it with the stick until it reared and struck in fury at his ankle. With unmoving bravado he tapped it, reproving it gently in the loving tones of a parent.

208

If you're going to get bitten by a cobra, I suppose a serum lab is the best place to go about it.

From a safe distance the cobra was a beautiful thing, its gently arching throat plated with golden scales below the grey hood, spread wide now in menace; the living pattern for a Pharaonic death-mask. With another flick of the stick Vlad closed his fingers round its head, behind the lethal jaws, and carried it into the next room. He pressed the bared fangs against the edge of a Petri dish until yellow venom, innocent-looking as sugar syrup, oozed on to the plate. Long after he had replaced the cobra in its cage, it continued to hiss and curse at him.

This room was the laboratory. A human skull rested on top of a filing cabinet. "Was that the last zoologist who worked here?" Having seen them handling the snakes, I wasn't entirely joking.

They kept serum ready for use, in case of accident. "But you have to be careful," added Yaz. "It's quite possible to die anyway. Different people react in different ways; it's like antibiotic."

"Have you ever been bitten?"

"Yes," said Vlad, "but my health is strong, and I got over it in a few days. I was off work for a month." It was just an occupational hazard, said his casual tone, as if he were a doctor who had caught 'flu from one of his patients.

While they finished feeding and milking, I went outside into the grounds. The wild corn underfoot, yellow-ripe already at the beginning of May, gave an autumnal feel to the landscape. On the hills the grass was burning up, brown with only a hint of green remaining, and the herds of ranging sheep trailed comet's-tails of dust.

Back inside, the kettle had just boiled, and Yaz was hacking generous slices off a chunk of honeycomb. "Badkhiz honey," he said. It was the nearest I ever got to Badkhiz Zapovednik.

They looked an ill-assorted pair - Vlad laughing, fair and Russian, Yaz quiet, dark and Turcoman - but clearly an inseparable team, the embodiment of continuing Turco-Russian *entente*. Both had earlier worked at Badkhiz, although Vlad had

209

left to try his hand as a businessman before being drawn back inexorably to the zoological work that defined him.

"It's very difficult here for scientists," he said. "When I finished training it was hard to get a decent job as a biologist. You could die from hunger before you found work." Currently, both earned five dollars a month plus accommodation.

But it was interesting work, for they were employed by the Kopetdagskii Zapovednik, the local Nature Reserve. A rich diversity of wildlife roamed the nearby hills: wild sheep, gazelle, kulan, and more. "I saw a leopard in this valley once," said Vlad. "It was eating a horse." This was Yaz' cue to upstage Vlad's snakebite.

"A leopard attacked me in Badkhiz. It caught me by the arm, but I yelled at it and hit it on the head, and it ran off." It sounded like a tall story; until, like an Agincourt veteran, he stripped his sleeve and showed his scars: deep furrows running the length of his forearm.

It was time to go. Tonight, they would return after dark to go into the hills and shoot small animals to feed the snakes. Three air rifles lay on a table, tools of their trade. But for now their time was their own.

"You know, we might be able to find some kulan to show you. Are you interested?" I jumped at it; the day was getting better and better. As we left, the croak of a frog came from a tin box, bizarrely magnified by the resonance of the container so that it sounded like the voice of a primitive god. I didn't ask to see it; the poor thing was probably the cobra's lunch.

The kulan excursion took us back down the gorge, where to my astonishment Vlad turned off the road... into Akhrana's yard. He drove right through and stopped fifty yards the other side. Yaz got out and scanned the hills with a very large pair of binoculars. After a minute he gave a yell of triumph, and pointed.

It was unbelievable. In full sight of the camelyard where I had spent a week was a bunch of pink dots on the crest of one of the hills. Kulan.

Vlad gave a sing-song whoop, his boyish features creased with delight. "Come on!"

We leapt back into the jeep and set off again. The lads were now as keen on the hunt as I, and they pitched the jeep up and down steep hillsides to get as close as possible. In the end a near-vertical slope defeated them, and we settled down on the grass to watch the herd from a distance of about a mile.

From here, with the powerful binoculars, we could see every detail of individual animals, picking out the foals and yearlings, matching the grey-pink colour precisely to that of the sands. Like the Przewalski horses I had watched two years before in Mongolia, they stayed on the hilltop by day, returning to the valleys to drink only at evening. "Up there," said Yaz, "the wind blows the biting flies away."

I couldn't thank them enough. "Just luck," said Vlad. "It was through God's help that you have seen them."

"But it was yours, too. I'm very grateful."

They gave me a lift back to Ashkhabad, for I had business with Obbly-Guli. Back in the city Vlad drove like a maniac, hurling the jeep too fast round the corners, tyres squealing. "You'll have to excuse us!" he shouted merrily above the desperate shriek of the engine. "We aren't used to the city. We're uncivilised people! We're scared here!"

They took me right up to the Hippodrome gates. Then, instead of turning, Vlad simply drove in a wide circle, bouncing the jeep over a flowerbed on the way out. The last I saw of them was a cloud of dust and a screech of brakes as they turned into the main road.

*

The next day started so dismally it could only get better.

Breakfast was a pan of cold, half-cooked rice, heated on Orazniaz' wood stove the night before, and left to stew wrapped in my sleeping bag. Tom was still very lame. The inside of his hind leg had filled behind the stifle joint, and one ball had doubled in size, making it look quite stupendous. There was probably deep-seated infection somewhere in the hip. I could have cured it in a week with a course of antibiotics. But in Turkmenistan, telephone numbers of dollars wouldn't produce

211

veterinary antibiotics. And I hadn't managed to catch Obbly-Guli the night before. Now, all my hopes rested on Akhrana, or Rep.

Things began to look up. Rep was in.

His house was one of the most prosperous on the kolkhoz; spacious and well-built, with the sort of covered rooftop veranda above the garage that wealthier Turcomans use for summer parties. A satellite dish hung from one of the walls.

While I waited for him, Rep's wife brought me *char*, or fermented camel's milk - a favourite summer drink among the Turcomans, like *kumiss* (mares' milk) among the Kazakhs and Kirghiz. It was clear, sharp and slightly fizzy, with a white sludge of curd at the bottom of the bowl. A tiny black and white kitten with china-blue eyes climbed my knees and peered at it hopefully.

Rep was a pleasant, warmly hospitable man of about forty-five, with a wise, humorous face; the face of a man who had seen everything and found not all of it displeasing. He listened gravely as I told him of my hopes and plans, and of the story so far.

"You mean Obbly-Guli couldn't find you a decent horse?" he asked incredulously; then added, "Yes, I think I can help." I held my breath, and tried not to hope too much. So far there had been too few chickens to count.

On the way to his Kalininskii farm, he stopped to pick up a woman from the next street. There was something familiar about her.

It was Jamilia's mum. She had come to the kolkhoz for essential supplies. "The men are supposed to be repairing a motorbike," she laughed. "I've had to fetch them some more vodka. Otherwise they'll never get any work done!"

The farm was just above the tamarisk stream, with the pink cliffs of the gorge close on one side and the high peaks of the Kopet Dagh far off to the other. Jamilia met us at the door, demure today in a long, green Turcoman dress; one of those admirable people who move with perfect equilibrium between two cultures, secure in both.

We walked down the valley to see the herd, and I complimented Rep on the condition of his horses. "Yes, they're OK here," he answered. "They're thin at Ashkhabad. But this grass is going already. Normally it grows for a month."

From inside, the tamarisk grove was an enchanted place. As Rep searched out his favourite horses, pink fronds brushed our faces, blending with the pink cliffs above them. The occasional call of an unseen mare to an unseen foal drifted through the bushes, punctuating the steady crunch of teeth on grass.

"This is Gerakle." It was the same grey stallion who had threatened Tom two days ago. The name sounded like a compound of two great steeplechasers, Arkle and Grakle, an idea which pleased Rep. "He won at the Hippodrome, and he's also been jumping."

His other two stallions were at the farm, in a yard where a collapsing heap of rusty iron and barbed wire fenced in a herd of Angora goats. Even Rep, it seemed, wasn't immune to a spot of dilapidation.

"This is Sinkar. Champion type!" So he was. The bay horse was a textbook of all the characteristics Geldy had described so fervently. The elegantly tapering head was topped with long ears that were almost hairless inside, and his mane and tail were similarly thin. The upright neck stood on a long, deep shoulder, and under the powerful rump the length from hip to hock was enormous. He was a real eyecatcher.

"And this is Arian. He's a grandson of Absent." The incomparable Absent, who had won a gold medal for dressage at the Rome Olympics, thus for the first time putting on the world map the Akhal-Teke, that obscure beast from Central Asia. Arian was palomino and, at close on seventeen hands, the tallest of his breed I ever saw.

"Four white feet, keep him all your life," I quoted to Rep, pointing to the four showy white legs. "Three white feet, give him to your wife, Two white feet, give him to your man, One white foot, sell him - if you can!" Clumsily, I translated "wife" as "woman", something which Rep would remind me of later.

Rep's other horses were in Ashkhabad. On the way there we called in at the camelyard. Akhrana's face fell when I arrived with Rep. He saw his potential deal, and with it my saddle, slipping from his grasp.

"That's not a horse; it's a donkey!" was Rep's verdict on poor Tom. I spent the journey back to Ashkhabad trying the explain the saga of Yusup, Obbly-Guli and and Tom. At the city outskirts, my heart sank as Rep turned off the road - and into the Hippodrome. After all the problems emanating from here, I viewed the place with unmixed loathing, and never wanted to see it again.

Today, though, was a different ball game. I was here not as someone else's liability but as a guest, viewing some of the best bloodstock in the country.

Kako, Rep's head lad, disappeared into the gloomy depths of one of the barns, to return with the best horse I had seen in Turkmenistan. He was jet-black, the colour that the Russians call *voronoi* - raven - and seemed to ripple over the ground with the lightness of a dancer, head high, every muscle of him conscious of his three-thousand-year lineage.

"He has won both his races," said Rep. "His name is Gagat. He is for sale, at two thousand dollars."

In the West, such a horse would have cost twenty times as much. My imagination began to run riot with fantastic ambitions. All perfectly vacuous. I would never get him out of the country, and I didn't even have two thousand dollars.

One by one, the horses were brought out by Kako or his brother, Shokhrat. "Khalach. Three wins. $1,500." A ravishing golden dun, the definitive colour of the Akhal-Teke. "Kizildon. Five wins. $2,000. Saparkhan, one run..."

Slowly, my tentative hopes sank again. Rep's interest in me was as a potential Western business associate. I was here only as a prospective buyer. Back to the drawing board. Nevertheless, I couldn't complain. It had been a wonderful afternoon.

I walked once more round inside the barn, taking a last look at the horses. When I came out into the sunlight, Kako was holding a horse I hadn't seen yet, brought from elsewhere. He was chestnut, golden as the sands of the Kara Kum, and he stood with his head high, neck curved so as to look right over his own back, scenting the horses in the barn.

"Will he do?" asked Rep.

XII

Suddenly, the Hippodrome was beautiful.

At last, I was leaving it riding the horse of my dreams. The long, brisk stride of the Akhal-Teke stallion felt like coming home. Ashkhabad's dismal suburbs floated rapidly past in a haze. When I reached the orchards I kicked on into a canter, and enjoyed for the first of many times the floating, slightly rocking stride of this aristocratic horse.

I crossed the railway at exactly the same place as before - no train coming, this time - and rode over the same dune into Anau, where we spooked the same two camels. This time, though, there was no need for a two-hour halt, just a half-hour breather on the far side of town. I rode up to Akhrana's yard after just three-and-a-quarter hours, half the time it had taken to do the same journey with Tom. The stallion bellowed when he sensed the other horses, to be answered by the now-familiar, strangled bray of the lame donkey. The camels had just been fed, so there was fresh grass; when he was stabled and fed I could at last draw breath, take a long look at him, and consider my change in fortune.

His name was Atamekan[*]. He was six years old, and had been racing until last week. This meant that he was fit, another bonus, and at nearly sixteen hands he would have no problems with carrying the weight of the saddlebags. His head displayed all the beauty of the breed, and had a white blaze running right down to the muzzle. He also had three white feet. Rep had pointed them out with satisfaction, reminding me of the rhyme I had misquoted to him - "three white feet, give him to a woman!"

It was all coming together at last. Even my supper - more cold rice, followed by some hard tack biscuits that I'd stocked

---

[*] "Atemikaan", I had scribbled phonetically in my notebook at the Hippodrome, and it was two years before I learned to spell his name. So he became Kaan.

up on in Ashkhabad, and which looked like dog biscuits but actually tasted rather worse - failed to dampen my new-found optimism. There remained only two problems before I could travel the road to Merv. I had to recover my money from Obbly-Guli so that I could pay Rep, and I had to get Tom back to Ashkhabad.

With Rep's help, I tackled the first that night. He kindly drove me back to the Hippodrome, coming with me to lend his weight should there be any argument. But the errand was wasted, for again Obbly-Guli wasn't in.

The second had to wait for morning. It was a day that started badly, for I had my first disagreement with Atamekan.

He was such a lamb to handle that I was careless, and led him out early to graze with only part of a bridle on, the bit hanging loose below his chin. He promptly decided to challenge Tom, and lunged at him aggressively. Somehow I managed to check him, whereupon he rose on his hind legs and struck out with his front feet. After what seemed like an eternity he returned to earth, whereupon I whipped the reins twice round his nose and bundled him back into the stable.

When I'd got my breath back, I had to admit that it was an impressive performance. Rearing, for these horses, wasn't an uncontrollable, dangerous tantrum. It was a game, an expression of *joie de vivre*, carried out with perfect balance and control; more Spanish Riding School than Calgary Stampede.

But it was a salutary lesson. I was reminded that, for all his gentle manners, Kaan was no quiet old hack but an Akhal-Teke stallion; and, more to the point, I had absolutely no experience of handling stallions. I would have to be very, very careful.

There was more drama when I set out to take Tom home. The chestnut pony broke loose and decided to come too. His friend the donkey brayed after him and then hopped in pursuit. I found myself heading a ludicrous procession of three equine waifs, all setting out determinedly for Ashkhabad. The two followers refused to be driven back. I tried to manoeuvre drainage ditches between them and me to head them off; but the pony leapt them with ease while the donkey hurdled them like a Grand National winner on his three good legs. It took the combined efforts of a dozen small boys to halt them at the kolkhoz.

The fields around buzzed with activity: men, women and children all hard at work, tractors scuttling up and down, loads of grass being carted hither and thither. Piles of fresh mulberry branches lay in the yards, ready to feed the silkworms that provide a cottage industry for the kolkhozniks. It was extraordinary how the country had passed from virtual winter to full summer in two weeks flat. The barley had been in flower for a week, and harvesting would begin in four more. Every puddle writhed with tadpoles, desperately trying to grow legs and escape before the hot sun fried their home into dried mud. Another metaphor for Turkmenistan, for everything comes down to water, here.

Round every corner was another dyke, another pump, another reminder that this luxuriant growth depended entirely on irrigation. No wonder that, throughout history, breaking the dams was the unvarying prelude to successful invasion in Central Asia. Take away the water, and the building blocks of society would collapse to rubble.

Even in spring, away from the irrigation ditches the foliage was drying already, crackling underfoot. Once again I cursed the problems that had made me waste so much precious time. Yet I had been astonishingly lucky, for, in dumping me on Rep's patch, fate had provided me with the way out.

In Anau Tom collected another follower; a cow, this time. He had missed his vocation, it seemed, in advertising equine aftershave. Worse was to follow when, near the Hippodrome, we passed a string of racehorses. A big black stallion broke away and lunged after us, his jockey fighting for control. For a moment, it looked as if poor Tom was in for a fate worse than death.

Obbly-Guli still wasn't at home to callers. Could he possibly be avoiding me? But half the Akhal-Teke *cognoscenti* were at the Hippodrome today, all wanting to know where on earth my nag had come from. I told them willingly; a spot of common knowledge might shame Obbly-Guli into honouring his bargain.

Sadiq was there, his face more inscrutable then ever as he looked at Tom. So was Alexei, a former event trainer.

"That's a *pogranichnaya loshad*, a border guard's horse," he told me. The Russians, he said, had imported tough, coarse-bred horses to patrol the mountains. I was oddly relieved; it gave Tom dignity, somehow, to be able to pin a label on him. Amused, too, to think that, even now, images of Soviet Frontier Guards pursued me. Olga would have enjoyed the joke.

I tethered him on the best grass I could find, with a parting hug, and hoped fervently that he would be looked after. I left a letter to Obbly-Guli with Rep, asking him to give my money directly to him.[*] I also left my tent; I'd already discovered that Kaan couldn't be tethered, so there would be no camping out.

Then it was time to trudge out of the Hippodrome for the last time, and find a taxi back to Kaan. I crossed the railway lines to the Anau road with particular care. It would be rather a shame, at this stage, to get picked off by the down train to Mari.

Back at Akhrana's, I gulped a rapid meal of half-cooked rice with tinned condensed milk, and a handful of those biscuits that were more a sentence than a menu.

And then it was time to hit the road.

*

It wasn't a dignified exit. Just as we left, Orazniaz rode the mare into the yard. Kaan was delighted to see her. Bellowing loudly, he lunged at her, and I had to yank him away and kick on hard. We left the yard at a spanking trot, our street cred in bits.

But now at last we were setting out on the track leading eastwards out of Akhrana's stables, a track I had gazed at and yearned after for a week.

It wound gently among low hills, the lowest foothills of the Kopet Dagh. Normally bare, the land was now covered with a very fine scrub of wiry grass. Here and there, in sheltered places, the wind had blown sand across the path, sand indented with the tracks of Akhrana's camels.

[*] In the end, despite further promises, her grudgingly gave back only about half.

The tracks split and joined and split again. When they turned away at right angles I left them and took a bearing straight across open desert, angled slightly north to bring us gradually towards the farmland, and the road. Apart from a broken fence surrounding a few acres that had once been cultivated, there was no obstacle. We could travel where the lie of the land, the compass or simply whim dictated.

The day would have been very hot but for a sharp headwind. It blew sand straight up Kaan's nose, and dried my throat painfully. This was emptier country than I'd expected, and for miles there was nowhere to ask for water.

It was hard going. After his initial enthusiasm, Kaan began to get rapidly disenchanted with the whole idea. I began to realise that being "racing fit", here, meant rather less than it would at home. In any case he was carrying more weight than he was used to. So I took it very slowly, and let him find his own pace. I stopped often, but it was hard to find good grass. It was hard to find grass at all. Now and again, in the bottom of an old water course for instance, there was slightly better growth, and he cropped with dexterity and an unfamiliar rhythm: six bites to every chew.

Now I could at last sit back and observe him without a hundred worries paralysing my mind. He was what Geldy would have described as the "dry" type, lean and wiry. Narrow in the chest, he possessed enormous depth of shoulder, and the underlying strength of his bony quarters and great length from hip to hock promised more power than was at first apparent in his tall, thin frame. His mane and tail were sparse, but his beauty lay in his head, with its fine, tapering lines and enormous glowing eyes.

His temperament, also, was typical. I'd long heard of the sensitivity and gentleness of the Akhal-Teke. So why do some say they are stubborn? Acquaintance with Kaan was already beginning to resolve the paradox. Very responsive to people, he loved receiving my attention, even though I was still a stranger. But I quickly found that he became very upset if I tried to coerce him in any way. The only answer to a difference of opinion was patience, a dogged sit-it-out approach until boredom induced him to see things my way. Fortunately he was the most amenable of horses, and our disagreements were rare.

In mid-afternoon we came on a patch of dunes covered with saxaul bushes. It was the only potential cover for miles; might there be kulan here? I approached carefully, looking for hoofprints in the sand or patches of dung - though I wouldn't have been able to identify kulan-dung if I'd trodden in it. But the question was academic, as the only sign of life was the odd lizard. I never did see kulan during all my travels with Kaan, and repeatedly gave prayers of thanks for Vlad and Yaz.

Soon the road appeared, and we converged with it gradually. On the verge was a good patch of grazing in a hollow where saxaul grew among a profusion of poppies. Not the best spot; but Kaan was oblivious to the traffic, so we stopped for a long break.

With the sun now frighteningly low, we crossed first the road and then the railway line, and came down to the edge of the irrigation. The first houses of a kolkhoz appeared in the distance. Muddy brown water ran in a channel along the fields' edge, and with enormous relief I allowed Kaan to drink a little from it, against Yusup's orders.

As before, distance was deceptive in this flat landscape, and it took forever to reach the kolkhoz. Remembering Olga's advice I asked for the Bashlik, and was surprised to be sent to a formal-looking administration building. Each kolkhoz, as I gradually learned, is run on the lines of a large town, with its own Civic Centre and an administration staff working normal office hours.

Of course, by now everyone had gone home. As I stood indecisively, a couple of men approached to ask what I wanted. I was looking, I croaked through a throat almost too parched to speak, for somewhere for my horse and me to stop overnight.

"No problem!" they replied. "Come and stay with us!"

It was a response that was to become very familiar over the ensuing weeks.

*

221

My new friends set off up the road driving their two cows, and I walked behind with Kaan. They led me through a heavy metal gate into a yard with a house at each side and a barn at the back. Four women and a gang of children came out to see what was happening.

The fact that Kaan couldn't be tethered caused some head-scratching. But, with great goodwill, the men untied and moved one of the cows to make a space at the back of the barn. They fenced Kaan in with wire netting and an old bedstead to serve as a door. In no time he had had a good drink and was happily chewing on a generous armful of feed.

Now it was my turn. "I could drink a bucket of tea!" I said, and they laughingly obliged, carrying me off to dinner and giving me a pot all to myself. I drank it dry three times, and scarcely noticed what I ate.

The household consisted of an old man, the obvious head of the family; his fat, buxom, jolly daughters, increasing in fatness, buxomness and jollity from youngest to eldest; the two sons-in-law who had first taken me in; and a tribe of grandchildren. I had a store of small presents in my saddlebags and brought some out, giving each of the children a plastic trumpet or whistle. They rampaged round the garden blowing with gusto, and soon the hoots of the toys was drowning out the various bleats, moos and baas of the animals. Kaan took all this cacophony with barely a twitch of his ears.

I was worried, though, that he hadn't got enough food. And he wasn't even eating what he'd got, which was mostly odd greenstuff from the garden: fat hen, plantain and so on. Reluctant to give offence by collecting my own fodder, I waited until after dark then sneaked out with a binbag and stuffed it with grass pulled from the verges. Unfortunately, one of the family spotted me as I crept back in. But by that time Kaan had found a cache of hay in the corner of the barn and begun to steal it, so I had an excuse for my foraging. It was a relief to see him get stuck into a really big pile of fresh grass.

The family were dismayed when I asked to sleep beside him. I was still very aware that I was unfamiliar with stallions in general and Kaan in particular, and wanted to keep a close eye on him. Also, I was worried that he might hurt himself on the various knobs of his ramshackle pen.

But my hosts refused to let me sleep on the floor. They brought out a bedstead and propped it up high on blocks, then piled it with about three mattresses and thick layers of bedding. So I lay in unimaginable luxury in the most comfortable bed I had had for weeks, and slept to that most soothing of noises - the quiet, regular crunching of animals eating contentedly.

*

I was so tired - and so comfortable - that I made a late start next morning. By the time I had taken Kaan out to graze a little, it was eleven and the sun was fierce.

I tried to offer payment for our night's lodging, but was refused.

"You are our guest!" they exclaimed.

Unwilling to give offence, I gave in and thanked them gratefully. "But my horse wasn't your guest!" I added. "Please, please could I at least pay for his food?" But this, too, was refused. Such generosity was humbling, especially as my hosts obviously weren't well off.

Today's ride took us through very different country from yesterday. This was the cream of Turkmenistan's farmland. All around us wheat, barley and lucerne rocketed skywards under the dual influence of hot sun and abundant water. Tracks criss-crossed the fields, and it was easy to leave the tarmac and travel on soft ground.

And there was abundant grazing. Frequently, water spilled from the irrigation ditches on to a patch of grass verge, and in such places the growth equalled that in the fields. I stopped to let Kaan eat his fill, taking the saddle off so that the air could reach his back; then saddled up again, and proceeded at a leisurely pace, enjoying the sight of such plenty after the parched hills of yesterday. Easy travelling; a piece of cake, I thought with satisfaction.

No such luck. After a few miles, our way was barred by a cornfield so huge that you couldn't see where it ended. We were forced to turn at right-angles, and make a detour which eventually dumped us back on the main road.

It wasn't all bad news. We stopped for lunch at an excellent spot, separated from the road by an irrigation ditch and shaded by a spreading willow tree. There was plenty of grass; better still, the ditch was filled with rushes, the same rushes that I had seen at the Hippodrome made into rough hay. To Kaan they were ambrosia; sweet, perhaps, like sugar cane? It made life delightfully easy for me, as he stood in one place and gorged while I lounged against the saddlebags, tether rope held loosely in one hand.

In the end he got a full stomach, became bored with eating, and began to fidget. So I cut short our break after two hours - in fact, I rarely got the four-hour stop I had planned to make in the heat of the day - and on we went. How marvellous to know that at least one horse in Turkmenistan was stuffed to capacity! I hoped that he was feeling a little happier about his new job than he had yesterday.

The worst of the heat had passed, and it was a lovely afternoon. All around, nightingales and cuckoos sang to each other. At intervals along the road were ladies selling raisins to the passing drivers. I stopped and topped up with a kilo, replacing the small amount of food I'd been allowed to contribute to last night's meal.

Trees shaded the road, so we continued parallel to it for the next few miles. Parallel, too, to the Kopet Dagh. Its foothills had vanished and the main ridge drew close, to present an absolutely solid, sheer face of constant height, stretching into the far distance until it faded in the heat haze. This towering wall was to be our companion for some days to come.

*

Murad Mohammedov couldn't have been more helpful. He was the Bashlik of Kolkhoz Yashil Depe, and had the answer straight away.

224

"We can put you up at the *ferma*," he said. "Take this road right to the end of the settlement, and I'll wait for you in the car and show you where to go next."

I was baffled. The ferma? Wasn't a kolkhoz all one big farm? But when I got there I saw what he meant.

The "farm" meant the dairy unit, which makes the kolkhoz self-sufficient in milk, butter and cheese. Murad led me into a complex of lean-to barns with iron-railed paddocks, occupied by fat, contented cows. Heads through the rails, they munched lucerne from concrete troughs running the length of the paddocks. I had never seen such plenty, such plump livestock, nor such tidiness and order, anywhere in Turkmenistan.

The skipper of this tight-run ship was Ashir, assisted by his wife Bagda and half-a-dozen stockmen of varying ages. In no time at all they had installed Kaan in a small enclosure to one side of the barn, with three young calves poking their heads through the rails to make friends. He was given a great pile of the abundant lucerne, and one of the stockmen even managed to find him some barley. Again, they refused all payment.

Ashir and Bagda had a great brood of children, from mid-teens down to a youngest daughter of about three with a fetching smile. I burrowed in the saddlebags and came up with some balloons, and soon even the elder ones were joining in the games. They broke off abruptly when an emergency was called: a clutch of chicks was escaping from their pen, and we rushed to catch them and shut them up again, building and rebuilding the gap with blocks and wire netting until Bagda called us in to supper.

Over the meal Ashir told me about his work. The farm stocked seventy cows, plus a few extra animals of his own such as the chicks, and the clutch of broody turkeys I'd stepped over when coming through the lobby of his house.

To maintain them he had a hundred hectares, of which he put sixty down to lucerne and grew cereals on the rest. Yashil Depe's main crop, though, was fruit - apples, plums and grapes. I'd ridden through the odd orchard or vineyard on my way here, but most were away to the north on the far side of the kolkhoz.

As before, I was anxious to sleep within sight of Kaan. Ashir and Bagda made me comfortable on the family divan in the yard. Once again I had a wonderful bed piled high with blankets; once again I wasn't going to want to get up in the morning.

Come to that, it was too lovely to want to go to sleep at all. Above, the stars were brilliant, while the moon, just past the full, followed them into the sky about midnight. All round me the lucerne was spread to dry in the moistureless night air, its smell like that of an English hayfield - only more intense. Yashil Depe, the Green Mound, was well named.

Kaan was pretty pleased with life here, too. He had eaten his way through a pile of fresh lucerne, followed by a pile of lucerne hay, followed by another pile of fresh. Now he was standing with his head halfway to the ground, looking completely mind-blown by the amount he'd had to eat. I was deeply content to see my Celestial Horse at last receiving his proper, historical diet of lucerne.

My own breakfast was Bagda's wonderful bread. It was the best I'd tasted in Turkmenistan, and I said so. She was delighted, and promptly pressed on me a great heel to put in my saddlebags for lunch. She also gave me a big bowl of steaming milk straight from the cow. It made a glorious start to the day.

Outside was a hive of activity; but gentle activity. There was much work to be done, but no pressure to do it in a hurry. The huge mountain ridge scowled over all; from its top the scurrying humans must have seemed like ants. Strange thought, that if I were one yard on the other side of that spine I would be in Iran, and would have to be covered from head to foot.

Life here seemed idyllic. But when I said so, over breakfast, I learned that things weren't quite so easy. To my surprise, Ashir wanted to get away.

The order and efficiency, so impressive, were achieved at high cost. "I start work sometimes at four in the morning," he said, "and go on till late at night." The responsibilities and the sheer volume of work was giving him gall-stones, and he couldn't go on much longer. He was building himself a house elsewhere on the kolkhoz, and once he could move out of the farm he wanted a job on the railway, using his original training as a construction engineer.

"You'll miss your cows!" I said, and he nodded. Such high standards couldn't be achieved without personal commitment. At heart, Ashir was surely first and foremost a stockman.

Before I left I took photographs of the family. I was rapidly understanding that it was going to be impossible to pay my way on this trip. The small presents to children were hopelessly inadequate to say a proper thank you for the kindnesses being heaped on me; and in any case my supply was already low. When I got home I would write a proper "thank you" letter and send a batch of photographs to all my hosts. It was little enough, but better than nothing.

There was another kindness still to come. Ashir's eldest daughter noticed a small tear in my saddlebags. She wouldn't let me mount until she had run for a needle and put in a few deft, strong stitches. I was hugely grateful; for by the time I had put it off a dozen times, it would certainly have been a dozen times as bad.

*

The main road and the Kara Kum Canal, respectively south and north of Yashil Depe, converged ahead of us at the town of Yashlik. I wanted at all costs to avoid the hard roads through the town, and was thankful to find a brand-new bridge which would take us across the canal and back into the farmland.

From its height, I took my first real look at Turkmenistan's main artery. Its waters flowed in slow procession within their straight banks, stopping to lick and slurp at a clump of reeds or a projecting earth wall; or dancing ponderously to the unheard tune of some underwater obstacle in a series of sucking whirlpools. An unattractive, functional being, man-made, yet master rather than servant. Thick, brown and turgid; and liquid gold to the kolkhozniks. Past and present mingled on its banks. Camels grazed on either side, and a herd of sheep and goats followed a tinkling bell-wether down to drink. Above them a line of pylons marched away to the modern town nearby.

227

The bridge meant a long stretch of tarmac, on which I dismounted and walked. I was seriously worried about Kaan's unshod feet, which probably presented the biggest threat to my chances of completing the journey.

Normally, the dearth of farriers in Turkmenistan isn't a problem, for the horses have feet quite hard enough to stand up to everyday situations; especially in a country without many roads. But travelling like this was a different thing altogether. There would be too many situations, like now, where I couldn't avoid tarmac. And Kaan's feet weren't even trimmed. The horn of a horse's foot, the equine equivalent of nail and claw, grows constantly, and needs regular cutting back. Kaan's feet were too long. Only time would tell whether they would wear down gradually without damage, or break and split in the process. If I was careful, there was every chance they would do the first, and harden up as well.

It wasn't the only worry. I was acutely conscious that he wasn't in long-distance training, and thin as well. I planned to take things very steadily the first week, rarely if ever breaking out of a walk. I had to turn him, slowly but as quickly as I dared, from a racehorse into a long-distance horse. It was a dicey business. One mistake - one sprain, one saddle gall - and the journey was over.

On the far bank we could step out briskly over a friendly earth track. The shepherd, an old man in a Teke telpek riding a donkey, was bringing his herd up from the water's edge, and stopped to pass the time of day. Generously, he pressed me to take a draught from his flask of tea, then gave me directions for going on. "Have a happy journey," he said as we parted. "May you live to be a hundred years, and may your road be peaceful."

Yashlik passed behind us. We followed the canal along a path which was turned to baked, rutted white mud by sections of dredging spoil and bulldozer scars. The sun beat back up mercilessly from the shiny earth, and the only relief came from the gradually increasing cover of tamarisk bushes, among which I hoped presently to lose ourselves for a bit of shade and an afternoon rest.

The Kopet Dagh ridge continued to tower over us, undiminished; we were still less than halfway along it. From here I could see that it was a very steep scree slope, topped by a cliff of several hundred feet. If the canal is an artery, then these mountains form the backbone of Turkmenistan. A backbone very much like poor Tom's; a pointed frame from which everything else hangs. And so there is an apparent contradiction, that this sharp edge, so clearly defining the frontier, lies right on top of the most densely inhabited part of the country. It is an uneasy juxtaposition: population and activity on the one hand, a highly sensitive border on the other.

The tamarisk groves were disappointing, giving little shade and promising better grazing than they delivered. Saddling up after an unsatisfactory half hour, I blocked out my obsessive eastward drive and made a beeline for some trees a mile or two away to the north. Kaan was tired, probably from the intense heat, so we settled down under them for a good, long rest.

Before long someone else had the same idea. A young man left his work in the melon field nearby to come and sit out the heat of the day. Presently he invited me to join him for tea.

Chari had no pretensions to a fancy stove. He simply made a small pile of twigs which burned furiously. From their wrappings in a piece of old sack he brought a couple of bowls, a heel of bread, and a curved pot encrusted with the soot of a hundred brews. In less than five minutes the tea was ready, and we drank, ate and drank again.

Then it was Kaan's turn. "There's a lucerne field beyond the melons," said Chari's friends, newly arrived. "Take him for a graze!"

"I couldn't possibly!" It would be little better than theft. "But everything here is communal," answered the young men. "It's meant for everybody. So it's up to us to decide who uses it."

So we picked a careful way among the melons and crossed a ditch to stand surrounded by the lush, tall clover. Kaan, ungratefully, preferred the reeds in the ditch. The chance couldn't be wasted, so I pulled lucerne to fill my binbag for his supper.

229

The melons covered acres, each row carefully protected by polythene tunnels. "Whatever do they want polytunnels for in this heat?" I asked Chari. "It brings them in just that little bit sooner," he said. A complex system of channels watered them, running right underneath the tunnels. It was the daily work of the lads to manage these miniature dykes, lifting a spadeful of earth here or depositing one there to vary the flow and give each row its fair share.

Now came decision time: push on or stay here for the night? Chari had friends in the nearby settlement, who he was sure would put us up.

We had come only a dozen miles all day, but it made sense to accept the offer of help. Both Kaan and I were tired from the exceptional heat. My hands and arms were red with white blotches, the skin all scaly from simultaneous burning and peeling, while my face felt like a bit of boiled leather. Worse, my hands were already becoming raw; partly from handling the very coarse tether rope in the last ten days, but also from pulling grass. My fingertips were so worn that I could only handle a bowl of tea with the heels of my hands.

So we rested until Chari had finished with the melons, then followed slowly when he jumped into his jeep and drove off to alert his friends.

The road swung west, and we followed a herd of cattle directly into the setting sun. Only a quarter mile; but how mulishly I fretted at the thought of backtracking even such a little way! North again; and now acacia trees lined the road, rustling and chattering with a thousand sparrows. Fifteen or twenty nests crammed each tree, making a sort of natural, Soviet-style apartment block for birds. At the end of this avenue was the village street, where Chari waited with a "yes" clearly written on his face.

The friend was absent, but his wife Mir and her younger sister Tsetok seemed quite happy to have a stranger landed on them at dusk. A space was made for Kaan in the goat pen by evicting its occupants. I left him happily attacking the lucerne and went on a successful foray for his night rations. Sure by now that I could leave him safely, I spent my first night indoors.

Mir was a little reserved, as if she minded my intrusion after all. She smiled, though, when I produced balloons for her toddler. The rubber wouldn't stretch at first; as we struggled to blow them up, we both lost all our dignity in a string of rude noises, and were soon giggling together like old friends.

She was one of the most beautiful Turcoman women I had seen yet, with a profile like that of Nefertiti; a girl who could have earned megabucks modelling in the West. So was her sister. Money, however, would never have tempted these girls to the immodesty of selling their looks. They were utterly content with their quiet rural existence. Tsetok had followed her sister here from Tedzhen, and was delighted with life in the country. "I've been offered good wages for a job in Ashkhabad," she said. "But I like it better here."

Inevitably, they bemoaned the financial situation. The family owned two or three houses, and were currently rebuilding the main one. But only dollars would buy the building materials they needed.

"We're a hundred and fifty dollars short, and where on earth could we get it from? No-one has anything but manats here. The usual wage is ten dollars a month. I could earn two hundred and fifty in Ashkhabad as a translator, if only I could speak English." But then she would have had to leave the village...

She washed my shirt for me, yet another small kindness. As I watched it drying almost visibly in the fresh night air, I resolved firmly that I must, absolutely must, get off early tomorrow. Especially as the plan was to go wall hunting.

*

Some months before, researching my journey in the map room of the Royal Geographical Society in London, I had come on something that made me sit up. A World War Two German reconnaissance map of Central Asia, startling in its Teutonic precision and attention to detail ("this well is sweet, this is brackish, this is definitely salt..."), showed a couple of stretches of embankment south-east of Tedzhen.

Alone, it would have meant little. But further west, on the south-east and south-west shores of the Caspian, are large sections of ancient earth and stone embankment collectively known as "Alexander's Wall". The name has no significance; the name of Alexander was as that of a god in these parts, and tends to be attached to anything of note - much as Britain is littered with Caesar's Camps and Arthur's Caves.

What was interesting was the possibility that this German map showed a continuation of Alexander's Wall some hundreds of miles further east. For millennia in these lands the settled, civilised world marched with that of the nomad horsemen; two extremes, meeting at the grating edges of two demographic as well as two geological tectonic plates. What if the ancient dwellers of settled Persia had had the same idea as the Chinese, and created a Great Wall of vast length to keep the barbarians out?

The thought simmered, coming to the boil in Professor Atamuradov's office in the Ministry of the Environment. On the detailed map he had used to show me the distribution of kulan, I had spotted not far east of Ashkhabad a short castellated zigzag marked "remains of ancient wall". Another bit! This couldn't be a coincidence.

I was about to enter the relevant area. The hunt was on.

*

But the next day brought its own concerns.

At last I'd managed to leave while the sun was still low in the sky. A few miles out from the kolkhoz, we followed a lane whose verge, shaded by acacia trees, dipped to a ditch filled with water. The combination of heat and wet had done its stuff, and the grass was like an English hayfield in June.

I could never afford to pass up good grazing. Although it was a bit early I stopped and prepared for a long break. Taking off Kaan's saddle, I found a small swelling on one of his vertebrae.

It was a pressure swelling, and meant bad trouble. Despite a numnah, or saddle-pad, the saddle was rubbing, where the gullet along its spine should have prevented it from even touching. Unattended to, the swelling would quickly become a saddle gall - something serious enough to cancel the rest of the journey.

I got out my Karrimat, and went to work with a penknife. When the saddle went back on it was over two layers of foam slab, the lower with holes cut where necessary to relieve pressure. From now on tacking up was a piece of precision work. I had plenty of practice, for at every stop, however short, the saddle came off to let the air get to Kaan's back, and I brushed him off to restore circulation and prevent the formation of knots of sweaty hair, which might rub.

We passed an old Soviet checkpoint, a red and white raised barrier next to a tatty wooden hut, now fallen into disrepair. Two girls waited there for a bus, their scarves pulled tightly round their faces with only the eyes exposed. They might have been figures from the Palestinian Intifaada.

The trees fell behind, and the country opened out again: real prairie farming, here, with great fields of wheat and barley stretching to the limits of sight. The size of the fields made for some major detours; too often the tracks ended in a T-junction against a barrier of wheat a mile wide, or gave out altogether in a dead end. We had a very nasty moment where careless irrigation had caused a torrent running straight down the dirt track. I tried the edges, and Kaan sank to his hocks in deep mud. So I let him choose his own way, and unerringly he found the best ground - straight up the middle, where the water was deepest but tractors had packed the earth hard, giving solid footing. It was strange to have problems with mud in a desert country, and frightened us both a little.

At least this track had led us due east for several miles. It couldn't last, and it didn't. The next T-junction wasn't at just a cornfield, but an aqueduct - a major waterway, deep and steep-sided, with a concrete channel along which the water raced and pounded with colossal force. Left or right? I turned right towards the road, only to find after a mile that the canal curved a further ninety degrees to the right - back the way we had come - with no sign of a bridge. So, grinding my teeth, I turned Kaan round and backtracked to the junction, and beyond. There had to be a bridge soon.

But this was Turkmenistan. Human mobility was a very low priority for the people who had laid out this system of waterways; they considered it a perverse habit to be discouraged. We plodded on and on, the crashing of the water alongside muffling my growing string of obscenities, until it seemed that we should have left the irrigation miles behind and be halfway across the Kara Kum. Behind us, those towering mountains lost none of their size or distance; they just sank a little deeper into the heat-haze.

Desperate loss of time and waste of mileage! The conclusion was inescapable, that in future I must throw in my lot with either the road or the canal and stick to it. It was just no good going through the farmland. And yet, I had to go through the countryside, to keep Kaan's feet off tarmac roads, and to stay near the best grazing. It was an insoluble problem.

At least this route was well provided with feed, for lucerne had seeded and grown all along the path. I jumped off, loosened the girth and removed the bit from Kaan's mouth, so that he could stock up on the hoof. Every time we passed a bush, we stopped and grabbed in equal measure; he to stuff it down and I to pull an armful which I could feed to him as we walked on.

A line of pylons slowly took shape ahead, shimmering in the mirage. A bit nearer, and I could make out an embankment. A road, or just another canal to box us in hopelessly? An old man in a Teke hat appeared on the horizon, leading a donkey. He must be walking on something, going somewhere. I could hardly bear the suspense.

We climbed the bank, and still the question was unresolved; there was a meeting of old and new waterways, a deep dry ditch and lots of concrete. A bit further, and I let out my breath in relief. Our "own" canal, the one which had fended us off for so long, here swung hard right. Although we still could not pass it, we could at least turn with it, cross the dry ditch and start heading in the right direction. Twenty yards up the ditch, I saw with exasperation, was a completely pointless bridge.

234

The old Teke had stopped under the only tree for miles, parked his donkey and made a fire of twigs for his pot. "Come and drink tea!" he called.

It was music to my ears. But I couldn't stop here. There was no grass for Kaan, who needed a good rest. He didn't much want to go on either, for he wanted to say hello to the donkey. Reluctantly we crossed the system of old dykes, and on the other side found gold: a hut and a shaded animal pen, the overnight pad of occasional shepherds. Fifty yards away, water had leaked from the aqueduct to nurse a patch of grass, good rich rye and wild barley.

Kaan pitched in with a good appetite, and was so happy that I left him loose while I collected a bagful of fodder. I suddenly realised it was very quiet, and looked round to see that he'd disgraced me. He was a hundred yards off, making for the donkey, and as I started after him he broke into a canter. For a hideous moment I had visions of him charging all the way back to Ashkhabad; but the old Teke caught him.

"Come on," he said. "Now you're back here, you might as well drink tea!" So we sat together under his tree enjoying refreshing bowlfuls, while Kaan fidgeted and stamped and did his level best to knock everything over.

He spent the afternoon in the animal pen with a good pile of cut grass, while I sat and watched him from the shade of the hut, drinking almost continuously. I need never have worried, after all, about losing the stove. It was the work of moments to collect a few twigs or dried stalks, make a hearth of three stones as Chari had done, and boil water in a billycan. The litre from my bottle was soon used up, but water from the hated aqueduct, left for half an hour to allow the silt to settle, made a perfectly good brew. It tasted slightly of charcoal, but so what; that masked any lingering flavour of mud.

We sat out the heat of the day in peace and plenty, and were well rested when it was time to push on. Kaan was raring to go, and impossible to tack up. In desperation I tied him to a bar of the shed; but he pulled back sharply, ripping the plank loose and hitting me in the face with it. When I finally climbed into the saddle I had a bloody nose and, for a time, saw four ears flickering at the end of his long neck.

We had another tantrum at a small water ditch. Finally consenting to jump it, Kaan leapt sideways, caught the saddlebag on a bit of projecting concrete and tore a great hole. This was one fire-eating horse today. At least I wasn't riding him into the ground.

Just as well, for although we were now travelling east again, we were as trapped as ever by the impassable canal on the right. More so, for after a few miles a second aqueduct swung in from the left to run parallel. If the two were to converge ahead... I couldn't bear to think about it. The eight or ten yards between were bog, from which pieces of rusting machinery stuck out like the hulls of wrecked ships. Little black dots wriggled among them. They were half-grown tadpoles - tiny, tiny froglets that squirmed in the filthy mud, or scattered from under Kaan's feet as we picked our squelching way along the edge.

At last, to my unspeakable relief, both canals simultaneously swung away, to leave open ground - and a good track ahead. Barring the way to freedom was the worst patch of bog yet; deep and slimy, the sort you could disappear into with no more trace than a couple of glugs and a few bubbles. But our luck had well and truly turned, for working at the waterway intersection was the first human being I'd seen for hours. He pointed out the best ground, and after a few nasty moments we were through, covered in black slime.

Free at last, we made good time at a brisk trot in the right direction. The luck lasted some miles, but it couldn't last forever. We struck the most impenetrable barrier yet: marsh - real, natural marsh, not just over-irrigation - stretching left and right and forever ahead, thickly packed with reeds above head-height. There was no alternative but to strike out to the right and south for the road, over open but, fortunately, good ground.

How long would it remain so? After a bit we picked up wheel tracks on a broadening path. Perhaps at last the gods were with us, I hoped, crossing my fingers against hubris.

I had learned my lesson. The wall could keep its secrets, and even the farmland its grass. From now on I was sticking to the road.

*

It was a small settlement, just four houses. But a few sheep and goats were coming in for the night, and each house had a stable or two. I caught up a couple of lads bringing two cows home, and they said that they could find a spare pen for Kaan.

It was low, with a narrow doorway. But Kaan was getting good at this kind of thing. Very, very carefully, with a girlish wiggle of his fine hips, he squeezed inside without even touching the frame. I spent the next hour frantically racing the growing darkness to gather food for him, rushes from drainage ditches and grass from the roadside. Hungry as he was, he was eating it almost as fast as I could bring it in.

Once again, not wishing to intrude, I intended to sleep outside with Kaan. "You can't," said my friend. "The mosquitoes are terrible." He was right; I had noticed them gradually getting worse over the last mile or two, and now Kaan was plastered with them. Before I staggered inside, numb with exhaustion, I sprayed him all over with Deet repellant. I hoped the problem wouldn't arise again, as I'd nearly emptied the bottle.

Rustam's family, along with the other three living here, worked the surrounding land to produce feed - barley and oats - for the Komsomol Stud, where his father worked. Posters of Akhal-Teke horses covered the walls of Rustam's room. On one of them, the horse was accompanied by a girl in a flimsy blouse showing lots of boob - rather unexpected, in this eastern culture.

Although I protested that I had my own food, Rustam's mother fed me generously. Yalya was a lovely, gentle person, with the innate serenity so typical of Central Asian women, her beauty having written itself ever more deeply into the soft lines of her face rather than fading with middle age. Her husband Tokhtamurad (the name, with its Mongol-Arab derivation, encompassed twelve centuries of history), a tall, greying man in an army jacket, was the sort of person you would instinctively trust your life to. What an irony, that Obbly-Guli was actually this man's boss; and how fortunate, I thought yet again, to have this opportunity of knowing the genuine people of Turkmenistan. Turkmenchilik ran naturally through the arteries of Tokhtamurad and Yalya.

In fact they and their small community were Tadzhiks, refugees from the civil war in their own country. Life in Tadzhikistan had become increasingly difficult until, four years ago, they had given up the struggle and come here. "It was no place to live," said Tokhtamurad sadly.

The family had two cats. One, an aristocratic black kitten, found her way into my room and spent the night in the crook of my legs, making it difficult to turn over.

Kaan was tired in the morning. But he stepped out bravely, and I loved him more than ever for it. At least his load was lighter; for I'd left my sleeping-bag with Yalya, together with one or two other inessentials.

My baggage was now pared to the bone: a single change of shirt, trousers and underwear; basic medical kit with some veterinary additions; toothbrush, soap and a small towel; a billycan with tea, sugar (sometimes) and a bag of rice or pasta; and a little drawstring bag of useful miscellanea - string, tape, needle and thread, matches, spare batteries, compass, a tiny torch... Items for frequent use - knife, map, dictaphone, camera, money, papers and the vital Russian dictionary - I stowed about myself in pockets, bumbag and moneybelt.

The sun was behind cloud, and a stiff breeze blew. But it was still hot enough to turn the reed-marshes into a mirage of shimmering water. There were great stretches of real water, too, parting the banks of reeds. This was natural oasis, where the meltwater running off the mountains had collected over a wide area. I thanked my stars that we weren't out there somewhere, trying desperately to find a way through it. The sound of the traffic was music to my ears.

Travelling up the road was no soft option, though. The good ground alongside soon deteriorated, and we had a very nasty moment when Kaan broke through the thin, dry crust into near quicksand underneath. I jumped off quickly and he managed to flounder clear, but he was very upset and shaken.

From then on this sort of deep ground was common. Where the surface was better camelthorn grew thickly, coarse shrubby stuff two or three feet high and covered in two-inch spines that raked Kaan's legs. We were continually forced on to the road itself, walking up the wide hard shoulder while the traffic, fortunately light, thundered past inches away.

At least we had now reached the end of the mountain ridge. Here the border swept down into the foothills and close to the road. I would have to watch my P's and Q's for a bit.

We reached some good grazing at last. It was time for a halt. I was thankful I didn't have to pull grass for Kaan, for my hands were in a bad way. Ripping up the coarse reeds last night had taken off most of the remaining skin, and I was now reduced to cutting fodder with a penknife. I must be getting soft in my old age, I thought angrily. Already I was down to holding the reins on my second finger; there was only one more to go.

Kaan's back, however, was holding up well. The skin over one vertebra was still raised slightly when I was riding, but went down as soon as I untacked. It didn't help that the saddle kept slipping backwards. This was partly due to the pull of the saddlebags; but more so because Kaan had the figure of an Olympic swimmer, with great shoulders tapering to a wasp waist. While he ate, I improvised a breast girth from a luggage strap padded with my sweater. From now on the saddle stayed in place, well forward; one worry fewer.

Another quarter-mile, and I spent my first money since Ashkhabad. A swaying mirage resolved itself into welcome substance: a chai-khana beside the road. I drank a pot of tea dry, while Kaan, his stomach still full, stood as quiet as an old mule. Passing the filling station alongside, I briefly regretted the stolen stove. I'd rather looked forward to riding my horse up to a petrol pump and asking for fuel.

Quite horrible country lay ahead: salt flats, with white ground blazing back up at us under a mid-day sun that had long since swallowed the few friendly clouds. The marsh had fallen behind and on both sides, as far as the eye could see, nothing grew except a few scrubby tamarisk bushes. Crystals of salt lay like a crust of ice on the surface of old water courses.

This was land which had never been under irrigation. How much of Turkmenistan's salt contamination was man-made disaster, and how much natural? The journalist Edmond O'Donovan had come this way after the battle of Geok Tepe, racing the Russians to their ultimate destination - and mine - of Merv. Travelling across this desert long before the days of the cotton monoculture, he noted the phenomenon. "Nitre... is specially abundant... the soil of the whole plain is more or less impregnated with it."

Plodding up the edge of the road, I was glad of the wild lucerne which grew abundantly. If progress was slow, at least Kaan could feed on the move. And move we must, for there was nowhere to hide from the sun. Some stunted trees a few miles ahead turned out to be behind the frontier fence, and I eventually had to settle for a brief rest in the shade of a workmen's hut.

There was something odd about my tea, apart from the slight scumminess. After a moment I pinned it down: it tasted salt. All around, the wind raised white dust-devils, sometimes real twisters, from the salt dust. You could see where the Moslems of these lands had got the idea of djinns.

In the late afternoon we re-crossed the Canal. I drew two good bucketfuls of water for Kaan and a third for myself, leaving it for the silt to settle while he filled his stomach with reeds. The sun was dropping, and it was time to think about somewhere to spend the night.

There was no village in sight. Worse, a line of tall fencing with watchtowers showed that the border was only half a mile away. As the light dimmed and the long ridge of the Kopet Dagh behind us reddened with the beginnings of a spectacular sunset, it seemed that I would have to bed down uncomfortably close to the pogranichniki.

Good farmland, rich with growth and frequent tracks, now enveloped us. To the left, and away from the frontier, we passed some wire animal pens. One of them had a hut alongside. There was plenty of foodstuff here for Kaan. This would do us nicely. I regretted ditching my sleeping bag, but the nights were warm.

A lane led from the road towards the hut. Halfway there, we met a man and his daughter coming home from the fields, laden with cut grass.

I opened my mouth and drew breath to ask him whether we might use the pen for the night. Before I could speak, he beat me to it.

"Come and have supper with us! There's a farm up the road where you can leave your horse! Come and stay the night!"

XIII

The jeep was bright red, and shone like a new toy in the morning sun. Whoever, I wondered, could afford such smart wheels in Kolkhoz Artik? I was still wondering when it pulled up sharply beside me, and out got the KGB.

It was naïve of me, I suppose, to have walked openly up the main street of a village so close to the border. But I badly needed to fill my binbag with grass for Kaan. Anyway, I had the precious visas which had cost so much effort. As I was scooped up and carried off for checking out, I had no worries. Again, naïve. This was Turkmenistan.

The boss, a quiet, courteous chap with a cuddly figure and ginger moustache, inspected my passport as if it were something smelly on a slide. His sidekick looked on superciliously from behind an expensive pair of shades, worth about a month of Olga's salary. He smirked with satisfaction when the boss told me the bad news.

Over one thing, at least, the Anau policeman had been right. My week's homework had resulted in visas which, while covering the whole oblast of Mari, only covered me for the city, not oblast, of Ashkhabad; and certainly not for Artik. It was the usual story: pay a bribe to get it right at the time, or a "fine" later if you don't spot the deliberate mistake. In my ignorance, I hadn't oiled the bureaucratic wheels. Now, my documentation was inadequate. And with the border this close, I was in extra deep shit.

I grovelled, explaining that I'd made several visits to the Foreign Ministry, and thought that my papers were in apple pie order. If the Ministry itself couldn't get it right, I asked, how could I, an ignorant foreigner, know they'd cocked it up?

The sidekick sniggered. Dollar signs lit up the eyeballs behind the Ray-Bans. I braced myself for a thumping fine, or worse. But I was lucky, for his boss was out of a different

242

mould. He knew and, it seemed, disapproved of the tricks. If I got out of the district first thing tomorrow, he said, then they hadn't seen me. Meanwhile, if I wanted food for my horse, I must go that way, not this.

A nice KGB man? Eat your heart out, James Bond. I thanked him gratefully, and he gave me a smart salute and turned on his heel to go. It was a pity that someone had left a pile of old wire lying in the road, and that it chose this moment to wrap itself round his leg and nearly floor him. He really had been exceptionally decent, so I turned away quickly and pretended I hadn't seen.

It had seemed a good idea to rest at Uraz' house for a couple of days, for Kaan and I were both exhausted after two very long and difficult days. Kaan was now comfortably stabled in one end of Uraz' barn, with cattle and sheep for company and a camel next door.

As for me, there was a warm welcome, and an even greater luxury than the three teapots I'd emptied on arrival. Uraz' daughter led me to a bath-house like a Siberian sauna. A bucket of scalding water simmered on the stove, while one of tepid stood on the duckboard beside it. I sluiced myself from head to foot, washing off the crust of salt and dust, revelling in cleanliness.

In the morning Uraz clapped on his telpek and went to stand with his scythe like Old Father Time by the road, waiting for the truck which would take him to the fields. His second daughter went with him, scarf wrapped around her face against the dust of the day's work. The rôles of children are well-defined in Turcoman society: eldest girl to keep house, other children to work the land, and the youngest son to take care of his parents when they are old. Uraz had produced four daughters before siring the son who would provide for his old age.

The domestic skills of the eldest daughter were quite dazzling. I marvelled at the intricacy of her dress's yoke, the most decorative part of a Turcoman woman's clothing. She showed me how she stitched the pattern on an old treadle sewing machine, deftly twirling a strip of cotton to conjure in seconds a series of perfect whorls and arabesques.

243

Meanwhile, the day's bread dough was rising in a large shallow tin. "*Tan-dur*" she said, indicating the earth-brick oven out in the yard, one of the pivots of Turcoman life. The baking process began with a fire of twigs, straw and dried dung that produced fierce flames leaping out of the top of the oven. When it had burned for a bit, the girl sprinkled water to damp the flames without killing the heat. Now for the bread.

First stamping each loaf with a circular dot pattern, she leaned inside, scarf tight round her mouth against the smoke, to place it carefully inside the rim. It stuck facing downward, defying gravity, glued to the wall as the flour struck the hot brick. Five minutes, and it was cooked. The youngest daughter and a neighbour joined us, and we sat in the sun juggling searing fragments from hand to hand until it was cool enough to eat.

Moist, crunchy and delicious now, it would be quite hard by the time today's remains were unwrapped from a piece of coarse sacking for tomorrow's breakfast. Still palatable, though, dunked in tea or soup. These three are the staple diet for the country Turcoman, with the occasional luxury of eggs or boiled milk when the hens are in lay, the cow in milk. Later in the year, there would be fresh vegetables. Uraz' garden was a workmanlike scale model of the kolkhoz fields, with its own miniature system of ditches and banks, and in the evenings his wife Sarai supervised its flooding until the last tomato plant was soaked.

I had chores enough of my own before I took to the road again. Most important was some extra padding to fit the saddle more closely to Kaan's bony ribs. Two more strips of Karrimat did the job, stuck to the inner lining with superglue and anchored with a few stitches of strong carpet thread.

I thanked my stars for that thread, because I needed it for constant running repairs to the saddlebags. These were just a pair of kitbags bought for a tenner from an Army surplus stall, stitched together by my friendly saddler and modified with loops and metal rings in strategic places; clipped to the girth with mini-karabiners and held stable under the belly with a luggage strap through the girth, they did the job perfectly. The problem was that the original kitbags must have been sitting in

244

an Army warehouse for years, for the fabric was already beginning to rot. I could have done with three cards of that carpet thread, not just one.

Before I left I cooked pasta and soup from my stores, to add to the family meal and return just a little hospitality. It was a long meal. After a day in the fields, Uraz shared my lust for tea, and we emptied pot after pot.

"*Pi, pi*!" he said whenever I laid down my bowl - "Drink, drink!" - sending a daughter to put the kettle on yet again. If I carried on like this, I thought, I would do nothing else all night.

Uraz wanted to know where I had found Kaan, and how long it had taken to travel this far. So I told him the long saga of poor old Tom, of Yusup and Obbly-Guli. To my astonishment, he knew Yusup. Just an extraordinary coincidence, or some other reason? "We Tekes know one another," was all he would say, shaking his head mysteriously.

Inevitably, the conversation turned to the current problems. "In the days of the USSR, the shops always had what you needed. Now, there's nothing, and no-one has money anyway. The only currency that's respected is dollars, and it's very hard to get dollars if you don't know the right person. If you just go into a bank and try to buy them with manats, they cost twice as much as if you have connections."

The local KGB, he said, had teased him about his foreign guest. "She should have plenty of dollars for you!" they had said to him. What, I wondered, was a simple kolkhoznik doing hobnobbing with the KGB? A lot of unanswered questions hovered about Uraz.

As ever, we made some price comparisons. The salary of the average Westerner was undreamed of riches; but the family were quite shocked to learn how much of this would be used to pay for gas, electricity and water, all free in Turkmenistan. The concept of income tax, VAT, council tax and so on was quite incomprehensible, whereas the idea of petrol costing a dollar a litre... exactly one hundred times the cost here - forty manats, or about one cent.

There followed a rather uncomfortable discussion about dollars. Uraz and Sarai desperately needed dollars; could I exchange some for their manats? I spared as many as I dared from my small store, but it left me dangerously short. They were disappointed.

Could I come back to Artik from England and visit them again? Could I bring a thousand dollars? Two thousand dollars? They thought that in the West, dollars grew on trees and everybody was rich. It was hard to explain that I'd brought as many dollars as I could afford on this trip, and I simply hadn't got any left.

I felt that I'd failed them, and it was an unhappy thought to take with me back to the road.

*

From now on, as that imposing ridge receded behind gentle foothills, the plain was littered with earthen mounds, perhaps fifty to a hundred feet high and four or five times that in diameter. Their dead, crumbling clay disguised living history; for these were old settlements, the accumulated debris of centuries, maybe millennia of occupation.

Occasionally, surrounding humps or the remains of a rampart showed how the township had spread beyond its original mound; one or two were enclosed by a square set of walls about five feet in height, scaled-down models of Geok Tepe. I had seen identical walls around modern farms. It was good to know that the old practices were still in use.

No-one I asked had any idea of the age of these settlements. "They are from the Old Days," was the usual answer. Fascinating, to imagine excavating from the top down, and passing backward through layers of history: Turcoman, Turco-Mongol, Seljuk, Arab, Sassanid, Parthian, Macedonian, Persian, Scythian.... although the period didn't necessarily label the occupants. Absorbing probably only a minimal amount of foreign blood as successive invasions flowed over and around them, they would have remained much the same people, ordering their lives to the same patterns, for thousands of years. It was a mode of life abandoned only in the last century, finally killed off perhaps by collectivisation, for Edmond O'Donovan noted in his book that people still lived on some of these village mounds.

Such dense occupation reflects the climate changes over the centuries. These plains were better watered in earlier times than they are now, and their fertility supported many more people in antiquity than was possible later; at least, until modern engineering reset the parameters.

Certainly the earth was silty rather than sandy, and it was usually difficult if not impossible to go across country. Dismounting and leading Kaan off the track towards the shade of a tree, I looked back to see him once more sinking up to his hocks as he struggled along behind me. We both stood still for a moment in indecision as he slowly disappeared into the ground; then raced each other back to terra firma, sweating and shaking with fear.

At least there was plenty for him to eat here. He was well rested after his break, but I hadn't been able to find barley or even lucerne for him at Artik, and he had eaten little of the grass I collected for him. So for the next few days I stopped at every patch of green.

Here, where a pump had broken and was spewing water in a great fountain to flood a patch of grass, he stood in a puddle up to his fetlocks and gorged on sweet, sappy rye. There, someone had cut a circle in a bank of reeds to create a corral with a narrow opening, and I was able to leave him loose, eating his head off without needing to move a step, while I went to a safe patch of bare earth to make a fire. He ate so much that he got bored and came to find me, and I had to look sharp to stop him knocking over the pot and escaping back towards the main road.

One afternoon, he had an excellent feast in the grounds of the Hakimlik where I had gone to look for accommodation. The Hakim was away, but his deputy, the *Zametitel*, was expected later. Meanwhile, would I please wait behind the building?

The fence had kept out the village sheep and goats, the grass was long, and the Zametitel was late. For three hours Kaan guzzled shamelessly, while I got out my billycan and cooked some supper. When we left, the garden looked as if it had been visited by an extremely efficient lawnmower; which, I suppose, it had.

The drawback - and there had to be one - of good grazing anywhere was the ticks. Good grass meant more animals visiting, and parasites went forth and multiplied. During one morning halt I removed sixty, a lot of them from places where most respectable horses didn't have places. It was a good job this was a quiet horse, I thought, as the revolting creatures sank their heads obstinately into his tenderest parts while I yanked hard.

Sometimes they swarmed up his legs like ants, keeping me constantly busy picking them off and grinding them under my heel. They were at once loathsome and ludicrous; perfectly oval with no features and eight equally spaced legs like an innumerate child's drawing of a beetle. They reminded me, as they climbed upwards with mindless determination, of the nasties in a computer game. As I zapped them mercilessly, I half expected them to explode in technicolour, with an electronic squeak.

Better grass and ticks, than no grass and no ticks. Over and over, I made good time for the simple reason that I had cut short a halt, afraid that Kaan would suffer from over-indulgence: a good problem to have. He began to leave a trail of green cowpats behind him, partly a result of the fibrous reeds but also from bingeing on spring grass.

Yet his bony frame stayed bony, for as fast as the calories went in, the travelling was leaching them out again. Try as I might, I could only rarely find corn for him. Lucerne, high in food value, made a good substitute, but that was often unavailable. Even so, he was visibly fitter each day; and able to go that bit faster... which left more time to eat.

It was a slow upward spiral. I hoped fervently it would continue. By the time this horse got to Merv, there was going to be more of him than when we set out.

*

To travel like this, receiving the hospitality of the local people, is a rare privilege; for it allows joining in a way of life which, in many respects, must have changed little over long years.

I can't tell this as I approach a kolkhoz. The square, block buildings with their tin roofs, laid out with Roman precision in a grid of streets, couldn't be farther removed from the haphazard cluster of felt-covered yurts, huddling together inside earthen walls, that comprised the Turcoman a'ul of a century ago. But the deeper I go within the village, then within the yard, and finally within the family walls - and thus into the prescribed rituals of Turcoman hospitality - the farther back in time I seem to travel.

They are miniature smallholdings, these family yards. The house and the animal sheds face each other across the vegetable patch, where a network of tiny canals mimics the irrigation system in the fields outside. The house cow is tethered in the corner. Her patch has long since been grazed bare and trampled to mud, with only a few tufts of wiry grass growing in the angle by the fence; but a tractor is coming up the road with a trailer full of cut grass, stopping at every gate, and soon she will have an armful of feed. So will the sheep and goats just brought in by one of the children, having spent all day on the edge of the desert. They haven't settled yet, and scamper round behind the broken hurdle or rusty netting that fences them in, nudging each other and bleating loudly. The noise doubles when the pen next door is entered by a large chestnut horse, an unfamiliar creature. Soon they will fall quiet, and the only sound from either pen will be the regular crunching of teeth on grass.

My saddle and boots are locked in an outhouse, and someone lends me a pair of sandals. From now on I shall wear these outside but shed them to go barefoot when I enter the house.

One of the daughters of the family comes to me with water in a silvery curved jug with a tapering neck. I cup my hands while she pours water, and splash my face and forearms several times until I have washed off the dust of the road. Sometimes I am invited to include my feet in the ablutions, and sit on the edge of the divan soothing their hot sweatiness with blissful cold water. The girl carries a towel draped over one arm, and courteously hands it to me when I finish.

Now she leads me inside, and we leave our sandals on the untidy pile in the doorway. Another girl is putting the finishing touches to the meal. Her kitchen table is a cloth on the floor, at which she squats with feet apart and both heels flat on the ground, her weight well back and squarely balanced. The soup boils on a gas jet behind her; the only other modern item in the room is the television, switched on now for the Mexican soap, dubbed in Russian and watched by half Turkmenistan.

If this is a poor house, there is no other furnishing in the room. If better off, there is a chest or two in the corner and maybe even a sofa against one wall - for the use of visitors, as the family prefers the floor. The essential item of furniture is the carpeting: fine Turcoman rugs or beaten felt, depending on wealth. In the middle of the room a cloth is spread, and we sit closely round it while one of the girls brings pots of tea and shallow bowls. Another brings a cloth bundle and unties it to reveal a pile of flat loaves. With the arrival of the large dish of stew, we each tear ourselves off a piece of bread, and dip into the communal bowl with a spoon and a hunk of bread alternately. Sometimes, as a guest, I have a bowl of soup to myself.

After, grace is said. All rub their hands over their faces in the symbolic gesture of washing, and then sit throughout the prayer with hands before them, palms upwards to receive the blessings fallen from Heaven. Then one girl removes the plates and another brings fresh teapots. Kneeling on the floor, she pours a ritual first bowl and empties it straight back into the pot; then another, and another. The first pouring is almost colourless, but the third shows bright yellow-green against the white glaze of the bowl. Now it is reckoned fit to drink. It tastes refreshingly of lemon. Green tea, say the Turcomans, unlike black tea, dilates the arteries and promotes heat loss. After a day in the saddle or in the fields, we share this aim, and even more so that of rehydration, and drink insatiably until bedtime.

This is the social hour, and the neighbours come in for a chat. The newcomers - usually men, for the women have done their visiting earlier in the day - approach each of the other men in turn for the two-fisted handshake of the Turcomans. It is a powerful gesture, but sometimes lacks the heartiness it deserves. Especially among the younger boys who are included in the ritual, it may be little more than a limp, rapid touch. Two down and eight to go, you almost hear them thinking.

When the guests have gone, we spread out to sleep through the other two or three rooms of the house. They all seem enormous because of their lack of furniture - just a chest or two. From these chests we lift down the bedding: sleeping mat, pillow and quilt. The women slip off their thick trousers, and their loose dresses double as nightgowns.

The morning starts early, for the workers leave for the fields soon after seven. After a breakfast of tea and bread (and a frothing, steaming bowl of boiled milk if the cow is in good form) the men don their telpeks, while the girls wrap their faces in white scarves, only their eyes showing. They pick up their tools, and go to wait in the road for a truck to take them to the world where tractors and polytunnels and fertilisers co-exist with hoes and scythes and good old-fashioned muck. I pick up my saddle and go to join the horse who will take me along well-beaten tracks among the goatherds, or along tarmac roads among the lorries.

It is time to rejoin the outside world, and to flirt intermittently with the twentieth century.

*

Kaakhka, the first sizeable town en route, was surprisingly large and suburban; not the sort of place where most people kept a few sheep and goats and had a spare pen. I chatted up everyone I met, but no-one said, "Come and visit us! Put your horse in our cowshed!"

"Try the hotel," someone suggested. It didn't seem the best place to turn up with a horse, but to go there was no worse than wandering aimlessly.

I couldn't exactly go inside, but the administrator's window opened on to the street, and I was able to lean through and speak to her while Kaan stood patiently on the pavement. I had hardly expected practical help here; but I should have known, from Olga's example, never to underestimate Turkmen receptionists. Maria was a Russian lady of sixty-three, with hair scraped back into a severe-looking bun in sharp contrast to her kind and humorous face. She was completely unfazed to find a horse turning up and asking for a bed.

"We've got a big yard round the back," she said. "Come and have a look."

So I tied Kaan to a telegraph pole and went to inspect his "room". The yard was huge and, even more important, completely secure; for the hotel was basically a truckers' hostel. Best of all, there was plenty of grass. Kaan couldn't be turned loose, however, for in one corner grew a magnificent rose bush, dripping with pink flowers. Maria was - quite justifiably - afraid that he would trample and eat it.

But at the other end was a ring of trees, which I could make into a corral for him. Now, however, came a blow, for on returning for Kaan plus baggage, I found that I'd left my long tether rope behind at the last kolkhoz. Some neighbours came to the rescue with a great coil of old rope, so thick that it might have last been used to tie up a ship. There was more than enough to wind twice round the trees, making a pen like a boxing ring.

Meanwhile Kaan wandered loose in the yard, while I kept a weather eye on the rose. He explored with great interest, ripping up huge mouthfuls of grass as he went, and finally settled by the pond, which was thick with his favourite reeds. No doubt there would be green cowpats again tomorrow.

Maria was quite unconcerned at these ravages in her garden. On the contrary; she even lent me a knife to cut feedstuff when Kaan was finally penned. Everything at last in order, she registered him in the books as a lorry, for which privilege I paid the princely sum of 375 manats, or about 7p.

Now it was time to see to my own hunger. After days of living on bread and soup - and of looking jealously at the empty drink cans thrown on to the roadside by careless drivers - I lusted for junk food. Tania, Maria's seventeen-year-old granddaughter, took me back into town to forage for Coke and chocolate.

Tania had come to Kaakhka to study, living with her grandmother and helping out occasionally in the hotel. Her mother lived in Ashkhabad; her father in the Caucasus, near Mineralny Vody - where just recently Chechen guerrillas had grabbed the headlines by holding a group of hostages for several days - on a farm where he kept horses. This explained the practised ease with which I had noticed Tania handling Kaan.

I was grateful to have her as a guide. It was late, and the kiosks I had noted on the way in were now shut. But she knew where to find the Late Shop. While the vendor gaped and Tania politely looked the other way, I loaded up with six cans of Coke and several bars of chocolate.

No way, though, would Maria let me go to bed on a stomach full of such rubbish. Calling me into her room, she sat me before a plateful of pork stew with lots of bread and tea. I was afraid I was eating her own supper, but she would hear no refusal. So I enjoyed my best meal for ages, before sleeping long and dreamlessly in a comfortable bed.

*

Kaan was well rested, too. Freed from his pen when the rope went back to its owners, he set off round the yard at a trot while I packed, keeping an eye on him through the window of my ground floor room. Tried to pack, rather; for his explorations always seemed to end in a beeline for the rose bush. Time and again I had to jump out of the window and head him off to the other end. It became a sort of game, and getting ready took forever. I couldn't be cross with him, for it was so nice to see his feel-good factor up to these tricks.

When we finally left, he towed me down the street at a great rate until we reached the little market, closed the previous night but now doing a good line in apples and carrots. The noise and bustle, not to mention the sight of so much food, put Kaan in a high good humour. As I tried to shop he rampaged round me in circles, while people scuttled out of his way and mothers with

253

babies gave me black looks. At last, suborned with titbits, he stood quietly while a tiny wizened old lady reached up to pour a stream of carrots into one saddlebag.

I was wholly delighted with Kaakhka. It had given me a kindly welcome and plentifully satisfied all my needs. Now, as we walked out through the suburbs, I warmed to it further.

It was a pleasant little town, green and shady with many trees. The air was full of the wonderful smell of damp gardens in summer, a scent overlaid with that of roses. The memory of Kaakhka's roses would be with me for a long time to come. Tania had cut a sheaf from the bush in the hotel yard and put them in my room; and just before I left the lady from next door, owner of the rope, had brought me another great armful. It was a shame to leave them, and I had pressed my nose into each head in turn before reluctantly taking them next door to Maria.

These were altogether more pleasant impressions than those of O'Donovan. Everything about Kaakhka gave him the creeps. "Not far from the Tejend swamp... partially covered with jungle, in which wild boar and leopard abounded, and tigers were not uncommon... At Kaka... intermittent fevers and consequent biliary derangements were terribly prevalent."

Hooray for the twentieth century. I wouldn't miss the tigers and leopards, and could do without the biliary derangements.

Fate, I was soon to find out, had other ideas.

*

Kaakhka hasn't always been a quiet little backwater. It was here, after a century of posturing, that British and Russian troops at last came to blows in one of the least known engagements of the First World War.

The Bolsheviks lost, but the British, fighting on the side of the Trans-Caspian government in Ashkhabad, suffered heavy casualties. Among those evacuated to Ashkhabad in a hospital train were two worthy successors to the Great Gamers. Captain Reginald Teague-Jones, with a round from a Bolshevik machine-gun in his thigh, lived to fight another day. His

254

comrade Lieutenant Ward, shot in the back by the "friendly fire" of trigger-happy Turcoman irregulars, wasn't so lucky.

Ward's excursion to Turkestan had been ill-starred from the start. Commissioned to blow up a major bridge on the Trans-Caspian Railway near Krasnovodsk, he had for extra secrecy been dispatched the long way westwards round the world; only to be followed to Canada by a bill from his agent addressed "Lt. Ward, en route Turkestan, Montreal". When he finally reached Central Asia, he discovered that his target bridge didn't actually exist. But in such turbulent times there was plenty to occupy a frustrated young officer, and before his untimely death in the Kaakhka engagement he had single-handedly arrested a shipload of German officers, come to gloat prematurely over the fall of Baku to the Turks.

It was to discover the situation in Baku, centre of the world's then biggest oilfield, that Ward's compatriot Teague-Jones was in Central Asia. After the Bolshevik Revolution the Russian Front had collapsed, leaving Baku, on the western shore of the Caspian Sea, open to the Turks. This posed two threats: the diversion of its enormous oil supplies to the Turks' German allies, and the possibility of a Turkish advance through Trans-Caspia - roughly, Turkmenistan - towards India.

Racing back and forth on the railway between Krasnovodsk and Ashkhabad and across the Caspian, Teague-Jones made three excursions to Baku, which duly fell to the Turks. By then he had found time to fall in with several attractive women spies - one of whom, in the best traditions, he eventually married.

Meanwhile a coup had toppled and liquidated the Bolshevik governor of Ashkhabad, replacing him with a Committee headed by the former train driver Comrade Funtikov. ("F-F-Funtikov", commented Teague-Jones, "when sober (was) probably a very good engine driver, but he was no earthly use as Prime Minister.") Teague-Jones now found himself, as Political Officer, the unfortunate go-between for this improbable and inept Committee and the even more directionless British authorities.

It was an unlikely alliance, and increasingly pointless. With no clear orders and - crucially - denied the money promised him to shore up the government, Teague-Jones could only watch as the administration collapsed and the Bolsheviks advanced. The Kaakhka affair had done no more than postpone their inevitable victory. At last the British withdrew, leaving the city to the Red Army and the Committee to its fate.

Teague-Jones' troubles, however, were only just beginning.

On the fall of Baku, twenty-six escaping Bolshevik Commissars had been taken prisoner in Krasnovodsk and, on the orders of the Ashkhabad Committee, shot by a firing squad. Two, at least, were personal friends of Lenin, who later blamed the British for their death. Worse was to come when Leon Trotsky accused Teague-Jones himself of being the "direct practical organiser" of the executions, claiming further that he had personally fired the bullets which killed the Baku Commissars.

Teague-Jones protested that he had not been responsible for the affair; that he had been in Ashkhabad at the time of the shooting, and had been no more than an observer at the fatal Committee meeting; but in vain. Learning that a *fatwa* for his death had gone out from the Kremlin, he covered his tracks and vanished completely, along with his Russian wife.

His new identity - "Ronald Sinclair" - remained intact until he published his memoirs in 1988, at the age of 99. He died the same year.

*

It was as well that I liked Kaakhka, for it was reluctant to let me go. When I finally threaded a way through the streets to reach the railway, it was only to get tangled in a mass of sidings and a large industrial yard.

I had been mostly following the railway for a couple of days now, having belatedly discovered that it was the best way of getting about. For much of the way a dirt track ran beside it, tarmac being unnecessary for the light maintenance traffic, and Kaan and I could make good speed on soft ground while travelling straight as a die in the right direction.

When at last we shed the town, we came straight on to open desert. The Canal was some eight miles off to the north-east, and the irrigation mostly beyond that. I had to weave from one side of the track to the other to benefit from sparse, infrequent patches of grass. Kaan became adept at picking his way carefully across the rails and among the sleepers.

Now there was an unusual hazard underfoot. For a distance of about three hundred yards the ground was suddenly thick with tortoises, urgently going about their business of eating, courting and mating - or all three at once. They have only a few short weeks to accomplish these needs before the fierce desert sun burns off all vegetation, and activity must cease. They were going at it flat out, oblivious of the huge golden beast looming above them, or the strange creature it carried.

This had all the makings of a very pleasant day... briefly. The first hint of trouble was when I started to feel a bit queasy. Tough; it was a pity that the day was going to be spoiled slightly, but it couldn't be helped.

Soon, though, I realised I was slowing up badly. While fording a shallow stream Kaan tried to roll, pawing once then folding his long legs and lowering himself on to his side before I'd reacted at all. I leapt off and whacked him urgently on the rump, and he jumped to his feet looking outraged, muddy water dripping off the saddlebags and running down his legs.

It was high time for a rest. I managed to keep going until I'd found a patch of bushes shading some good grazing next to an isolated tomato field, and called a proper halt.

Now I began to get really worried, for the problem developing was dysentery. I had been dehydrated at the end of every day on the road at the best of times. This spelled serious trouble.

By now I was too feeble even to walk with Kaan while he grazed. I just wanted to curl up and sleep, and bitterly cursed myself for having lost my tether rope two days before. I took the bit out of his mouth, looped the reins round his neck and lay under a bush while I tried to recover a bit.

Nearby was a small building, a shack for the tomato growers. A teenage girl and boy came to say hello and offer tea;

but for once I had to refuse, explaining that I had trouble with my stomach and couldn't eat or drink. Kaan, meanwhile, was eating for both of us. All was well until a horse neighed, close by. Kaan's head shot up; and before I could get to my feet, he was galloping in the direction of the sound.

It was a grey horse, a few hundred yards away and closing fast from, as luck would have it, the far side of the tomatoes. As I struggled through the shoulder-high growth, continually stumbling into wet patches and losing my shoes, I prayed that it was a mare. When Kaan reared into sight above the tomatoes, boxing with his front legs, I realised I had a stallion fight on my hands.

Terrible visions crowded in, of having to tell Rep that his horse had broken a leg, or been torn to pieces in an avoidable incident. Fortunately both horses were hampered, Kaan by the reins which had come loose and twisted round his leg, and the other horse by hobbles. Dodging the flailing feet, I fought to unbuckle the bit and force it back into Kaan's mouth, so that I could control him.

The other horse raced round us, trying to renew the fight. But help was on the way, for the boy from the settlement came running. He carried a heavy stick, which he flung at the horse with a stream of curses. It clearly knew the rules, for without further trouble it turned and galloped off into the distance.

Our progress back to camp was a comic affair. I could hardly put one foot in front of the other, while Kaan was still highly charged up, and dancing round me in circles. It was like the demonstration of a country dance: two steps forward and dos-a-dos. Kindly, the boy took charge, taking Kaan from me and leading him back.

It was time to go, and the sooner the better. There was no question of staying here with the other horse still loose. More to the point, my strength was failing fast through sickness and dehydration, and I had to get somewhere safe before it packed up altogether.

Tying Kaan crudely by his reins to a bush, I sorted my gear. Then, too exhausted to move at once, I sat for five minutes while I drank the last of my Coke and gathered some energy.

It was five minutes too long. As I tacked up, the grey horse suddenly returned at the gallop. Kaan went beserk, raging round the bush and trampling on the saddlebags. My friend from the shack again came out and helped, and somehow between us we managed to get the saddlebags over the horse and me on top.

We beat a hasty retreat, jumping the irrigation ditch with a grand leap. It was the final straw for my stomach, and as we slowed to a walk I parted company with everything left inside.

After that I felt briefly better. But I was getting feebler by the minute. I'd probably lost most of the liquid I'd taken in that day. I began to feel the real fear of any desert traveller: that of baking to a crisp before I could get to water, and safety.

The next village couldn't be more than about seven kilometres, and I plodded on as best I could. But I had to keep dismounting every ten minutes or so from necessity. Eventually, inevitably, I couldn't get back on.

I couldn't even stand up any longer. Reins over my elbow, I crawled to a post and sat propped against it. Kaan by now had burned off his tantrums and stood quietly without trying to get away. There was no grass here to tempt him; for once I was glad of that.

Even in the desert, you are rarely alone for long in Turkmenistan. Soon an old man came by with a few sheep. With perfect courtesy he averted his eyes from my predicament, and I couldn't screw up the strength to call out to him. Ten minutes later, though, he came back, and this time I managed "Please... help..." like some frightful character in a Victorian penny novelette.

He came and took charge of Kaan, which solved my most pressing worry. He must have called someone, for after a few minutes a couple of girls arrived. They sat me up and helped me to drink, then rummaged in my luggage to find my medical kit and give me a fix of Enterosan. I was wondering what to do next when the main protagonist arrived on stage like a hurricane.

She was a small, fiercely capable woman who at once took control. "I know what's wrong with you," she said grimly. "One of my daughters once had your problem!" Much later, when we had come to know each other well, she told me that one daughter had come running, shouting, "Mum, come and help - there's a Russian woman got drunk and fallen off her horse!"

She sat me up and began to knead my body and arms, a sort of halfway job between a massage and a pummelling whose only effect was to bring about the return of my last remaining Coke. In the middle of the puddle, I saw with despair, were the two Enterosan tablets - also my last - disintegrating horribly. For a second, I had to fight the urge of my addled brain to pick them up and put them back in my mouth.

Somehow, the three of them shovelled me into the saddle and set off to take me the several kilometres to their home. As the woman led Kaan off at a brisk walk, I wittered feebly about my baggage.

"Don't worry," she answered. We've got it all. It's quite safe." And then she added, "This is Turkmenistan!" Even in my befuddled state, I felt a stab of guilt for the times I'd used those words, or heard them used, in anger and contempt.

Houses hovered on the horizon. For an age they hung there stubbornly; then at last began to get nearer, and bigger. Kaan was led across the main road and round to the back of the small settlement, where I was lifted off. I made feeble motions to try and loosen Kaan's girth, but the woman stopped me. "Don't worry. We'll see to that." One of her many children came and led him away.

"Don't worry about him," she repeated. "I told you - this is Turkmenistan!"

*

Aina was forty years old, although her thin, lined face, with its startling blue eyes, made her look older. A strong-willed, matriarchal figure, she organised her seven children with formidable efficiency. Six, I should say, for her eldest son Hemra was away doing military duty on the Afghan border. His place in the household was occupied by his wife Maisa, a gentle, shy creature two months away from giving Aina her first grandchild.

260

Two hours'pit-stop in Mari. The hoarding, reading, "He who is alone - that person is without strength. But in friendship he will obtain strength", might have been written for Kaan and me

Stopover in Mari's Central Park

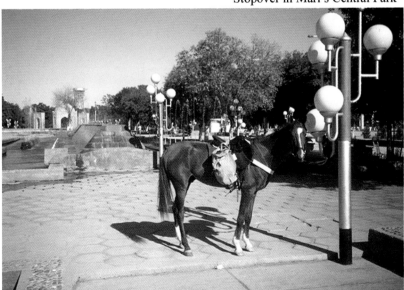

End of the road: Kaan and I pose for the obligatory tourist snapshot by the mausoleum of Sultan Sanjar, ancient Merv

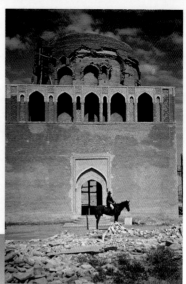

Moonrise over the ruin of Little Kis Kala

Camels, mainstay of the Silk Road, graze on the approach to Merv's first incarnation: the city founded by Zoroastrians in the 6th Century BC

below
Present-day inhabitants of Sanjar's Merv

Kaan takes the quick way
home to Ashkhabad

Two years later:
Kaan's chance of
escape came just
in time

Final journey's end
in a Herefordshire
paddock

Aina couldn't have been taller than five feet, or heavier than seven stone, but as she half-carried me into the house I could feel her tremendous, wiry strength. Within moments she had stripped me of my soiled clothing and dressed me in a clean Turcoman dress. She also offered me trousers, which I refused because of the heat. She must have been concerned at my lack of modesty; for now and then, when she thought I was showing too much leg, she leaned forward and unobtrusively twitched the dress down over my ankles.

She propped me on cushions in a corner of her living room and fed me a constant supply of tea. I sipped carefully at first, then more and more urgently as the hours passed, and I became sure I could hang on to it. Despite my protests Aina sent for the village doctor, who checked me over, gave me some more tablets for my stomach, and firmly refused any payment.

By the evening I could make it across the yard on my own two feet to the privy, and take a look at how Kaan was doing. He was tethered rather precariously with a bit of baler twine to a barbed wire fence; but he had a pile of feed, and seemed to be standing quietly enough.

That night he shared a pen with Aina's goats, which huddled in terror when he was led in to join them. At the end of the pen was a stack of iron bins, and they climbed on top, hard feet clattering noisily, to look down on him quizzically. I had no barley, but made him a feed from the Kaakhka carrots, mixed with the torn up bits of half a loaf that a kolkhoznik had given me a couple of days before. I prepared it as unobtrusively as possible, afraid that Aina would be scandalised to see such food being wasted on a horse. It was a scratch meal; but he wolfed it gratefully.

The feed situation was a worry. Although he was depleting Aina's hay pile with alarming speed, he wasn't really getting enough to eat. It wasn't possible to ease the situation by taking him out to graze; for the village was right in the middle of open desert and the nearest grass, said Aina, was seven kilometres away, well beyond where she had picked me up.

Kaan spent the next day variously tethered to the barbed wire, a concrete post, and a combine harvester immobilised by two irreparably collapsed tyres. Twice he broke free and ran off, a misdemeanour which earned him an extra ration of hay to keep him quiet. I wanted to leave as soon as possible, before he ate Aina out of house and home. But my legs continued to wobble, and it was a couple of days before we could move on.

This was the best opportunity yet to engage in Turcoman village life. Apart from the fact that block houses had replaced yurts, and that news of the outside world came from the TV, life in the village of Karakhan was much as it must have been for centuries.

It was in some ways a hard life, but seemed also a relaxed and happy one. Mod cons took the form of gas and electricity. There was no running water, but there was a well sixty yards away; you dropped a shiningly clean galvanised bucket to a depth of about eight feet, and drew up water so pristine you hardly considered boiling it - until you thought about biliary derangements.

Baking was the day's main labour. Aina mixed the dough for her excellent bread in a shallow tin about three feet in diameter, and knelt on the floor to knead it for a good twenty minutes, the sinews standing out on her thin, hard wrists. A similar tin was used for the washing, no small task when done by hand for such a big family.

Other housework, though, was minimal, not least because the rooms were largely empty of furniture. At night we slept on mats arranged in a row in the bedroom. Making the beds in the morning was a simple affair of stacking the bedding on top of the two large chests which were the room's only other contents. Sweeping the floor with a brush took scarcely longer than it would have done to vacuum - especially with several daughters to rotate the task between them.

Above all, life for the women of Karakhan was immensely sociable. Constantly in and out of each others' houses, they spent a lot of their time helping each other, playing with their friends' babies or just gossiping over bowls of tea. And not only the women; in the evenings when the men were home from the fields, they too came in and out, mingling freely with the women. Over all was an atmosphere of enormous good fellowship, a deep sense of community that we of the West have forgotten, with our closed doors and often uncommunicative, television-orientated home life.

Aina's house was particularly busy, for much of the village came to inspect the foreign visitor. Aina herself was much in demand as interpreter; for while she was fluent in Russian, few of her neighbours spoke much. It no longer came as a surprise to find one more thing that Aina could do better than everyone else. Such were the comings and goings, that it took me at least a day to work out who were Aina's own children. Two girls of about eight, with unusually short, fair hair, were so alike as to be indistinguishable. Dunegözel and Makhri were always together . To Aina's delight, I took them for identical twins. In fact, Makhri was her sister's child.

Gradually, though, I began to know them all by their resemblance to each other, if not to Aina. One young boy plus five tall, beautiful girls. How, I wondered, had the tiny Aina produced this tribe of Amazons?

It was after the evening meals, purely family affairs, that I was able to pigeon-hole everyone. As night fell and the temperature dropped from fierce heat to a pleasant warmth, the low table would be carried out into the yard and hoisted on to the family divan for a leisurely meal. We sat cross-legged round a communal bowl of soup with meat, beans and vegetables, eating with wooden painted spoons or simply dunking bread. When it was quite dark, everything was carried back indoors and the social life was resumed around bowls of tea until late into the evening. This was the time for the old suitcase full of photographs to be hauled out of a corner, and its contents spilled on to the floor. From among the faded prints a sixteen-year-old Aina gazed out from a face of haunting beauty. Wistful eyes under dark brows gave her a Queen-Mother-look. The likeness now to her daughters was unmistakable.

Their stature, however, remained a mystery. (Aina's husband Byashim, currently away on business and whom I met later, was little taller than his wife.) Only the tiny Maisa matched her mother-in-law.

Shyly, she told me how she had come to marry Hemra after a romantic Brief Encounter at Ashkhabad railway station. "We saw each other by chance," she said, "and we knew at once that we loved each other."

"So you are free in Turkmenistan to marry as you wish?"

"Of course. We choose our own husbands."

On my second morning Aina's former schoolteacher came to visit. Looking to be in his mid-fifties but actually over seventy, he was a striking man with an aquiline, rather ascetic face; a face that might have sat comfortably upon a mediaeval abbot, or an Oxbridge don. He had been teaching for fifty-four years, he told me, and Aina had been one of his best pupils. The two, it was clear, respected each other deeply.

She told him about our first meeting, and how she had thought that she was picking up a drunkard. "I suppose you were too ill to remember much about it," she said, looking at me anxiously to see if I remembered her rough handling. I promised her that the whole episode was a complete blank.

The schoolmaster spoke of shoes and ships and sealing wax, but sadly in very difficult Russian. I bitterly regretted my limitations, for I was sure I could have learned much from this fascinating old man. But when I asked him about the ancient wall I was searching for, he saw how desperate I was to understand, and made his language as simple as possible for me.

Once or twice, I'd spotted possible candidates for the wall marked on the Royal Geographical Society map and again on Professor Atamuradov's. In this land of banks and dykes, though, an ancient earthwork could look like a modern irrigation barrier, and vice versa. A few questions along my way had brought only blank looks. I'd more or less dismissed it as a figment of my imagination. This might be my last chance to find out if there was anything to it.

"Oh, yes," he answered at once, and I held my breath. "There is such a wall. It runs twisting around and through the Akhal Oasis from beyond Dushak right up to Bacharden, Kyzyl Arvat and beyond. It's called the 'Merz'." No-one, he said, was quite sure what its purpose was. There were three theories: a road, a dyke to retain water inside the oasis, and a military defence.

From Kyzyl Arvat to the Caspian was a geographical stone's-throw. I was certain, now, that this was all part of "Alexander's Wall". All that remained was to find it. That afternoon, I saw its location from a distance. On the horizon to the south a city mound wobbled in the heat-haze. "That's old Karakhan," Aina told me. "It sits right on the line of the Merz."

It was time to think about moving on. With a little spare energy at last, I gave Kaan a thorough grooming, followed by a tick session. The children joined in enthusiastically, finding sharp sticks and squashing the bugs as fast as I pulled them off. Then it was my turn for a clean, and I had a thorough bucket-bath in Aina's bathhouse, helped by Dunegözel - for once without her "twin" - and Sarai, a bright, laughing child of about ten who was Aina's fifth child.

That evening, I gave each of Aina's children a ride on Kaan. The bush telegraph hummed, and no sooner had we begun than the entire child population of the village came running, and lined up expectantly. Kaan did his stuff magnificently, despite being short of exercise and rather hungry - enough to make most horses irritable. My heart went out to him again, as I watched this thoroughbred stallion behaving with the patience and gentleness of a riding school pony.

Sarai and her younger brother Orazmurad took charge. They understood at once how to settle each rider comfortably, adjust stirrups and check against feet thrust dangerously far through. At last, every child had taken a turn, even the youngest toddler, safely held by Sarai. Now Aina's teenage daughters were persuaded into the saddle, and rode, laughing, round one circuit of the yard.

"This village will remember you for a long, long time," said Aina.

"I will remember you for far longer," I replied.

To my disappointment, Aina herself refused to ride. "I'm an old woman!" she said.

"Rubbish! You're younger than me!"

"No," she continued to shake her head. "It's immodest for a woman of my age to do something like that."

Strange; one would have thought that characters like Aina made their own rules. But even she was servant to the customs of her society. I realised that even after living here for two days, and becoming so close to this family in the process, I had only scratched the surface of Turcoman village life. There was still so much to learn.

*

Before I left, early the next morning, I gave the children small presents.

For Aina herself, I had nothing remotely adequate. But in my belt was a pair of silver earrings, worked to an intricate filigree pattern, that I had bought in Turkey some years ago. No gift could ever have expressed my thanks to this wonderful person, but they would do for now to remember me by.

I knew her well enough by now to realise that it would be difficult to persuade her to accept any sort of gift. So I wrapped them in a tissue and, literally as I was riding off, leaned down and tucked them into Aina's pocket. "A memento," I said, fudging - for once deliberately - my Russian, to get a laugh and cover the moment.

Then I was off, heading into the desert at a swinging canter, and leaving her world with rather more style than I had entered it.

XIV

"No, I haven't heard of the Merz," said the lady from the Hakimlik as she poured me another bowl of tea. "But the Archoin will know if there is anything to be seen near here. The Archoin is a very keen historian. I'm sorry he still isn't back."

As far as I was concerned, he could take as long as he liked. The Archoin was also a keen horseman, and grew lucerne in the garden of his Hakimlik. Kaan was at this moment, by invitation of the hospitable staff, stuffing himself with the said lucerne. The Archoin wouldn't mind, they assured me. I hoped they were right.

The route from Karakhan to Dushak had crossed desert with hardly a blade of grass. We had plodded on and on under a blazing sun, with no more grazing for Kaan than the odd patch of shrivelled growth by the roadside. The mirage turned some lumps of bulldozed earth into a promising looking row of bushes which dissolved when we reached them. When Dushak itself came into view, it seemed for a long time to levitate above a white haze. Even on the outskirts, where one might have expected irrigation, little grew but camelthorn, on which a herd of camels appropriately browsed. The tiny market sold only a few imported goods; T-shirts, chewing gum, the odd packet of pasta, but not a carrot in sight. So the Archoin's lucerne was a gift from heaven.

His title fascinated me. The small settlements had a Bashlik, the towns a Hakim, but nowhere had I heard of an Archoin. The word was intriguingly similar to the title of Archon given to the city magistrates of ancient Greece. Could this be yet another legacy of Alexander, a word which had lingered in local memory of former authority, which the present mayor, the lover of history, had resurrected?

After two hours the Archoin arrived. He was a very pleasant and friendly chap, and at once invited me to stay at his house.

267

His courtesy, however, deserted him when it came to horses. Seizing Kaan by the jaw, the Archoin wrenched his mouth open to look at his teeth. As I gathered my things and prepared to tack up, he grabbed the saddle and whacked it down with a flourish, making poor Kaan wince and screwing up the numnah underneath.

There followed a rather difficult and embarrassing hour, when he tried to override everything I did. "Give the horse to those boys!" he told me. "They will take him to my home. You must come in my car!" It was kindly meant; but it was imperative that Kaan be kept off the tarmac, which the lads wouldn't have understood. Tactfully I protested that it was better not to let children handle a stallion. After all, he didn't know about Orazmurad and Sarai.

"That's no stallion!" he retorted. "It's at least ten years old!"

When we reached the house, it became apparent why he was so dismissive. His horses, although in excellent condition - indeed, the fattest I ever saw in Turkmenistan - were not thoroughbred, but *pogranichnie*, the rough horses used by the army, like Tom. Having an Akhal-Teke turn up on his doorstep, and one ridden by a woman at that, had put his nose seriously out of joint.

The Archoin's brother came to meet us, yanking the reins out of my hand and dragging Kaan off roughly. "Don't worry," said the Archoin. "My brother knows all about horses. He's a real 'cowboy'!" That was just what I was afraid of.

Open disagreement broke out when they decided to tether him. Three times I explained that he couldn't be tethered, showing them the remains of rope burns from when I'd tried unsuccessfully and he'd tied himself up. Three times they listened politely, then firmly told me, "Don't worry. It's perfectly safe to tether horses." How can you know? You're a woman, and a foreigner. What's good enough for our horses is good enough for yours. Don't be difficult.

Pushing me aside, they tied Kaan to a tree, with the same rough handling as before. So I simply sat down and explained politely that if he was to be tethered, I must stay here and watch him, ready to disentangle him if necessary.

The two men finally realised I was serious. After some scratching of heads, they came up with another idea. Mounting his own horse, the brother led me and Kaan to a lovely spot on the edge of the town, where an old mud-brick barn stood among trees by a pond. The Archoin kindly followed with a boot-full of hay and a padlock for the heavy iron door; although he shook his head in despair when I bothered to fill a bucket of water for Kaan.

Once away from horses, Nurnazar Djumanazarov was a charming, courteous and informative host. He lent me a tracksuit so that I could shed my dusty, travel-stained clothing; then, similarly dressed after changing out of his mayoral suit, settled down over pots of tea to tell me all about the Merz. "Would you like to see it? It's not far away." I jumped to my feet at once. He drove me out to a spot north of Dushak where its course crossed the road. And so at last I found myself actually standing on the ancient wall.

Not that there was much to see here: just an earth bank a few feet high. No wonder that only the most obvious parts of it actually showed up on the map. But it was very ancient, said Nurnazar. Old city mounds, like that at Karakhan, stood along its length. Just nearby was one which had been stormed by Alexander - thus ran local legend.

You could see several from here - another reminder of the once greater fertility and natural wealth than the land possessed today. Just this morning I had passed one of the bigger ones, Altyn Depe, or the Golden Mound, so named for the abundance of gold found there by archaeologists.

Yes, the land had been fertile once, said the Archoin, confirming that the Oxus had once flowed much farther west. "In parts of the Kara Kum, you can find water only twenty or thirty metres below the surface. In the Sahara, on the other hand, you could dig down hundreds without finding a drop."

Back at Nurnazar's home, we had supper on the floor in front of the television. The news at the moment was full of the State visit of Iran's President Rafsanjani, come to open new road and rail links between the two countries. Endless footage of Rafsanjani shaking hands many times with Niazov, to the background of patriotic music, were followed by a shot of the Iranian President's departing plane - rather a faithless mode of transport in view of the reason for his visit. As he left, in flew the Presidents of Kirghizstan, Uzbekistan and Kazakhstan for a Central Asian summit. Niazov was having a very busy social life.

As might be expected from a government representative, the Archoin was an enthusiastic supporter of Independence. "How crazy that a country should not have its own laws, its own army, its own government! That it should be run from thousands of miles away! For years, the Soviet government exported all Turkmenistan's raw materials, without building a single factory to process them here. We've had to start absolutely from scratch, building our own factories, new roads, a decent international airport. Everything, right from the bottom up! Of course things are hard now," he conceded. But he was bullish about prospects for the future.

Immensely proud of his country's present, Nurnazar also possessed an insatiable thirst for its past. A former sports teacher, he had become increasingly absorbed in local history and folklore. He had written a book on folklore which was shortly to be published. Unfortunately, he said, his duties as Archoin prevented him from working much in that field or, indeed, from spending much time with horses. Perhaps the last wasn't such a bad thing.

For, among much useful information about the road ahead, he continually gave me negative instruction over Kaan. The lesson was resumed the following morning on the way to the barn, the Archoin gradually discarding the persona of courteous intellectual for that of didactic know-all, as the distance between him and the horse decreased.

"Why are you travelling so slowly?" he asked, without listening to my answer. "Why do you want to take two days to get to Tedzhen? You're to stop at Kazarana for lunch and then go on to Tedzhen in the evening. Don't forget the Akhal-Teke can easily do a hundred kilometres in a day." So it can; well-fed, in training - and shod. "It's quite all right to ride on the road.

The hard shoulder is soft enough for him. Don't worry if his feet hurt. That won't do him any harm."

The one thing that might have increased our speed was some of the barley which he fed abundantly to his own horses, while I looked on heartily breaking the tenth commandment. I reminded myself sharply how we had scrumped his lucerne.

"Why do you wear those boots?" he went on. "You mustn't. They're too hot." I dared not mention my morbid fear of snakebite, which had led me to sweat inside their protection. "And your saddlebags are too low..." He stepped in and yanked the saddle forward officiously, disarranging my careful layers of Karrimat so that I had to undo the girth and start again from scratch.

Yet snatches of Jekyll popped up from Hyde's skin, as if they could not be suppressed absolutely. "Come back if you have time. I'll drive you out to the Zapovednik. I'll show you where to find the kulan..." A very kind and hospitable man, and very well intentioned.

*

He was also very knowledgeable about the history of his land. So his assertion that the Turcoman people had been here for six thousand years was one to take seriously.

"Unlike the other Central Asian peoples, who are Turco-Mongol, they are Indo-European." This contradicted other opinions; in view of the language, the culture, indeed the name, of Turkmenistan's people, and their history, it was a bold theory. I wished later that I had asked him to elaborate.

Did he mean the city dwellers, the long-term inhabitants of the fringes of settled lands to the south, as opposed to the incoming nomads? For while the first may well derive more of their blood from Persia and its neighbours than from Turkestan, the nomads were undoubtedly Turkic, their history well mapped over the last millennium and a half.

No-one is absolutely sure where the Turks originated. The union of a young man with a she-wolf - the mythical version - serves as well as any; while scholars argue over their possible

271

descent from the Hsiung-Nu. They first appear in history with Chinese references to the Tiu-Kiu, or T'u Chueh. The mid-sixth century found them living a nomadic life in the Altai Mountains of Mongolia, from where they erupted in 552 AD to throw off their Juan-Juan overlords, with Chinese help, and conquer the whole Mongolian plateau. On the Khan's death his two sons split their patrimony and continued to ride respectively east and west.

The Western Turks, with a momentum foreshadowing that of Genghis Khan, overran most of Central Asia, splitting the empire of the Hephthalites (more Hsiung-Nu descendants) with their Persian allies. Their eastern cousins were less fortunate, now defeating, now ruled by, the Chinese; although the vast area that was now Turkestan became briefly reunited around 710 AD under the Khan of the Eastern Turks.

Early fragmentation of such a huge empire was inevitable, as the Mongols were to find in their turn. To the west, the Arab invasion swamped Transoxiana, printing Islam indelibly on the Turks. To the east, the Uighurs, first of the Turkic sub-tribes to dominate their kinsmen, overran Mongolia. By the time that Genghis Khan was born into the small clan called the Mongols, many of the tribes in what was to become Mongolia were partly or wholly Turkic.

From now on, competition among the Turks threw up a succession of ruling clans. Such were the Seljuks and the Khoresmshahs; such, with the process resuming after the Mongol invasion, were the Timurids, the Moghuls, the Uzbeks and Ottomans. The Kirghiz and the Kazakhs are just two more branches of the extended Turkic family. Then there are the Yakuts of Siberia, the Azeris west of the Caspian...

And what of the Turcomans? No-one is sure when they attained a separate identity; no-one confidently names the father of their tribe. They themselves differ. Some restrict the name Turcoman/Turkmen to the oasis-dwellers around the Kara Kum, the inhabitants of modern Turkmenistan; while others apply it to the whole family of Western Turks, tracing their descent to the patriarch Oghuz Khan.

But it was they who in their turn became guardians of the Sacred Horses of Central Asia; they who preserved the age-old traditions of horsemanship handed down by the Scythians, through such as the Hsiung-Nu, to the early Turks of the Altai mountains, those horsemen who carved out empires and peopled half Asia with their seed.

*

I had to wait until Nurnazar was well on his way before I set off myself, as I was leaving by the track alongside the railway, against his orders. It gave us a quick route out, and even provided a good patch of grazing for Kaan's breakfast.

It was the Trans-Caspian Railway which made Dushak into a town worthy of the Archoin. In 1881, when the Russians were still forcing its construction eastwards towards Ashkhabad, O'Donovan found only "a long, low rampart, enclosing a rectangular space about a hundred yards square... Within was an irregular, muddy encampment, where pit-like hollows were half-filled with reddish-brown liquid of pestilent odour - the drainings of the camping ground of camel, buffalo and human being. Amid this stood what at first sight appeared to be gigantic stacks of corn, but which proved to be the huts of the inhabitants. They were composed of great sheaves of giant reeds..." Five years later the railway had arrived. Dushak ceased to be a Turcoman encampment, and became a town.

Perhaps it sucked in its people from the surrounding village-mounds, which littered the plain beyond more thickly than ever. More and more obsessively I wondered about the people who had lived in these villages two, three thousand years ago and more. Were they nomads who had given up the saddle for the hearth, beating their arrowheads and bridle bosses into ploughshares? Scythians perhaps, Saka or Sarmatian or Massagetae, or even the dreaded Hun? Or were they southerners, farmers who had drifted north and now periodically huddled behind their earthen walls on their earthen mounds for fear of those very nomads? Did they despair as the encroaching desert gradually swallowed the rivers which fed their small communities, leaving them to shrivel and die? Had their women lived bustling, sociable lives, like Aina and her friends?

I craned for a sight of the Merz, for it was in this region that I'd first spotted it on the German map. But even this far from the irrigation, dykes and banks seamed the desert, and tamarisk and camelthorn hid its contours.

There had been no cultivation for about twenty-five miles. But the Kara Kum Canal was converging with the road, and the distance held green patches. A motorbike passed, its sidecar piled high with fresh-cut lucerne.

The farmland, I was gradually realising, lay mostly to the north of the Canal. The ground was so flat that it was hard to have any concept of "downhill"; nevertheless it was the lie of the land that dictated the Canal's course, and the fields it watered must lie, if not necessarily lower, then at least within the height compass of a simple pump.

Crossing the Canal, therefore, meant re-entering farmland. This was welcome, for I was increasingly worried about feed. Other worries were temporarily suspended. Kaan's feet, which earlier had been wearing down frighteningly fast, had now shed their surplus growth and looked to have stabilised. He was sore, as ever, on hard ground or stones - in fact, contrary to the Archoin's advice, if I must take him on roads he was happier on smooth tarmac than the rough hardcore alongside - but perfectly comfortable on anything else. His back, though still bony, was pristine under its cocoon of plastic foam. I had my eye on his back legs, for sometimes one or both fetlocks were swelling slightly overnight. It seemed no more than the slight "filling" that arises from standing in a stable after a hard day's work, and it disappeared after the first few miles each morning. He was perfectly sound.

For all the Archoin's instructions to go faster, our steady pace was in the best Turcoman traditions, according to Conolly. "Their pace is alternately a *yoortmah* (or gentle jog-trot) and a long walk; every hour or two they halt, and let their horses graze... and occasionally give them a mouthful of corn... they get over much ground in a few days, and their horses' steady endurance of fatigue is wonderful." Yes, the Akhal-Teke could

274

gallop for hours when necessary - on a raid, for instance - but why hurry just to prove the point?

The morning saw a major landmark, for we passed from one of my maps to the other. The mountains were peeling off to the south, taking the Iranian border with them. They had been our constant travelling companions until now, and their departure left me feeling rudderless. We crossed the Canal at last, and doubled back to find shade under the bridge.

It was a five-star spot. I didn't care much for the shaking and rattling of the rusty girders whenever a lorry passed overhead, but was grateful for the abundant grazing and an endless supply of water. While Kaan strayed from grass to reeds and back to grass again, I tried something new: "Yuppi", a pink powder which had come from Chile via the Dushak market, and which combined readily with the Kara Kum Canal to make a change from endless green or black tea. It was a thoroughly international drink; for the water had come, via the Oxus, from the snows of the Hindu Kush. It was nice to think that Chile and Afghanistan could co-operate to hit the global market.

Our next halt wasn't so happy. Back in the irrigation, we passed through miles and miles of fruit trees with little other vegetation. When I finally found a thick patch of reeds in a ditch, I had offsaddled before realising that we were right at the entrance to an army barrack.

Some teenage conscripts came out to look us over. They nudged each other and giggled, but were pleasant enough. The trouble came after they'd left, and from another quarter. A young tough, stripped to the waist for his work in the fields, swaggered over. I gave him the time of day, but he had only two words in his vocabulary. He used them over and over again.

"*Odin raz*." Just the once. He made its connotations obvious but, to keep the peace, I wilfully misunderstood.

"One time, my first time, in Turkmenistan, yes." Again and again, as politely as I could, but with mounting irritation to put over my own message. He persisted, adding something in Turcoman; then switched to sign language, making gestures first suggestive, then obscene.

It was his bad luck that I was at this moment drawing a bucket of water from the ditch for Kaan, and that Kaan wasn't thirsty. The lad got the lot in his face. Too late, I cursed myself for not aiming lower.

It got rid of him, but instead of going back to the fields he headed for the barrack. As he went, I tacked up Kaan in case of trouble. When five youths came out of the building and started in my direction, it took only a moment to throw the saddlebags over and hightail it out of town. They looked harmless enough, but I wasn't about to take chances.

For it was becoming clear that, on one instruction at least, the Archoin had won. I'd passed one settlement quite early in the afternoon, so small that I couldn't decently ask to stay there. Anyway, more people were working in the fields around me than I'd ever yet seen in one place. Surely, among all this agriculture, there would be a kolkhoz nearby.

But there was nothing. Perhaps that was the reason for the number of small reed huts along this stretch of road - places for the workers to lie up through the heat of the day. They wouldn't need shelter if their homes were close by.

Anxiously I stood in the stirrups and scanned the horizon. Nothing, nothing and more nothing. From now on the journey became increasingly nightmarish, as I raced to try and reach Tedzhen before dark, pressing the pace more than ever before. Kaan showed his class, tired but pushing on gamely, giving me everything he'd got.

Under more relaxed circumstances it would have been enjoyable travelling. Firm tracks running parallel to the road spared us the usual penalties of tarmac, camelthorn or deep ground. The sun sank behind the distant reeds in a brilliant red sky, reminding me of Otmoor. Homeward bound kolkhozniks shouted cheerful goodnights to me from motorbikes tottering crazily under mountains of greenstuff.

It was quite dark when the first lights of Tedzhen appeared, winking in ones and twos then filling the horizon. Used by now to the deceptive distances in this extraordinarily flat land, I was unprepared for the effect of darkness on the phenomenon. Unable to hurry any more, we plodded on seemingly for ever.

Towards the end I dismounted and walked on in a fatigue-induced trance, my mind detached from my body, only Kaan's steady stride beside me keeping me going in a straight line.

It must have been close on ten o'clock when we entered the town and staggered into a transport café. It was only a van in a lorry park, but lorries need water and drivers need food. It turned up trumps with two buckets of water for Kaan and - the ultimate luxury - two cans of Coke for me.

At that time of night there was no option but to try the hotel. Chari, another customer at the roadside booth, offered to take me there.

"Are you your parents' fourth son?"

"Yes - how did you know that?" I told him of my friend Chari at Yashlik, who had explained the traditional names. "It must be a hospitable name!"

Doubly so here. This Chari was to travel to Ashkhabad tomorrow, to be treated in hospital for chronic stomach trouble. "I've been ill with it for five years. This is my eighth time in hospital."

"Then please just point me in the right direction and go straight home!" But he insisted in walking me all the way there. This, I thought gratefully, was Turkmenistan.

I would never have found the place without him. It looked exactly like all the other buildings in Tedzhen: a long, two-storey building fronting straight on to the street. Chari went and roused the receptionist, and came back to tell me the good news. "Yes, they can take your horse." Quietly he wished me well, turned and walked away.

"Goodbye!" I called inadequately at his departing back. "I hope your health improves..." He was already out of earshot.

Directed to take Kaan to the back, I sleepwalked round the block and arrived at a very solid wooden gate. Keys rattled in padlocks, hinges creaked, and we hobbled in.

As I unsaddled Kaan, I was dimly aware of a large yard with enough grass to keep starvation at bay until morning. And no roses; here he could stay quite loose and graze freely. The night watchman and his lad slept outside, and would see that he came to no harm.

I was thankful to leave him to their care, for by the time I had washed him down and seen him comfortably settled, it was nearly midnight. My cold shower was blissful, and my rather grubby bedroom better than a suite at the Hilton.

*

There was no lying in the next morning. The moment the Hakimlik opened I was knocking on the door, urgently asking where I could buy lucerne and barley.

A minion took me upstairs to an inner sanctum where the local big cheese sat behind a desk at the end of an impossibly long room. Behind him on the wall hung a huge Turkmen carpet. Niazov glowered downwards from a photograph and sideways from a marble bust. I wondered if I was meant to approach on all fours, as to the Emir of Bukhara.

The Hakim looked at me as if I were an insect which had lodged in his underwear. I explained my errand, and he sighed and reached for the phone.

"What is your hotel called?" They were the first words he had spoken. I didn't know. There was, after all, only one hotel in Tedzhen.

He looked down his nose, and I felt myself shrink. Putting down the phone, he said, "Your feed will be delivered to your hotel in two hours." Insect or not, I wanted to hug him.

Now I had time to linger in the rinok. It was the biggest since Ashkhabad, and well stocked with local produce. I wandered dazed among the stalls, feeling like Oliver Twist in a chocolate factory, unable to believe such plenty. After weeks of living on bread, tea and soup, I would have killed for fresh fruit and vegetables. I bought cucumbers and cream cheese and light rolls of soda bread, and when I found a stall with the first of the season's strawberries, I thought it was Christmas and birthdays all rolled into one.

Back at the hotel I ate bread and cream cheese and strawberries, then cucumbers and cream cheese, then bread and cucumbers, until I had run out of permutations and my stomach

278

ached. As I swallowed the last mouthful there came a knock at the door. The really important stuff had arrived: Kaan's food.

A lovely, burly teddy bear figure backed a van into the yard and shovelled out a mountain of dried lucerne followed by a sack of barley. When I tried to pay he shook his head.

"No. You're a guest in this country. We look after guests here. The Government provides this for you."

I had one last try. "We have a custom, too, at home. When someone does you a favour you buy them a drink. Will you at least let me do that?" But he shook his head resolutely, and, as last night, I could only stammer a stream of hopelessly inadequate thanks as he drove off.

He left Kaan standing bemused in the middle of a feast, stuffing down lucerne as if he had never seen so much food in all his life; which, poor lad, he probably hadn't.

There was so much kindness here. Everyone was enormously interested in Kaan, and enormously nice to him. I went out to sit and enjoy watching him eat, but instead had to set to work again on the ticks. Immediately, out came the Russian receptionist Viola Mikhailovna - always addressed in full to distinguish her from the Turcoman receptionist Viola - with some strong insecticide. Together we sponged his legs, watching with vicious glee how the little monsters shrivelled and fell off. Meanwhile Viola found me a tin bucket and unlocked the laundry room so that I could boil the barley. Whenever I went out to fill Kaan's water bucket, I found that someone else had beaten me to it. And nobody complained that I had turned my bedroom into a feed and tack room.

The two receptionists couldn't have been more different. Viola was tiny and feminine, with dyed ginger hair falling loose over the collar of her green Turcoman dress, and an impish, Listen-With-Mother smile. Viola Mikhailovna was a broad Russian matron, hair dyed dark brown and scraped back into a severe bun to expose a forehead fit for a professor of Special Relativity .

There was an air conditioner in my room, a surprising luxury. I kept it on constantly, battling with the warm steam that drifted in from the neighbouring rooms. One of these was the shower room, a dank dripping cave with an empty light socket and a dense population of cockroaches. The other was the kitchen, where both gas rings burned night and day. This was common practice, the waste of free gas being better economics than the waste of a match which must be bought. Turkmenistan, with three burned-out springs and three exceptionally hot summers behind it, was happily flying the flag for global warming.

The town itself, underneath the usual superficial scruffiness of crumbling concrete and jumbled wires, was neat and pleasant. So, I imagined, might an American mid-western town have looked in the thirties. On the nameplates of the main street Makhtum Kuli had displaced Lenin, but Pushkin had survived. Niazov popped up everywhere in marble, stone or on paper; his statue in front of the cinema made a threesome with hardboard cutouts of Loony Tunes characters. Accidental, or someone's deliberate irony?

Viola Mikhailovna bemoaned the inadequacy of the local library, its lack of decent books. "In the winter," she said, "I sew. In the summer, I just want to read." She was mildly ashamed of her current book, a Russian translation of a steamy western novel. "It's all I could get."

The bookshelves in her home sagged under the weight of Dostoevsky, Pushkin and other giants of Russian literature. In my honour she had cooked pelmeni. I couldn't admit that what I wanted most of all was more fresh fruit and vegetables.

It felt strange to be in a Russian house again, and eating off a table. When I unwisely said so Viola Mikhailovna and her neighbour, who had come over for lunch, began to disparage Turcoman customs.

"Can you imagine - they sleep on the floor in one room, all laid out in a line! And they have so many children that sometimes the fathers have to ask the mothers what all their names are..." I couldn't listen silently; it would have been unpardonable disloyal to all my earlier hosts.

"The Turcomans are wonderful people," I replied. "Everyone I've met has been terribly kind and hospitable to me." The conversation abruptly ceased, and I was afraid that I'd been

280

rude. It was the eternal dilemma of the guest: honesty versus good manners. But as I left Viola Mikhailovna thrust a sheaf of roses from her garden into my arms, and I was forgiven.

The roses scented my room as I sat stitching the saddlebags yet again. The rest of my equipment was holding up well. The synthetic saddle was especially successful, being lighter than leather and more tolerant of the hot, dry conditions. On the makeshift breast girth the last of the Karrimat had long replaced my roughly wrapped sweater. Aina had stitched a double thickness of it for me; after watching my fumbling attempts with impatience she had taken the needle from my inept hands and finished the job herself, her thin, strong fingers making short work of it.

Kaan had barely left his pile of lucerne for a day and a night. Now, he was getting almost bored with it. In between meals he took long, luxurious rolls in a patch of sand, or wandered round the yard. His desire for human company usually brought him to stand by the back door of the hotel. Everyone made a fuss of him, but not unnaturally the two Violas got upset when he deposited on the path, and I had to keep running out with a shovel.

The evening before I left, the weather was so oppressive that I found myself subconsciously looking for a thunderstorm. "This is Turkmenistan!" I had to remind myself. Sure enough, though, a few drops of rain began to fall, and I prayed for a downpour to make the grass grow as we took to the road again. The next leg of the journey, from Tedzhen to Mari, was a long one.

*

But it was barely damp as I said my goodbyes the next morning. At least the cloud cover kept the temperature down.

The town was just waking up as we set off. Workers on the early shift were making their way to the cotton factory. A few children roamed the streets, while their mothers swept outside their doors and sprinkled water to lay the dust.

281

"*Devushka, prodaosh*?" Hey, girl, is he for sale? I heard it two or three times from laughing groups. Viola had told me that, somehow, the media had heard of our journey, and last night's television news had mentioned us. Perhaps that was why Kaan was attracting more attention than usual.

He felt fresh and rested this morning. He sprang forward when I asked him to trot, despite the weight of the remaining barley that he had to carry. What a difference, I thought as I cantered towards the river on a fresh, pulling horse, from the way the pair of us had limped exhausted into Tedzhen.

The Tedzhen River is one of the great oasis rivers of Turkmenistan. Despite lending much of its water for irrigation upriver it was still wider here than the Kara Kum Canal. It ran thick with mud, like brown custard: the pattern for the great rivers of Central Asia. The river banks were home to colonies of bee-eaters, delicate birds with iridescent plumage and the streamlining of a Stealth Bomber. They wheeled in squadrons above the dirty water, slicing through the air in a row of blue-green flashes like djinns before returning, suddenly mortal, to the clay of their nest-holes.

We crossed on the old bridge, a small boy with his herd of sheep showing us the way. Off to the right, the traffic roared across a new steel structure. Two centuries ran side by side just fifty yards apart.

It was a busy road, leading not only to Mari but also to Serakhs and the Iranian border. Luckily, I was able to turn off it a few miles out of Tedzhen. From now on we would be travelling mostly on minor roads. At the corner was an unexpected truck stop; a clutch of rickety stalls selling snacks and canned drinks.

It was probably the last chance of junk food before Mari. I sank a can of Coke in smart order and bought a packet of "proper" biscuits to add to the hard tack left over from the Dushak market. Kaan gave a great, gusty sigh as I put it into the saddlebag, but in all honesty it weighed only a few ounces.

He soon forgot the extra weight when rapid hoofbeats sounded behind. A young lad drew abreast on a bay part-bred and pulled up smartly beside us. Kaan danced sideways, and as the lad put his horse into a flat-out gallop I let him follow at a sharp canter. A hundred yards ahead, the boy drew rein and looked back in disappointment. He wanted to race his horse. I shook my head and gestured to the saddlebags. One day, I promised myself, I really would let Kaan out and see just what he could do. But not today, with twenty pounds of dead weight and a lot of miles ahead.

So I thought, anyway. The lad joined another horseman and the two peeled off to the left. Kaan cantered on peaceably for a moment, then mutinied. These were the first horses he'd seen for days, and he wanted company. Without warning he bored left, straight towards the road. It took all my strength to wrench him round, away from the traffic, and drive him to safety. The effect of the altercation was galvanic. He must have feared that I would punish him for it; for with breath-taking acceleration he went into overdrive. For the first time I experienced the full power and speed of an Akhal-Teke. The thrill made my skin prickle, and I was tempted to let him run. Then I remembered the full saddlebags. The fun would have to wait until later.

I'd long considered the riddle of the Akhal-Teke's speed. How could this lean, wiry horse, with muscles designed for endless aerobic exertion rather than brief, oxygen-guzzling speed, be the second fastest breed on earth after the English Thoroughbred? You might as well expect an Olympic marathon champion to be a national standard sprinter as well. But, in Kaan's sudden burst, I had the answer. I'd felt the gentle, floating canter morph into a raking, workmanlike stride of enormous length. In a moment of revelation I saw how the working parts were superbly designed to move together; how the high-set neck gave more freedom for the great shoulders to extend; how the long back coiled and uncoiled like a greyhound's; how the length from those high, bony hips to the low-set hocks gave extra leverage to propel the whole machine forward. Geometry, not biology, was the secret weapon.

The exertion had darkened his neck with moisture. It was the first time I'd ever seen him sweat, except under the saddle.

Maybe this was one component of good performance under desert conditions: an ability to maintain body moisture, to lose heat in some other way. In fact the leanness of the Teke, its greyhound build, are engineered by thousands of years of evolution to lose heat fast in murderously high temperatures.

Not that it was hot, today. The clouds hid the sun and occasionally even sprinkled a little rain. Travelling was a pleasure. I began to realise for how much of the journey so far I had been obsessed with the need for water and shade.

And there was good going underfoot. Salt crusted the surface, and occasionally Kaan's foot cracked through a layer of it as you might crunch through a frosted puddle. But the ground underneath held his weight. Leaving the road, we followed a good track beside a finger of the Tedzhen River, on its one-way trip to oblivion in the Kara Kum.

This was natural marshland, with a rich variety of life. Besides the usual cuckoos, their voices competing with those of the frogs, there were herons and a sort of wading bird, somewhere between avocet and oystercatcher. Terns flew overhead, perhaps coming from the Khauz-Khan, an enormous reservoir to the south. "Don't go anywhere near the Khauz-Khan," Viola Mikhailovna's neighbour had warned. "There are very bad people there." I had gathered that there was some sort of institution: a prison, perhaps?

I saw my first non-torpid snake here, a dull brown rope wriggling out of our path like a sidewinder. It was a sharp reminder that this is a country full of snakes; I'd been getting rather blasé about them.

We covered a brisk twenty-five kilometres that morning. Gradually the good track gave out and the camelthorn encroached. Kaan picked his way through with increasing distaste, occasionally stopping altogether and turning his head to give me a dirty look. Just as it became completely intolerable we reached another junction, guarded by a *GAI* - Police - post.

Opposite was a deserted chai-khana made from an old railway carriage. The door was locked, but all the amenities were outside: a tin awning and trees for protection against the sun, which was beginning to shine again; an unusually clean canal, edged with reeds and excellent grass; and a sort of raised platform, half divan and half treehouse, reached by a ramp.

Kaan lunched well on barley followed by reeds, his reins coupled to his noseband for a makeshift tether. I spent the afternoon on the platform, lying just above his head out of reach of ants or ticks.

All it needed to make the day complete, I suddenly decided, was a swim. Stripping off no further than my shirt in deference to the nearby GAI post, I slid down the bank and splashed in the clear water, taking good care to keep my mouth tight shut against biliary derangements. I kept a weather eye on Kaan; but the old rogue saw his chance. As I was hopping on one foot getting my shoe back on, he somehow slipped loose and set off back the way we had come. I had visions of walking back to Tedzhen, but a friendly policeman stopped him. He delivered Kaan back to me along with a stern lecture about my carelessness in losing him, while I listened meekly.

We turned off on to the minor road and continued through farmland, similar to the country I'd become used to around Ashkhabad. There were settlements every few miles, as Viola Mikhailovna had promised. Men, women and tractors were busy in fields still surprisingly bare. There seemed to be nothing visibly being grown, but a lot of work going into not growing it.

I had yet to learn the whims of cotton. Needing a temperature of 35° C just to germinate, it appears very late in the spring, then grows furiously. I was now entering the cotton belt, and from here to Mari and beyond more than half the land was given over to it. This was why, in late May, so many fields still appeared barren, why so much work showed as yet no clear end.

As the day wore on, truck after truck began to pass. Their human cargoes, packed in the back like sardines, shouted and waved to me. I waved back, feeling like a child waving at passing trains. There must be a village ahead. I hoped they weren't going all the way to Mari.

A double trailer load of lucerne passed, and turned into a yard ahead. This looked promising. I followed, and found only a line of derelict concrete buildings, barren of all but dust.

But the hay was near; I could smell it. So could Kaan. He was, these days, wised up to the idea of scrounging his supper, and thoroughly approved of it. Noses twitching like Bisto Kids, we followed the scent round the end of the concrete and found ourselves in a ferma, where the lucerne was even now being shovelled off the trailers into troughs.

As I dismounted, the boss drove up in a battered old car. He wound down the window and, before I could utter a word, he cried, "Yes! Yes! Put your horse here! Come and stay with me!"

He got out of the car and led the way towards the lucerne, Kaan outpacing us both.

*

The farm belonged to Kolkhoz Kurban Durdi, and Sem was its dairy manager. His tanned face seamed with wrinkles, a chuckle always hovering somewhere deep in his throat, he was a dead ringer for Sid James.

He was busy this evening. The cattle were due for their weekly insecticide dose. There was no fuss here about face masks or protective clothing. Sem wielded a hosepipe connected to a tank and pressurised by a tractor, spraying organo-phosphates with a verve fit to have won him a gong from an Iraqi military academy. The cowering cattle massed at the end of the yard, until with yells and sticks the farmhands drove them twice through the jet of liquid: once for each side. Fascinated and terrified, I watched from a safe distance, and upwind.

Another unit up the road needed the same treatment. We piled into the car, with Sem's thirteen-year-old son at the wheel. The boy drove like Jehu up the road, looking over his shoulder to talk to his dad and nearly taking us all over the bank.

At the other farm were the dairy cows; plus six magnificent bulls, all living harmoniously in one pen. Sem's wife was there,

286

forking hay. She wouldn't let me help, so I sprawled on a corner of the haystack, enjoying a moment of leisure and watching a re-run of the spraying.

Mucking in with the farmhands were local lads, aged perhaps eight to eighteen. These were hangers-on, there for the fun of helping with the animals - or just for something to do. Later in life, they would go their separate ways; some to be employed at the farm, some to go to the town, to college, to move away. But for now they were a fraternity, with a common purpose. It was a familiar scene, one independent of place and - to a lesser extent - time; one that might have come from the pages of Housman, or Hardy.

Life in rural England must have been very much like this a hundred years ago, when it was at a comparable level of industrialisation, of sophistication. I felt a pang of nostalgia for an England that doesn't really exist, and maybe never did, except in one's imagination - or that of the poets. "Only the wanderer abroad knows England's graces..." mused Ivor Gurney from the trenches. It was easier for me to imagine this rustic idyll from thousands of miles away than it was in the right place, but from the distance of a hundred years.

When the last cow had been sprayed and the last calf fed, the boot was crammed with fresh hay, a churn of milk was balanced on the back seat, and we set off. Sem stalled the car three times then powered away like a rally driver, bouncing over the potholes and treating a gravel patch as a skid pan. It was easy to see where his son had learned to drive.

We stopped at the first farm to deliver bread, onions and milk to the night watchman, who was preparing for sleep on top of his wagon. He had already brewed his tea, taking water to fill his blackened pot from the same ditch where I had filled Kaan's bucket, and boiling it on a tiny fire of straw and stalks. Kaan, meanwhile, had finished every grain of barley and was getting stuck into the lucerne.

At Sem's house we were met by his daughter, a striking figure with jet-black hair falling over a brilliant green dress. She brought us tea as we sprawled comfortably on cushions, surrounded by cats. The younger son followed, holding a white-tailed pigeon.

"How does that get on with the cats?" I asked Sem.

"Oh, they all live together," he replied cheerfully. Just as he spoke one of the cats made a dive at the pigeon, which took refuge on top of the bedding chest, feathers ruffled in outrage. Tearfully, the boy chased the cat out of the room.

Order restored, we enjoyed a wonderful supper of chicken stew. I revelled in the change of diet, but hoped the chicken hadn't bitten the dust in my honour. For Sem, though, the real point of entertaining a guest was the excuse to get out the vodka.

Every time he proposed a toast, he expected me to match him and drain my glass to the bottom. That was, roughly every three minutes. From time to time he nudged me to raise my glass and do the honours.

"To friendship!" "To Turcoman hospitality!" "To Akhal-Teke horses!" My subjects, uninspired as they were, seemed to satisfy him. Not, though, my capacity.

"This is what a good Turcoman would do!" draining his glass. "You must do the same!" To press the lesson home he took a refill and threw it down, screwing up his face with distaste for the rough liquor and drinking cows' milk kumiss as a chaser. As the evening wore on, the creases bit deeper and deeper into his face, and his smile broadened like a slice of melon.

By ten, I longed for bed. Towards eleven, Sem suddenly stood up, weaved an unsteady path outside, and hollered for me to join him. When I got there, he was sitting in the car.

"We're going to a wedding party," he announced. "Get in!"

I couldn't. With the best will in the world, I couldn't. Wobbly with fatigue even before the vodka, I was now absolutely legless. As for Sem, it was a miracle that he was still moderately vertical. He could have fuelled the car just by sneezing on the carburettor.

He dismissed my excuses and tightened the screws. "You'll offend my friends if you don't come!"

His friends, I pointed out, didn't know I existed. Besides, it was academic. I simply couldn't stand up any longer.

Crestfallen, he got out of the car. He wouldn't go without me. My name, it was pretty obvious, was mud.

*

He had rather less to say for himself the next morning. In fact, I don't think he said a word all the way to the farm. Perhaps he was concentrating on his driving; for he handled the potholes with unusual care.

Sem wasn't the only one who looked like a ghost this morning. Kaan had found a patch of cement dust at the back of his pen. He had rolled long and carefully, and was now covered in white powder. His bony hips were particularly thickly covered, accentuating his thinness. My heart gave a lurch as he walked across to me.

The water ditch was full of black wriggling dots; a batch of tadpoles had hatched overnight. It made for a long job drawing a bucket of clean water.

Make the most of the water, Sem warned as his voice cracked into action at last. "The day after tomorrow, you must cross a bad patch of desert. There's no water for forty kilometres. Before that, there's a kolkhoz called 'Baz'. That's where you want to stop tonight."

It was hard to believe in the deserts just ahead and behind. Grey skies and abundant greenery almost made me think myself back in England. Large infrequent spots of rain plopped on to Kaan's neck and soaked into the saddlebags. Was the weather an accident in this fertile belt, or did something in the lie of the land hereabouts draw more rainclouds to speed the growth?

Canals scored the ground every two or three hundred yards. In the fields between them tractors raced up and down, huge tractors the size of earth movers, balancing crazily on a single front wheel. Here the cotton was king, and man and machine hurried to do its bidding.

I dared not stray far from the road for fear of being boxed in by water. As usual, the headlands of the fields were either deep ground or a jungle of camelthorn, by now so well grown that it brushed not only Kaan's legs but my own, clawing at the

289

saddlebags. Presently marsh closed in again, and we had no alternative to the tarmac. Hordes of mosquitoes began to follow us.

By mid-day we were back on good, firm ground, under skies that were thinking of clearing but so far not doing much about it. Cotton fields had given way to waste ground covered with tamarisk in a wonderful range of colours - pale lilac to deep carmine to pastel pink - and throbbing with cuckoos. A pity we had to keep weaving like drunkards to avoid the worst of the camelthorn. If I ever got this horse back to England - a hope which was growing in my mind with every day that passed - I would forget about such things as eventing or long-distance riding, I thought irritably, and put him in for bending races.

With brazen opportunism I stopped and offsaddled for lunch a hundred yards from some buildings, under the only decent trees for miles. Sure enough, it was less than half an hour before one of the monster tractors came down the track. "Come and drink tea!" said the driver.

I followed him up the track to where his friends were gathering for the afternoon siesta on a divan under the trees. One of them jumped up, took his sickle and disappeared into the fields. In ten minutes he returned with his arms full of lucerne for Kaan.

Bargadi was a tiny settlement where these half-dozen men lived to work the cotton on a rota system: ten days on, five days off with their families in Mari. It was poor; their huts were railway carriages and their divan made from an old truck body. But it wasn't entirely comfortless. Despite the cleanliness of the water ditch they drew their water from a well; while if you looked closely at the fire, on which three blackened teapots simmered continuously, you could see that it wasn't twigs, but a half-buried gas jet that burned so furiously.

After we had pooled our bread and raisins over several pots of tea, some of the lads rolled over and fell instantly asleep. The rest smoked, continued drinking and chatted desultorily. Life was good, said my host Kushun, and getting better. "We've got a great president! Things are better than they were five years ago."

"How are they better?"

"We're free, now. We have an independent government. Nobody meddles or interferes with us. We have free gas, cheap petrol. We can sell our surplus, which we weren't allowed to do before."

Would Murad, the kolkhoznik from the Chardzhou train, recognise his own land? But this was cotton country, and rich. Until the oil and gas could flow more freely abroad, cotton was the fulcrum of Turkmenistan's economy, and first in the queue for such subsidies as the straitened government could afford.

"A couple of Americans came here last year, reps for John Deere. Our *Raion* bought seventeen combine harvesters. They cost a million dollars."

"How much?!"

Kushun was embarrassed; he wasn't sure if this was true, or whether he'd been repeating the inflated figures of hearsay. But the cotton must be doing pretty well, I thought, if the Raion's account books dealt in that many noughts. For the first time I began to understand a little why the country's farmland continued to produce so much white gold, while animals starved and people queued for bread.

The hours passed, the sun burned less fiercely, and one by one the sleeping men awoke. "Stay with us!" they pressed. We've got plenty of lucerne for your horse."

It was tempting. I had grown roots into the divan, and didn't want to move. But a few good hours of daylight remained, and Kaan was well fed and rested. Besides, sharing the place with six men could make problems. It was time to move. The lads shovelled a last armful of lucerne into my saddlebags and saw me off reluctantly.

A few miles up the road, the signalman on the brand-new Turkmenistan-Iran railway was equally hospitable. "It's not far to Baz! You've plenty of time! Come and drink tea!" But it was, and I hadn't, so I didn't. He had no objections to a photograph of the historic new line - a liberty which not so long ago would have cost me my film, if not my camera - and even held Kaan for me while I took it.

291

At long last the irrigation stopped abruptly, and sand dunes rose beyond a final ditch of clear water in which some young men waded and splashed. A solitary farmhouse stood just off the road. I could see some kind of big settlement well ahead; that must be Baz.

"Come and be our guest!" cried the swimmers from the farmhouse. I can't remember why I refused; only that it was a bad decision.

XV

Baz wasn't a kolkhoz. It was a yard, big enough to enclose several football pitches. A broken concrete fence enclosed a rectangle perhaps five hundred yards by half a mile. It was quite empty except for some buildings hugging the near corners, a few bits of rusting machinery, and a row of agricultural conveyor belts lined up with geometric precision.* A light burned in the window of a railway carriage by the gate. I knocked on its door, and raised the porter.

He was an unprepossessing old man, with an Uzbek skullcap perched above hollow unshaven cheeks. He stared at me blankly for a long moment; then leaned away from the door to release a stream of green liquid from the corner of his mouth. I had interrupted his evening fix of nas.

Should I beat a hasty retreat to the farmhouse I'd just passed? Surely there was nowhere here for Kaan, and I was less than enthusiastic for myself. But the porter had already called the night watchman, and it was too late to escape.

Yes, they decided, we could stop here. There was a pen where Kaan could stay, and they even managed to produce an armful of greenstuff for him from some unlikely corner of this concrete prairie. He was installed and eating before I realised that there was a serious problem.

On and off, we had been plagued by mosquitoes. I'd spent much time and energy slapping horseflies, huge creatures an inch long and engorged with Kaan's blood, exploding under my hand to splash his legs with red splodges.

But the mosquitoes here were something else. Like a Biblical plague or a horror from Hitchcock, they landed on Kaan so thickly that you could barely see an inch of his coat for them.

The Deet was long finished, but I still had a bottle of Viola Mikhailovna's tick fluid. With a double strength batch and a

---

* Baz was actually a cotton collecting and processing station.

293

sock as a sponge, I was soon splashing OP's around with a flourish that would have done credit to Sem. I went all over Kaan twice, with my mouth clamped shut and my throat tight against inhaling. The result was miraculous. All but a few hardy or suicidal mozzies lost their appetite, and I called down all the blessings of heaven upon Viola Mikhailovna.

Then it was time to look to myself. I have a well-founded terror of strong insecticide, and wanted soap and water fast. To my astonishment the old man, who was being so nice as to shame my first impressions of him, offered me a "shower".

It was only a cold tap rigged above a duckboard in a ring of bushes, but it did the job. I washed every inch of myself, my hair and my clothing, including the sock three times, and breathed again. And if that was the old man lurking behind the bushes, I was too tired to care.

I slept in his railway carriage that night; if "slept" is the word. Although I hid under my slimy towel from the mosquitoes, they found their way underneath and bit hard all night. The porter kept his radio on at high volume, himself sleeping like a baby through the noise. When the station finally closed down at four in the morning and only the crackle of static disturbed the peace, I dozed a bit. But broadcasting began again at five. I wanted an early start anyway for fear of the desert to come, so I wearily got up and went to see whether the mosquitoes had left anything of Kaan.

The old man was up, sitting on his sleeping mat and brewing tea when I came back. As I blew into the steaming bowl, trying to cool it quickly and swallow as much liquid as possible before leaving, he told me a little of the way ahead.

He was behaving awkwardly today, not meeting my eye, the geniality of the night before completely gone. I wondered if I had offended him. When I thanked him and got up to leave, he stopped me.

"*Nado platit*," he said. You have to pay.

I was surprised, because I had already brought up the subject the night before, and he'd refused; but also relieved, that for once I was to be allowed to pay my way. This explained his odd manner. He was embarrassed at asking for money.

"Of course!" I replied, and brought out a handful of manats. He waved them away.

"I don't want any money," he said crossly; then again, "nado platit."

Curiouser and curiouser. Before I could open my mouth to ask what he meant, he moved crabwise on to my sleeping mat and began to paw at me.

I thrust the manats into his groping hand, and fled as if all the wolves in Turkmenistan were snapping at my heels.

Well, I had wanted an early start.

*

By now, Kaan and I were veterans when it came to crossing desert landscape. But a new experience awaited us when we set out that morning.

Until now, the "desert" we had been used to was uncultivated, uncultivable wasteland; too high to reach with irrigation and too poor even to try, too dry to grow anything except a few blades of grass for a week after a sprinkling of spring rain. Desert by definition, almost by default.

Ahead, though, was the real thing. The finger of desert that reached out to separate the Tedzhen and Merv Oases was vintage Kara Kum, an extension of the Black Sands that stretched for three hundred unbroken miles between Ashkhabad and Kunya Urgench. Rolling waves of sand broke against the walls of Baz, low dunes bound by stunted saxaul and chopped off short to leeward in crumbling vertical drops, their windward slopes pleated into ripples like a beach when the tide has gone out.

Desert, but not deserted. The sand had been heaving, it seemed, during the hours of darkness. The sharp angle of the rising sun picked out tracks on every inch of ground. Tiny, spidery tracks; sizeable paw-marks - a jackal, perhaps; the herringbone pattern of a sidewinding adder; and a curious continuous groove like a bicycle's wheelmarks. While I puzzled over the last, its mystery was solved. A fat scarab beetle, out late and hurrying for home before the kites had it for breakfast, laid a perfect bicycle-track across our path. That, and an obscene hairy spider, were the only life I saw all day.

Good paths ran among the dunes, so we could leave the road and even pile on some speed before it got hot. As we cantered over a rise farmland again lay before us, sudden as an oasis, unconvincing as a mirage. So much for Sem's desert, I thought, with the slightly fake disappointment of one who has been let off the hook.

In fact, it was worse going: back to detours around ploughed ground, dykes forcing us on to the road to find a bridge, camelthorn degrading the headlands. When we finally reached a chai-khana in the late morning I was horrified to learn that, far from the twenty-five kilometres I'd estimated, we had only done fifteen; for a further twenty-five remained to the town of Shatlik, our destination.

Those twenty-five kilometres are burned into my memory of the journey. Burned literally, for as the sun reached its height, we hit the desert for real. Sem's warning was not after all exaggerated, and the dunes we had crossed at dawn were just an aperitif... if such a liquid metaphor may be allowed. For after one last dyke for Kaan to drink from, the waterless sands of the Kara Kum swallowed us up.

There was no chance of rest, for there was no shade, no water, no grazing. At least we were spared the road, for a good track forged its way straight as a die between the dunes. We plodded along it for hour after hour through the unchanging landscape, while the sun beat down relentlessly. From time to time I dismounted and walked, for we had knocked off a good few miles over the last three days, and Kaan was getting sore on the harder bits of ground. Walk a bit, ride a bit; it was the only variation available in the ongoing trudge.

The shimmering heat-haze, or the curvature of the dunes, or maybe just my rambling brain, made for an odd illusion. The track seemed to be slightly uphill all the way, the horizon ahead just a few feet above eye level. Yet when I looked behind me, it was just the same. We seemed to be walking across the bottom of a bowl, a wide, shallow bowl in which some power kept us constantly at the bottom, the rim unattainable.

296

At last buildings broke the horizon, tall enough to show above the undulating sand. This was the aerodrome marked on my map which, according to my reckoning, we should have reached hours before. It was marked immediately next to Shatlik, and the trek was nearly over.

I didn't know just then how staggeringly inaccurate was my map, one of the world-wide series of Tactical Pilotage Charts compiled from US spy-satellite photographs. If this one was typical, it was a good thing that the Cold War never heated up; the Americans would have missed the bulls-eye and nuked the open desert every time. It showed the aerodrome far too far to the west - the reason for the confusing distances at the chai-khana - and Shatlik itself was actually miles further on.

It appeared at last in the distance, a beacon drawing me in but never getting any closer; the usual phenomenon of distance in Turkmenistan. They say that at sea, the horizon is six miles away. It must be about the same here, so flat is the land. And six miles, in our current state of exhaustion, took a bit of covering.

At least Kaan still had some life in him. As I tightened the girth to ride the last half-mile into town, he turned his head and bit me. It was completely out of character. He was as disenchanted with life, at that moment, as I was myself.

We had both, I thought grimly, had quite enough of the bloody Kara Kum.

*

Shatlik was no oasis. It was a dormitory town, its *raison d'être* being Turkmenistan's potential crock of gold: the vast gas-fields hereabouts. The hotel had no friendly yard for Kaan.

There was nothing for it but to try the Hakimlik. The local doctor, who lodged at the hotel, kindly offered to drive me there. I would much rather have gone with Kaan, who in attracting the usual attention might also have won himself an invitation; but it would have been rude to refuse. Anyway the Hakimlik was a mile away, and we were both rubber-legged. So the administrator, a lounging youth with a vacuous smile, took Kaan to graze, while I climbed into the doctor's old black Russian car.

The Hakimlik was closed, and the Hakim not expected before tomorrow. At least we found a kiosk selling cold drinks. I sank five large glasses in quick succession, and they went down my throat as if I were pouring them into the sand.

We tried the local ferma, a big impersonal yard about as far removed from Sem's or Ashir's set-up as a battery chicken unit from a garden hen-house. The boss, a big, coarse man with small, cold eyes in a face like a brick wall, might have passed for a crooked bookmaker. No, he hadn't anywhere suitable for a horse, or if he had Kaan might jump out, or escape, or... No chance to ask if he had any barley for sale, for the doctor, who had taken charge, was conducting the conversation in Turcoman and whisked me off again.

He was by now regretting the quixotic impulse which had saddled him with me. He wanted to get home, or back to work. I for my part would gladly have relieved him of my presence, which was beginning to embarrass us both. But Turkmenchilik insisted we see the thing through together. And he had another idea which might settle it quickly.

Not that quickly, though, because his car refused to start. He had to push it down a bank before we could leave the farm. Eventually we limped into a chai-khana a kilometre from the hotel, whose owner had a few cattle - and a spare enclosure.

It was the most dismal and dangerous place yet. Coarse, rusty wire mesh threw spikes out at odd angles, including vertically from the ground. Iron bars half-buried in the sand poked sharp edges up to knee height. Getting in and out was a question of uncobbling a length of the wire mesh and bending it back. Yet I had no choice but to agree.

It was now getting late. I fetched Kaan quickly, pausing to rip some grass from a ditch and stuff it into the saddlebags to tide him over until I could hunt down some proper food. That was my next problem, and getting more urgent by the minute.

Now I struck my first bit of luck. On the edge of town was a GAI post. If in trouble, ask a policeman. Disillusioned as I was with Officialdom, I reckoned I had nothing to lose.

I called in, introduced Kaan to the man on duty, and told him about our journey. In no time the whole squad had come out, friendly and chatty, from the glass box that served as an office. "Feed? No problem!" they said. "There'll be a feed wagon coming past in a moment. We'll send you some down!"

Sure enough, no sooner had I got Kaan penned than a tractor and trailer turned into the yard of the chai-khana. Jumping into the back, the driver began to fork out a mountain of fresh grass, reeds and lucerne. "Stop! Stop!" I cried ineffectually, as the stuff kept flying out and the mountain grew. "More! More!" shouted the owner of the chai-khana, seeing his own feed problems solved for the coming week.

At last the tractor man left, refusing my attempts to pay him. Immediately another tractor arrived for a repeat performance. Blessing the policemen, I couldn't help thinking of Guljemala and her "Korruptsia!". I was afraid we were on the receiving end of a sweetener to the police. Had they stopped the driver, with a deal: "You do us a favour, and next time your papers aren't quite in order, we'll do you one!" Whatever the case, principles wouldn't feed a hungry horse. I couldn't help a twinge of amusement to think that it was probably the unhelpful farm boss that we had robbed.

At last I left Kaan before a pile of grass, his tack safely locked away in the chai-khana, and tottered back to the hotel. The evening wasn't over yet, though.

My gear had been locked away somewhere, and I still hadn't fixed up my room. But the administrator was nowhere to be seen. Someone went to find him, while I slumped in the passage. He eventually appeared, wobbly-kneed and reeking of alcohol.

Earlier, he had looked after Kaan for me, and I was grateful. Now, he plunged his account into the red by trying to collect his dues. Shutting the door of my room behind him, he went through the motions of trying to corner me, too drunk to see that he wasn't welcome.

Two goons in one day; one geriatric, and the other plastered. What a compliment; perhaps I should see an image consultant. It was the last straw, and by the time I'd heaved the youth out forcibly and locked the door, I was shaking from anger as much as fatigue.

But Shatlik's hotel wasn't all bad. When I had recovered my temper enough to look around, I was speechless.

It wasn't a room, but a suite. There was a sitting room newly furnished with expensive Turcoman carpets, separate bedroom, bathroom, and an anteroom with a fridge - working. All this for the princely sum of three thousand manats a night, about seventy-five pence.

I soaked my mosquito bites in a long, cold bath, had a good supper cooked in the communal kitchen, and slept deeply in the most comfortable bed for weeks.

*

Vladimir Ivanovitch Leshchenko emerged from under the bonnet of his car and straightened up with a grunt. He looked more like a character from Steinbeck than a Russian mechanic; grizzled hair under a baseball cap, kindly face hidden behind a pair of round spectacles and a pepper-and-salt beard, lumberjack shirt and old jeans stained with oil. He also had a dry sense of humour, which at first I wrongly thought was irritation at being plucked from his work to try and find barley for a troublesome Englishwoman.

After some difficulty getting it started, we climbed into the battered old car together with Vladimir Ivanovitch's workmate and his wife.

Unlike her husband, Eleonora Andreevna looked Russian to the core; living among the Turcoman people seemed only to emphasise her Russian-ness. With a sense of kindness and generosity towards strangers far beyond the call of duty, she was rapidly turning into my guardian angel. I'd stopped her in the street to ask the way to the rinok. She had immediately turned round and taken me there, and led me round each of the kolkhoznik stallholders asking them if I could buy barley.

The response had been negative, the advice unvarying. "Go to a kolkhoz and ask."

"Come on," said Eleonora Andreevna. "My husband has a car. If he's not too busy, he might take us out to a kolkhoz and see if we can find you some barley." She guided me between the drab blocks of identical flats to a tract of wasteland with a row of sheds along one side, where her husband ran his garage business.

Vladimir Ivanovitch's first thought was, like mine had been, to try the ferma. But the hard-eyed bookie was adamant. No, they couldn't even spare me a few kilos of barley. They simply hadn't got any. We turned to leave, but the car refused point-blank to fire. As we got out and push-started it, I had a feeling I'd been here before.

We took the road north out of town to the local kolkhoz, passing a brand-new industrial complex fetchingly done out in orange and blue. "The new cotton factory," commented Eleonora, "built with Turkish money."

Plenty of new buildings were going up on the kolkhoz, too; tidy, solid block-built houses with shiny corrugated roofs and first-floor verandas like Rep's home. It seemed that King Cotton was being generous to his subjects.

The car turned left and right through the grid of streets, and pulled up at a house where a warm welcome awaited the Leshchenkos. While Vladimir went off with his friend to trawl the village for barley, Eleonora and I sat on the divan drinking tea with his wife. Obviously close friends, they had a lot of news to exchange. Just as well, for it was a good half-hour before the men came back, triumphant. We jumped into the car and went off to see what they had found.

The corn was poor stuff, at a price which made Vladimir prickle with outrage. I would gladly have paid double, even though it was full of wheat, straw and cow dung. As the last few grains trickled out and the stream slowed, I caught the unmistakable glint of broken glass. No wonder the budding capitalist still had this unusable rubbish left; it wasn't fit to manure the garden with. But I couldn't say a word after the colossal effort of the Leshchenkos. So I held my tongue and paid up. Perhaps I could sort out a few clean grains.

Back at the chai-khana, Kaan had so far managed not to impale himself on any of the iron spikes. Vladimir and Eleonora watched with satisfaction as he attacked the carrots I'd bought at the rinok. Then, still brimming with kindness, they stayed to help me look through the barley grain by grain until we had extracted the glass from enough to give Kaan a good feed.

After another hour or two, I had enough of it picked through to take back to the hotel and boil for his next feed. While I worked the son of the house, a lad of about sixteen, came and asked about Kaan.

"Can I have a ride on him?" he asked, inevitably.

I had been acutely conscious, throughout the trip, that in riding a Turcoman horse I was enjoying a privilege not available to most of the Turcoman people. Whenever possible I shared that privilege, as at Aina's; but my first responsibility was to Kaan, who was not to be exploited without consideration.

After the recent mileage he needed a complete break. I was particularly anxious that he should have a full day without either his feet or his back being touched. So I told the boy, "Yes, but not today. Tomorrow, before I leave." He was disappointed, so I explained.

"He's done a hundred and twenty kilometres in the last three days. He's very tired now, and his feet are sore. Today, he must rest."

In fact Kaan was in surprisingly good form, all things considered. As I brushed him off, I examined his back closely. The hair on either side of his spine was rubbing a little thin, but so far there was no sign of chafing. The hard layer of muscle now building over his ribs gave him extra protection. The excess growth had all gone from his feet, but cleanly, with no splitting; the remainder was hard. He would never be able to travel far on tarmac, but I had no fear now of his going lame before journey's end. Best of all, although he was still thin his coat gleamed, infallible sign of good health. A rich metallic sheen, characteristic of the Akhal-Teke, threw back the sun like a mirror.

I felt pretty satisfied as I plodded back to the hotel, my own time to rest come at last. As well as Kaan's carrots, the market had come up trumps with the same treasures as at Tedzhen. I had a self-indulgent late lunch of rolls, cream cheese and cucumbers washed down with Coke; and put what was left into the fridge, hardly able to believe such luxury.

302

I'd only been lying on my bed for five minutes when there was a knock, and one of the guests put her head round the door.

"Your horse is outside."

*

It was the boy from the chai-khana. He had helped himself to Kaan, cobbled the tack on somehow and ridden him up the kilometre of road. Now he was sitting on him outside the hotel, waving at me as if he had done something clever.

On my sprint to the fire escape - the quickest way down - the whole range of ghastly possibilities had raced through my mind like a speeded-up film. Kaan had somehow broken out of his pen, he had torn himself on the wire, he was even now oozing blood, rust and tetanus, he had galloped loose through the town, he had come down on the road and broken his knees or collided with a lorry....

"Don't worry!" cried the lad brightly, when he saw the thunderclouds gathering on my brow. "His feet are fine. He came galloping up the road really fast!"

The saddle, which he was supposed to be keeping safe for me under lock and key, was on skew-whiff, the girth straps twisted, the crucial foam pads missing altogether. The bridle was actually upside down, browband behind the ears and reins somehow attached to the noseband. I should be thankful, I thought fleetingly, that he hadn't put the bit in Kaan's mouth and then swung on it all the way up the road.

I was incandescent. I couldn't bear it, to think what pains I had taken to keep this horse fed, fit and comfortable, only to have him thus abused. I cursed the boy, keeping up a flow of invective for several minutes without repeating myself, while a remote corner of my brain remarked cynically how my Russian had suddenly improved. By now a crowd of hotel guests was gathering. They had all heard about Kaan, had seen me trudging endlessly up and down to look after him, had good-humouredly shared the hotel stove while I boiled barley. The poor lad found public opinion hard against him, and hung his head while they tutted disapproval. I did feel sorry for him, and eventually made my peace with him; but much later.

All the way back to the dismal pen, Kaan was once again wincing whenever he stepped on hard ground. I left him with my two little luggage padlocks holding his wire door. Not that they gave much protection - you could have sliced through them with a nail file - but to make a statement. My saddle stayed in my hotel room.

In the end I got about an hour's rest; then it was time to go out and do the evening feed.

*

It may not have had the usual equine amenities, but it was a friendly hotel. On my second day the bibulous administrator was replaced by a fiercely efficient looking Russian lady, helped by a gentle girl with a young daughter who, her mother said proudly, learned English at school. The little girl was too shy to talk, but later knocked on my door with a bunch of roses from the garden - trade mark, I was beginning to learn, of hotels in Turkmenistan.

Apart from myself and the doctor the guests were all women, staying here while their husbands worked in the gas fields nearby. They were a sociable lot, migrating in groups between each others' rooms, carrying into this town hotel the social pattern of their village lives.

In a rare moment of leisure, the doctor called me into his room. He had previously spoken of his digestive problems, and the need to eat *trava*. The word meant "grass", but was used here of anything green and growing, and usually referred to animal feed. I'd assumed he meant green vegetables. Now, I discovered otherwise.

Tables filled his room. On them lay trays and trays of dried herbs. The doctor was a medical herbalist.

He moved from tray to tray, fingering the contents lovingly and explaining the use of each.

"You know," he said, pointing to a particular batch which he used as a sedative, "you could do with some of this. Your nerves are too tight." I'd have liked, I thought irritably, to meet the person who could spend the last weeks as I had, and arrive in a state of blissful serenity; and nearly said so. But that would only have confirmed his diagnosis, and I zipped my mouth.

What I really needed was sleep, and I got twelve hours of it that night. But in the morning I felt worse rather than better, having lost the momentum which was all that had been keeping me going. By now a complete vegetable, I took three shots at getting to the chai-khana. The first time I forgot the barley and the padlock keys, the second time just the barley.

Kaan, though, was in great form. I led him out to stretch his legs, and he rolled long and lazily in a patch of sand. His coat shone like polished bronze under the brush, and he was full of beans and raring to go.

This afternoon we would start on a crucial leg of the ride, taking us to Yazberdi Aga, a friend of Yusup's at Kolkhoz Chkalova just outside Mari. Yazberdi, said Yusup, would be able to arrange Kaan's eventual transport by lorry back to Ashkhabad. I carried a letter of introduction in my inside pocket.

If this transport materialised, a major worry was lifted off my shoulders. Better still, Chkalova would be our Base Camp for the last leg to Merv, just two more days' ride away.

*

All the hotel staff, the doctor and a deputation of the lady residents came outside to wave us off.

Kaan and I weren't quite finished with Shatlik. Eleonora and Vladimir had invited me to visit them before I left. So, having stopped to ask the way, I found myself led by a group of children to the Street of the Gasworkers, one more gem from the romantic imagination of Soviet town planners.

I should have guessed that to go visiting here wouldn't just mean standing in the street and waving up at the flat. Before I knew what had happened Vladimir was in charge of Kaan, now grazing on rich grass, while Eleonora took me in to meet the family and sit down to a huge meal.

If yesterday I had thought Vladimir like a character from Steinbeck, then his elder son resembled Caleb from the film of *East of Eden*. A youth with a slightly sulky, cynical air, he wore a bush shirt open to the waist and his hair in a fifties-style quiff. He even looked like James Dean.

Over the pelmeni, Eleonora told me a little about herself. Her story was a fascinating cameo of the trials and tribulations of the Soviet Union over the last six decades. Born in Mongolia, she had moved in her childhood to Moldova, where her father had died in 1946, "of starvation", she said with a heart-wrenching dignity. It seemed intrusive to ask whether this was part of the collectivisation debâcle, when quotas in excess of total agricultural output caused millions to starve; but Stalin featured in the story, as if to explain all. The remaining family had then moved to Siberia, where they had managed to scratch a living.

Eleonora had lived in Uzbekistan before coming here, hoping for a fresh start in a frontier country. Now, she found the rug pulled on her by her departing countrymen. Her pension was eight dollars a month.

"Surely," I said feebly, "Turkmenistan will become much richer when the oil and gas can be exported." But it was only a polite formula, something almost irrelevant to these people's pressing and immediate problems, and we both knew it.

"Of course," she said, "things were better under Soviet rule. We were all one people, then. Now, we are the odd ones out in a country of Turcomans. Then, everything was conducted in Russian. Now, it's all in Turcoman, and I don't speak Turcoman." Just like the former Turcoman experience, but in mirror image.

"Now," she continued, "you have to know people to get the things you need." Perhaps it was her acute awareness of that fact that had led her to be so astonishingly kind to me, a stranger who knew no-one to pull strings.

Below, in the street, Vladimir and Kaan were collecting a crowd. Word had got round, and every child in the neighbourhood had gathered to see the horse. They milled round him, the bolder ones reaching to stroke every bit of him.

Imperturbable as ever, he ignored them and placidly went on eating.

It was as Pied Pipers that we left Shatlik. A horde of some fifty children came too, one after another peeling off and waving goodbye, until there remained just half a dozen to wish us on our way at the final corner.

There followed a glorious ride through a perfect evening. Even the roads were kind to us, their edges gentle with sand instead of harsh with grit. It was the only reminder of our long march through the desert. All around was lush farmland, in which late workers plugged the last irrigation channels, and homecomers strode with shouldered scythes. This greenness was the gift of Merv's parent River Murghab, and we began to cross its first spurs, deep grey greasy ditches smelling of sulphur.

Kaan was enjoying himself. Well rested and well fed, he was as fresh as a daisy, joyfully cantering on whenever the road allowed. Even so, the sun was down by the time we turned on to the lane leading to Kolkhoz Chkalova.

The moment of truth was nearly here. My mood swung wildly between optimism and anxiety. Would there be a welcome for us? Would the lorry back to Ashkhabad materialise? Did the stable even exist, or was it merely another figment of Yusup's vivid imagination?

"*Konzavod?* Where's the stud?" I asked as we passed a group on a street corner. "Straight on!" they answered.

From then on, I didn't have to ask. Kaan scented the large concentration of horses and turned right at the crossroads with certainty, his pace quickening. For the last half-mile he trumpeted our arrival, shouting his head off until my ears ached.

As we turned up the long driveway leading to a mass of sheds and paddocks, indeterminate in the gathering darkness, figures emerged from the main barn and stood waiting. I dismounted wearily, and before I had even made my explanations or requests for help, Kaan was taken from me, led into a box, unsaddled and fed.

I needn't have worried about a welcome, I thought. This was Turkmenistan.

*

Utter contentment washed over me as I walked Kaan round to cool him off; a deep satisfaction born of the gradually dawning realisation that we were almost home and dry. So much for Aleksandr and Yusup, who had reckoned I would never even make it to Mari. So much for Akhrana's doubts and Sasha's warnings and Obbly-Guli's contempt. Even had we been unable to totter another step and realise my personal goal, we had achieved public success, and I could thumb my nose at the Jeremiahs. And total consummation was within grasp, for Merv itself was now a scant twenty miles away, and Kaan for one was still full of running.

It was a beautiful night, the stars brilliant, the crickets and the frogs in best voice. Everything was wonderful.

Kaan was pretty pleased with life, too, for after weeks on his own he was back with the crowd. He skipped irrepressibly on the tanbark of the training gallops. The stable boys had put on him a bridle of rawhide with a gaudy glass jewel on the browband, more fitting to the occasion than my own plain tack. A full circuit had almost calmed him down when he reached the mares' enclosure. He erupted, standing on hind legs and clawing the sky. In the dark it was somehow more daunting, and when he got his foot over the rein I was terrified he would break free and humiliate me in front of the lads. In the end, though, we managed to arrive together, with Kaan dancing round me like a lunatic.

These lads made an outstanding team. The eldest, and night watchman, was a typical horseman, small, wiry and efficient. With a shock I now saw that he only had one arm. The other two were younger, and after a few minutes a tall, stocky youth of about twenty joined them. The head lad, he took Yusup's letter, crumpled and sweat-stained now, to find Yazberdi Aga, while the others, with infectious enthusiasm, carried me off on a tour of the stables.

It was too dark to make out anything more than dim shapes. I looked forward to seeing the horses properly in the morning. Meanwhile, I could guess at the high standards here by simply handling them, feeling the soft, sleek coats, the well covered ribs.

The pot had almost boiled for tea when a new face appeared. It belonged to Djuma Yazberdiev, Yazberdi's son, now owner of the yard. He made light of my apology for turning up without warning, and whisked me off to home, family and supper.

Djuma was a hydro-engineer by training, and had subsequently moved into local government. Horses had always obsessed him; not surprising, for his father had worked all his life at the nearby Mari Konzavod, and was a fascinating old horseman. Djuma and his brother Sukhan had grown up steeped in horse culture, and raced at the Ashkhabad Hippodrome in their youth. Surely not so long ago, for neither could have been much over thirty. With sultry dark eyes, heavy lashed, they were ravishingly good-looking and alike as two peas.

Djuma had taken over the yard in 1991, the year of Independence, and had at once set about building it up. Gradually he had assimilated most of the best stock from the Mari Konzavod - helped, no doubt, by his father's eye for a good horse. I was thrilled to find that he knew Kaan and had seen him race. Having left Rep's yard with little time for details, I knew nothing of Kaan's racing career and pumped Djuma shamelessly. Perhaps I shouldn't have; I learned that Kaan was not a very good racehorse, for he was one-paced, or unable to accelerate in a finish. (The Russian idiom for this was exactly the same as the English.) Perhaps age had dulled his speed - six is middle-aged for a flat-race horse - for I later discovered that he had been assessed as Grade I at two and three years old.

I went on to ask, in general terms which I was sure never deceived Djuma for a moment, of the possibilities of exporting horses from Turkmenistan. The prospect of leaving Kaan behind was becoming unthinkable, and I had begun to toy with the idea of bringing not just one but several Akhal-Tekes to England and testing the market.

It was quite feasible to export, he thought. "Some Germans come now and then to buy horses here." He hadn't sold abroad himself, but maybe with only three stud stallions, twenty brood mares and a total stock of forty, he didn't yet have the surplus.

"I would like to exchange, rather than sell," he said. "Horses for saddlery, veterinary goods, food supplements." What a

309

market there was here, I thought, for some enterprising saddlery firm, robust enough to take on the bureaucracy and import these desperately needed goods into a completely empty market.

Djuma was a man of many faces, as his bookshelf testified. Among his text books were Russian translations of Guy de Maupassant and other foreign classics... and books on Turcoman folk music.

Just as enthusiasts were collecting and writing down the folk music of England, Scotland and Ireland around the turn of the twentieth century, the same thing was happening at the same time in Turkmenistan. Much had been saved, said Djuma, that otherwise would have been lost for ever under the influx of Russian culture. He reached to the top of the bookcase and brought down his *duttar*, a two-stringed instrument about the size of a viola.

I was enthralled. "Please, would you play something for me?"

He was very, very good. His fingers moved over the instrument with the easy agility of the virtuoso, seemingly far too effortless for the complexity of the music he performed. But by now I would have been most surprised had it not been so.

*

By daylight, Djuma's horses met all expectations. His best stallion was the eighteen-year-old Mele Per, nearly seventeen hands and of the classic Akhal-Teke colour: golden dun with a metallic sheen like a newly-minted penny - the colour of the Kara Kum, say the Turcomans, which fades if the horse is taken far from the desert.

Dozing in the box Mele Per looked his age: slightly sway-backed, his limbs thickening. Led out into the fresh air, he instantly shed a decade. Head up and ears erect, he looked every inch the horse who had partnered Geldy Kyarizov in the Ashkhabad to Moscow *probeg*, the marathon ride of 1988. Handling him was the tall youth, Djuma's head lad, who I only now realised was a deaf mute. Djuma communicated with him easily in sign language.

In a remote corner of the main stable block, two old carriages gathered dust. Carriage driving is unknown in Turkmenistan, and I wondered about their history. Playthings of some Communist mogul, perhaps, amusing himself by aping the aristocracy he despised; or a relic from pre-Soviet days? My interest delighted the lads. Within moments they had harnessed a horse, and we set off around the kolkhoz. It was a merry party, with the boys whooping and whistling until heads appeared at windows, while I sat back enjoying the feel of making holiday, the relief from tensions and responsibilities.

When we returned, an elderly man with a sharp, ascetic face was waiting. This was Yazberdi, come to drive me into Mari to visit Olga's family while Kaan had a few days' rest before the final stage.

After all those miles on horseback, it felt strange to be going into Mari by car. Babushka's house, hard by the railway, was easy to find. It was a lovely little house with a big garden, beautifully tended, where immaculate vegetables shared the plot with flowers. You could see at a glance why Babushka was an indispensable extra when it came to planting at Olga's dacha.

"Where have you been? We've been so worried about you!" scolded Babushka and Dedushka. Olga's father was another Vladimir Ivanovitch; it was easier just to call him "Grandpa".

Apologetically, I pleaded truthfully that my Russian wasn't up to phone conversations; and, anyway, I could hardly get Kaan into a Post Office - the only place to find a public phone. Cutting me short, Babushka carried me off to the bathroom, and dressed me in borrowed clothing while I washed out my own disgustingly filthy things, last washed only the day before but without soap.

Then came food, and, this being Olga's family, no shortage. There was hot soup followed by cold soup, pots of tea sweetened with honey - Katya had told me that Olga's elder brother, Zhenia, kept bees - and bread with home-made jam.

And, thank God, not a pelmen in sight.

*

In the summer of 1881, after a forced march across the final section of desert, Edmond O'Donovan finished his journey a couple of miles beyond Babushka's house. Over the centuries Merv had, as it were, moved westwards to meet him.

In the desert, rivers change course. An old channel may silt up and new ones develop; floods following heavy rain or exceptional snowfall in the mountain sources may carve out a new path; in an earthquake zone, as here, a main stream may be suddenly blocked. As the rivers migrate, so must the cities which depend on them. Since the Persians founded Margiush there have been many cities bearing the names Merv, Meru, Merouw or, as now, Mari - the last being roughly ten miles west of its glorious ancestor, the one-time Queen of Cities.

The Merv of O'Donovan's day was by then only a camp of a couple of hundred yurts enclosed by a mud wall, just across the River Murghab from where Mari stands today. Its inhabitants were a mongrel lot, part Bukhariot, despised by pure Turcomans. Even today, the Tekes and Yomuds will tell you dismissively that the easterners are "half-Uzbek". A century ago they were more forthright. "If you meet a viper and a Mervi," they warned, "kill the Mervi first."

With the townspeople quivering in anticipation of the Russian war machine, O'Donovan walked into a hornet's nest. Was he an honourable guest, or a Russian spy? Of course he claimed to be British, but of course he would. The elders sent urgently to the authorities in Meshed to check his credentials. Meanwhile, he was kept under guard in a yurt, wondering whether they planned to cut his throat at once or save the fun for later, while a stream of visitors crowded into his quarters to gawp at him.

At last the courier came back from Meshed with the all-clear. O'Donovan was cautiously released, permitted to attend the *Majlis*, or Parliament of Elders, and questioned voraciously. Was it true, they asked him incredulously, that the Padishah of England was a woman?

He might, the Mervis were now beginning to calculate, be of use to them. First, they showed him some ancient cannon. When he had modernised them, he was promised encouragingly, he would take command in the forthcoming action against the Russians.

Before long, he was to get a better offer.

There was only one way, the Mervis knew, that they could save themselves from the Russians: surrender voluntarily to the British first. But would the British want them?

The British army was currently engaged in one of its periodic adventures in Afghanistan, preparing to meet the threat of a Russian advance on India - a threat which, having exercised the minds of soldiers and politicians for most of the century, had never been closer to achieving reality than now. The British had fortified Herat, just two hundred miles upriver from Merv and gateway to the mountain passes through to India. The Mervis, their imagination fired by wishful thinking, were beginning to elevate the young Irishman from press reporter to Representative of the British Empire. Perhaps he could call up the cavalry.

Against a background of civil unrest, O'Donovan found himself made a Khan of Merv, joining two others: the hereditary khans of the Tokhtamish and Otamish clans that comprised Mervi society. Before long he was promoted above his colleagues to First Triumvir, and invited to lay the law down from a public soap-box.

"I followed the advice of old diplomats," he said, "and talked for a long time without saying anything." But he included two vital pieces of advice: give up raiding, or the Russians would be down on Merv sooner than ever - and tell Queen Victoria of their aspirations to join her Empire.

For it was imperative that the British learned of the situation, which had all the makings of a catastrophic diplomatic incident. The hastily cobbled travesty of a British flag had been hoisted at O'Donovan's yurt, and only some rapid thinking and good Irish eloquence stopped it being raised over the town itself. Meanwhile an iron was prepared to brand the local cavalry horses with "VR", surmounted by a crown; although, as the iron reversed the image and was used upside down anyway, the results were less provocative than they might have been.

313

But provocative they were. Russia regarded Merv as within her own sphere of influence. Moreover, her inexorable advance was bringing relations with Britain dangerously close to flash point. Any suggestion that Britain was laying claim to Merv, however farcical, might be seized on by Russia as an excuse to go to war.

So O'Donovan trembled, and laid plans for his escape. The Mervis would not release him willingly, for they saw him as their trump card. He sent privately and urgently to Teheran. After agonising weeks his *carnet de passage* arrived in the form of an official letter from the Ambassador, disingenuously summoning him to return and report to Queen Victoria without delay.

The Mervis couldn't disobey their newly elected sovereign. With regret they permitted O'Donovan to leave. As they had feared, they never saw him again. Within two years the city was in Russian control. The Great Game was entering its final chukka.

The implications for British India were terrifying. Now only Afghanistan stood in the way of the Russian advance. At Westminster, the Duke of Argyll coined the term "Mervousness". The stock market slumped.

And the Russians continued to encroach. With the diplomatic double-speak that had characterised all their advances in Central Asia, they blandly assured the world that they had no designs on India; meanwhile their army crept southwards up the Murghab, driving the Afghans back from one town after another. They "advanced stealthily, playing their old game of Grandmother's Footsteps," commented Peter Hopkirk in his classic *The Great Game*, "carefully observing Britain's reactions to each move forward, while maintaining long-running correspondence with London over the Afghan Boundary Commission as though nothing untoward were going on."*

War had never been closer. Diplomacy raced belligerence with desperate urgency. Lights burned in Whitehall and the Kremlin. The Afghan leader Abdur Rahman responded with

* © Peter Hopkirk 1990. Reproduced by kind permission of Hodder and Stoughton

statesmanlike and un-Afghan restraint to the incursion into his territory, while his British allies braced themselves in Herat for the ultimate collision.

The collision never came, for diplomacy won the day by a short head. Some horse-trading with villages and passes sealed a bargain, and one of the most contentious borders in history was finally drawn in ink rather than blood.

As for O'Donovan, his experiences hadn't dimmed his passion for adventure. He went on to cover the wars with the Mahdi in Sudan, where he tragically lost his life.

Before leaving, he rode out to the east to view the ancient remains, the original Merv.

"I climbed to the summit of a ruined building, half dwelling house, half fortalice, whence a commanding view was obtained over the crumbling expanse of cities. A feeling of oppressive loneliness comes over the spirit as the eye ranges across that voiceless wilderness, so deserted, so desolate, yet teeming with eloquent testimonies of what it had been of old. The heart of Zenghis Khan himself would feel exultant at the absolute, hopeless lifelessness of those sites, where great cities had stood and myriad populations swarmed... It was strange to think that a few yards of dam upon the Murgab, some trenches dug by illiterate toilers, had once made these present deserts vernal, and had entitled this Golgotha of cities to the proud name of Queen of the World. Who knows but that again, when the hand of the raider has been stayed, and the merchant is once more permitted to follow his avocations in peace and security along these formerly frequented tracks, history will repeat itself, and Merv once more take its place among the nations of the earth?"

XVI

Tall, loose-limbed and with thinning sandy-brown hair, Zhenia at first glance resembled his brother-in-law. Only at first glance; for his relaxed, easy temperament couldn't have been more at odds with Sasha's eternally restless spirit.

It was the perfect temperament for handling bees, and as if to emphasise the fact he did so without any protective clothing. He barely used his smoker - which he fired with cow-dung - gentling the bees instead with a few squirts of sugar solution.

"They're very quiet bees," I commented, following him along the side of the trailer. This meant crossing the flight path of eighteen hives at a distance of a couple of feet. Zhenia did so without a thought, while I fought the temptation to drop to my elbows and crawl.

"It's the heat, the sun," he replied easily. "While the nectar is flowing, the bees are happy. If it's not, they're more difficult. They're more difficult in Russia - and of course in England - because the weather isn't so good."

Turkmen beekeepers are slick operators. Most, like Zhenia, keep up to forty colonies on a single trailer, stacked in outward facing double rows. Following the nectar is thus a simple operation of hitching up and driving to wherever the flow is best, according to the seasons. At the moment they were on the lucerne, said Zhenia, jerking his head towards a carpet of purple flowers beyond the dyke. Shortly the camelthorn would flower, producing good nectar. (Thank God, I said to myself privately, the bloody stuff is good for something.) The main crop came from cotton, which seems to be as oilseed rape to British beekeeping: the biggest volume of honey, but pale and hard.

A sleeping area, equipped with gas stove and medical kit, completed the outfit. This meant that someone could be here full time to guard the bees. For this was a profitable business, and vulnerable. Zhenia and his friends from the surrounding trailers would take it in turns to stay here and keep watch. Tonight was Kolya's turn.

Kolya was sitting with Zhenia's wife, Galya, drinking tea with honey. This was Galya's last visit to the bees. In just eight days' time she and Zhenia were to join the exodus of Russians from Turkmenistan. She dreaded the upheaval.

"But what can we do?" she said. "There's no work here any more. There's no future." They were irrevocably committed; the tickets were bought, the furniture sent ahead to Tula, a major city "just three hours by *elektricheskaya* (electric train) from Moscow": rather nearer the hub of Russian life than at present.

"We haven't got any work there," she added, "neither Zhenia nor I." It would be a brave move, the exchange of one set of uncertainties for another.

A friend of Kolya's came over to join us, another man with only one arm. (The gatekeeper to this area was a one-legged man. How many people around Mari, I wondered, have a full set of limbs?) This man's son was also on the point of emigrating to Russia. "It's a constant trickle," said Zhenia. "Every day seven or eight people leave."

The signs were everywhere. On the way here we had passed an airfield where a few fighter planes, in varying stages of rust and decrepitude, surrounded a derelict building. "That used to be the pilots' barracks," said Galya. "It was a wonderful place, beautifully fitted out. I used to go and visit friends there. Now it's completely empty. After the Russians left people went in, stripped it, and broke all the windows. There's nothing for us Russians here now."

"The kolkhozes are the best place to be at the moment," was Kolya's opinion. "Three or four years ago they were having a very hard time. But they're doing well now." It was something I'd seen over and over again for myself, in the flush of new building and - in the cotton belt at least - the outlay of capital on new machinery.

As we sat lazily talking, the heady scent of lucerne blossom filled the air in drifts, like a swirling mist. It was easy to see why the bees were so contented.

317

Kolya's head suddenly appeared over the edge of the dyke with a triumphant shout. The nets he had laid had caught three fish. He donned oilskins and waded out to retrieve them, shouting in dismay as the deep water flooded above the overalls and into his clothing; then scrambled back up the bank to kill and gut them at once. Soon the sizzle of fish frying joined the constant hum of the bees.

A land flowing with fish and honey. It was possible to live well in Turkmenistan, if you only knew how.

*

"They didn't know when they were well off!" Dedushka's face grew red as he warmed to his theme, namely the current state of affairs in Turkmenistan.

"The Soviet Union was good for everybody, Turcoman and Russian. They were benevolent rulers." I watched him with a double degree of fascination; partly for the sentiments he expressed, and the conviction with which he expressed them; partly because the features displayed in the seventy-year-old face were so precisely Olga's, except that they were set - for the moment at least - in a mask of exasperation, rather than Olga's habitual tolerance and amusement.

"What about Afghanistan?" I ventured when he paused for breath.

"They ruled benevolently there, too. The Soviet Union was good for Afghanistan."

They unleashed an avalanche of horror that has ripped the country apart ever since, I wanted to say, but my Russian wasn't up to it. Besides, Dedushka had recently suffered heart trouble, and his current agitation was frightening. So I agreed politely with all he said, until the conversation could be steered into quieter waters.

His bitterness, after all, was understandable. With their pensions eroded to nothing by inflation and their elder son about to leave, Olga's parents had seen their well-earned retirement racked with fear and uncertainty by events that had turned their country inside out.

318

"We would really like to go with Zhenia," Babushka confided. "But we're too old. Besides, Kolya is our younger son. He'll look after us." They planned to sell their house and go to Ashkhabad, taking over Olga's flat as soon as the dacha was ready for her family to move into. A terrible shame; for the Mari house, with its quiet street and big garden full of flowers, was one of the nicest I'd seen.

The flowers weren't for decoration. Every day Babushka cut a huge bucketful, and walked the half-mile along the railway to the central market. In the morning she took me with her, and while she set up her flower stall I wandered among the well-stocked tables, then went to explore the city.

Central Mari was cheap and cheerful and, best of all, wet. Memories of the Kara Kum were fresh, and I delighted in the park fountains, sitting almost under the jets and viewing the world through rainbow spirals until mind and body felt pleasantly damp.

On the way to the bus station, I looked in at the department store to buy perfume for Babushka. Trawling the upper floor on an impulse, I found what I was looking for: a couple of metres of thick, heavy curtain material in gaudy stripes. To the mystification of the girl at the counter, I asked her to cut it into four pieces. It meant that much more to carry through a long day on foot, but it was to be worth the effort later.

The day's expedition to Turkmen Kala, the "Turcoman Fortress", was in effect a journey from one Merv to another. Settlement in the Murghab's oasis was a fidgety, nomadic affair, dictated by the frequently changing course of the whimsical river. As irrigation techniques progressed, man parted the river ever further upstream, spreading its waters ever wider. In the nineteenth century alone the main site had shifted ten miles westwards, from the town today called Bairam Ali to Merv's penultimate existence: the Turcoman camp visited by Abbott and O'Donovan, just east of modern Mari.

Doing research at the "Geog" I had copied on to my map what appeared to be the largest dam, the largest reservoir on the course of the river. This must be the heart and soul of the oasis, the foundation stone of Merv's recent history. I hoped to see it.

I left the bus at a shady crossroad in the middle of Turkmen Kala, and walked east out of the village through streets of low houses screened by vine-covered trellis. This should bring me to the river just below the reservoir and the start of the dam - if they were indeed reservoir and dam.

But the irrigation dykes forced me out of my way, and it was well into a baking afternoon when I finally made it to the river. Strange, to sit on bone-dry earth with a brown stubble of grass that pricked like straw, amid the desiccated flatlands adjoining the Turkmenistan desert, and watch the spring meltwaters from Afghan peaks racing past.

There was no sign of any reservoir. I began to wonder if it existed. Twice I'd met people in these deserted fields, and asked the quickest way to the lake. Both had answered, with the vagueness of those who never venture far from prescribed paths, "What lake? I don't know of any lake." Now I asked a third man. "There is no lake," he said with certainty, as I pointed north. It was hopeless. The map at the "Geog" must have been wrong, or out of date. I threw in the towel, and gratefully accepted his invitation to tea.

The Danatarovs were a large family, even by Turcoman standards. Presiding over the teapots sat an elegant elderly lady with long silver plaits escaping from her headscarf. She was mother to eight and grandmother to twenty-one. "We're all her daughters-in-law," said the eldest of the numerous young women squatting around the cloth. I sprawled under the awning chatting, to the background noises of babies crying and water crashing over the concrete dam behind the garden, until the sunlight filtering through the vine leaves faded to a more bearable level.

They set me on the shortest route back to Turkmen Kala. Coming to a road, I levelled my thumb hopefully at the infrequent traffic. And now the day was retrieved, for along came a knight in shining armour - or, rather, a smart jeep.

Settarmurad tutted at the story of my frustrations, and at once set about mending them. Generously abandoning his plans for the evening, he drove me south from Turkmen Kala to

Kolkhoz *Krasni Oktyabr* (Red October). "There is a museum there, which I think will interest you."

He went to rouse the owner, and soon an elderly man, rubbing the sleep of his afternoon nap from his eyes, was unlocking the door and inviting us in.

Garyandaya was a retired schoolmaster who had spent thirty-five years acquiring his collection. It had begun as a handful of artefacts to show to his history students, and had gradually taken over his life. "It's not enough just to teach about history; you must show people," he said. "That's how I came to start."

He was a fierce old man, with piercing brown eyes and a hooked nose. When I stopped to make notes, he berated me: "Come and listen!" But every now and then his face would soften as he recalled the origin of a particular item, or the enthusiasm of a distinguished visitor. "President Niazov came to visit last year. He brought twenty-five ministers with him and stayed three-and-a-half hours." Then he would shake himself, becoming didactic and peremptory again. He must have been a frightening schoolteacher.

There was a Turcoman yurt, fully equipped right down to the painted chests and treadle sewing machine. Its wooden door, warped and bleached with age, still bore the faint traces of mediaeval carving. An assortment of gourds, used for storage, recalled the shape of the duttar. The early farming implements might have come from the Heritage Museum two hundred yards from my own home.

Recent culture was there, too. Among photographs of local and not-so-local heroes, a full length portrait of Stalin scowled down over a collection of Russian samovars. A collection of documents recalled Turkmenistan's earliest days in the Russian Empire. It was a fascinating, and unique, exhibition; an entire social history of Turkmenistan contained under a single roof.

Afterwards, Settarmurad drove me back to Turkmen Kala and dropped me by its citadel. It was only a small mound. But from its summit I could trace the mud-brick ramparts of what had once been an extensive walled village, nearly the size of Geok Tepe.

It was quite high enough to give a very good view of the surrounding countryside. Too good; for out to the west I could see the lake, the lake that everyone had told me didn't exist, winking at me mischievously in the evening sunlight.

*

I shrank from the thought of riding a horse through Turkmenistan's second biggest city. But all routes were arterial. So through Mari we went; straight through the middle, that being the line of least resistance.

Almost immediately after leaving Chkalova, Kaan and I ran into a road block. Four convicts had escaped from jail, and the police were stopping every car, checking back seats, searching boots. A rather goofy young policeman, kicking his heels while his mates did all the work, waved me over.

"Can I ride your horse?" he asked.

"Sorry, no. He has a long way to go."

He scowled. "Passport, please!"

It was in my moneybelt, at my back and under my clothing. I didn't fancy disrobing in front of an audience, and said so.

"Passport!"

My patience broke. With a snort that would have done justice to Kaan, I turned my back on him and rode away.

"I don't think your pal has enough to do!" I snapped at his colleagues, who were checking three cars at once. It was foolishly provocative; but they were obviously fed up with him too, for they grinned back and let me through. I was lucky; for with dodgy documentation I should have been more polite.

But the fact was, that near the end of this arduous journey I was almost too exhausted to be able to cope with people - any people, aggressive or not. As we entered the packed streets of Mari, Kaan drew much interest, until I felt besieged and began to snap at people irritably. Get a grip on yourself, I told myself angrily. You're a stranger in their country, a stranger doing something eccentric. It's perfectly reasonable to ask what and why.

322

It was high time to chill out. I fled from the streets into one of the city parks. Here there were no hustlers, no traffic; just pleasantly shaded paths and the refreshing splash of fountains. And an ice-cream stall. As I tied Kaan to a gaudy lamp-post and sat licking an ice-cream, the world slowly turned the right way up again. Even the heads turning towards Kaan, mostly on the shoulders of quiet pensioners used to seeing nothing more from their park benches than the odd poodle, ceased to threaten. Kaan, for his part, stood demurely, far too much a veteran of the road by now to be surprised at any surroundings. In fact he was too relaxed; for he casually stopped, lifted his tail and committed an atrocity on the scrubbed paving stones. There was nothing I could do but flee once more, putting as much distance as possible between ourselves and the steaming pile.

In the end, Mari wasn't too bad. It wasn't a very big town, there was comparatively little traffic, and the streets were wide. And there was grass: plenty of it, in parks and on street corners, well grown without competition from sheep and goats. We stopped for two hours where a leaking drain had watered a patch of waste into rich growth. It was satisfying to watch how Kaan now grazed steadily and leisurely, instead of ripping up the grass as if were the first he'd ever seen, and might be the last.

If he hadn't put on as much condition as I'd hoped, he was still looking better than at the start. Hard muscle bulged on his neck and quarters, and the chestnut coat overlying it shone gold in the sun, gleaming with good health. Circumstances may have prevented us from setting any records for speed, but in all other respects I'd tested the toughness of the Akhal-Teke to its limit, and not found it wanting. On a hoarding behind Kaan was a slogan: "He who is alone is without strength; but he will obtain strength in friendship." So I had. I could have wished for no stronger companion on this journey.

And I needed all Kaan's strength, for little remained of my own. My body felt like a husk sucked dry, and my will, which had driven us both thus far, was tottering dangerously. There had been many difficult moments on this journey, but it was on the busy streets of this hostile city environment that I came closest to meltdown. By rights it should have been Kaan who faltered, out of his natural element. But it was he who strode resolutely ahead, and I who shambled behind, engaging my brain briefly when a taxing decision must be made - like "left or right?"; then dropping it gratefully back into neutral.

We escaped Mari at last, weaving a path between the road and the railway and trying to keep as far as possible from both. The canal lay ahead, with a choice between the main road bridge and the old crossing to the side. The latter wasn't inviting, with crumbling concrete slabs, no parapet, and a general air of being about to fall into the canal. But old Soviet engineering triumphed over modern Turcoman driving, and I chose that one. On the far side was a pleasant little park, and we sat out the remainder of the mid-day heat there before tackling the last ten miles to Bairam Ali, the town which was Merv's eighteenth century incarnation and which lies close to the ancient site.

There were firm tracks at last across the farmland, and for a bit we ate up the miles at a sharp canter. What an irony: now that Kaan was fit and hard enough to make use of his speed, we were nearly at journey's end. Every few miles city mounds rose, testament to days when the dams were in order, water was plentiful and the oasis as wide and fertile as today.

At sunset we came home with the cows to Kolkhoz Lenin, just outside Bairam Ali. Poor Urazgeldi, the Bashlik, was perplexed when I turned up on his doorstep. Changing rapidly back from evening tracksuit into daytime formals, he led the way to the ferma at the far end of the settlement.

Urazgeldi was concerned about his farm's biosecurity, asking me twice if Kaan had any infectious illness. "He's come all the way from Ashkhabad," I reassured him. "He couldn't have done that if there were anything wrong with him!"

Nevertheless, Kaan was required to pass through a disinfectant pit at the farm entrance. It was slimy, evil-smelling and very black in the dusk, and it was I who paddled in it while Kaan stood on tiptoe at the edge, at the full stretch of the reins, quite reasonably refusing to get his feet wet. At last he was excused, and allowed to climb along the bank at the side.

I left him installed in one of the usual iron-railed enclosures, in front of the biggest pile of lucerne yet. He would need all the food he could get, for tomorrow was the Big Day, the day we would ride to Ancient Merv.

*

After days of peeling back the successive generations of Merv like the layers of an onion, Kaan and I were about to penetrate to the core.

Sprawling across the very heart of the Merv Oasis, the ruins of Ancient Merv stretch some five or six miles from the small, circular fort erected by Zoroastrian Persians in the 6th century BC to the great citadel of Bairam Ali Khan to the south. The Persians called their city Margiush, and it was as such that it passed into the possession of Alexander on the fall of Darius' empire. His heirs, the Seleucid dynasty, built a new city, naming it Antiocheia Margiana: Antioch on the margin of the world.

It was soon to pass from margin to epicentre. With the coming of the Silk Road Merv, now Parthian, became a crucial stepping-stone across the Central Asian deserts. For it lay at a crossroads: east to Bukhara, Samarkand and on to China, west to Persia and Rome, south to Herat and the riches of India, north to Khoresmia and, later, the growing markets of Rus.

Parthia did well out of the Silk Road. Alone among the great empires that controlled it, she denied passage to foreign merchants, ensuring that her own carriers did a good trade at non-negotiable rates. By the time Merv passed to the Persian Sassanians early in the 4th century AD, it was a thriving commercial city with a cosmopolitan and dynamic mix of peoples. Here one of the earliest Nestorian bishops tried to convert his flock from Buddhism or the still-prevalent Zoroastrianism to Christianity; here the first local experiments were made in growing cotton, anticipating by one and a half millennia the future economy of Central Asia. Here, later, metallurgists employed a sophisticated method of steelmaking, otherwise unknown except from early Chinese and Islamic manuscripts.

Such days of tolerance and diversity were numbered. By 700 AD the warriors of the Prophet had advanced the Arab

325

Empire to Persia, and within a few years they had crossed the Oxus. They settled the Merv Oasis with fifty thousand Arabs and universally imposed Islam. Merv became their eastern capital, second only to Baghdad in the Islamic world.

But the foundations of this world were weakened by a fatal flaw: the dispute over succession to the Prophet . The resulting breakaway of the Shi'ite sect was cataclysmic, a fundamental schism that has divided the Moslem world to this day. The unity of Central Asia was one of its victims, and the region fragmented into separate oasis-states; until Alp Arslan ushered in its Golden Age.

Under "the Valiant Lion" the Seljuk Turks, who had come south from the Aral Sea area to take possession of Merv only a generation earlier, carved out an empire reaching from the eastern Mediterranean to the Oxus. Khoresmia, Afghanistan, Persia, Anatolia, Syria and Palestine fell like dominoes to Alp Arslan. Even the mighty Byzantium gave way before him; for at the fateful Battle of Manzikert in 1071 he routed their army and captured the Byzantine Emperor.

Alp Arslan may fairly be claimed as the first oriental to reshape western history, for profound consequences arose from this victory. The Byzantines, unable to recover from such a blow to their self-esteem, appealed to the Pope for help in protecting Christendom against the encroaching heathen. By Christendom they meant only themselves. But the force they unleashed developed its own momentum and aspired to a more glorious end: the liberation of the holy places of Palestine from the Turks. Thus began the First Crusade. It was the beginning of a movement which would give Byzantium more headaches than help and, ultimately, destroy it.

Alp Arslan survived his victory at Manzikert by only a year. Campaigning across the Oxus, he was fatally stabbed by a captive he was about to pardon. "Oh ye who have seen the glory of Alp Arslan exalted to the heavens," ran the inscription on his tomb, "repair to Merou and you will see it buried in dust!" The tomb remained for a century and a half, to be destroyed in the greatest catastrophe of Merv's history.

In 1221 Genghis Khan sent his eldest son Tolui to attack Merv. Tolui destroyed the Murghab dam, paralysing the city, and spent six days drawing up siege weapons. On the seventh day the Mervis' nerve broke, and they surrendered on promise of their lives. Disarmed, they were herded out on to the plain and systematically slaughtered. Each Mongol soldier, the historians record, was given a quota of between three and four hundred heads to despatch.

There was no way back from such utter destruction. When Merv finally staggered to its knees again, rebuilt under Timur's son Shah Rukh, it was no more than a poor imitation of its former self. And it was two miles away to the south, for perhaps ghosts still walked on those bloodstained plains.

*

There it was: journey's end. A collection on the skyline of baked brick towers, mausolea and citadels, jutting from behind earthen walls like broken teeth from pitted gums.

The weather was on our side today, cloudy and cool. Kaan had looked at me with distaste when I'd arrived with the saddle, and had indulged in an enormous stretch before setting out.

His feet were a bit sore after yesterday's city streets, and he plodded rather slowly down the first long section of tarmac. But the kiosks on the edge of town were open early, and he cheered up when I bought a kilo of biscuits. By the time he had eaten half the bag, his stride had lengthened a good deal.

I also bought a litre of some vile fizzy drink; choking stuff, but today for once I was travelling without saddlebags, and must carry my liquid internally. Behind the stall was a running tap, and - the bucket being with the bags back at Kolkhoz Lenin, where we would return for the night - I cast around for some container to fill for Kaan. There was no need. While I searched, he stepped casually up to the running tap and sucked directly from it. Would he ever cease to surprise me, I wondered?

Cutting across the edge of Bairam Ali, I took to the fields. At once the great mausoleum of Sultan Sanjar rose above the surrounding mud-brick ramparts, a lighthouse drawing me in as it had generations of travellers.

Had they, I wondered, chafed as I now did at the restricting irrigation ditches? Only a mile remained, but we covered at least three times that much as we zigzagged back and forth to find a way through.

I watched my step, for they say that around Merv are the remains of *qanats*. These subterranean irrigation channels used to be common in Central Asia and Afghanistan. Gustav Krist, here in the nineteen-twenties, found them so numerous that the vertical access shafts were a serious hazard.

But it was the account of John of Plano Carpini that made my imagination tingle. Carpini was an Italian monk who travelled across Asia as envoy to the Mongol Khan in 1245. In the report he wrote for the Pope on his return, he combined sophisticated and detailed descriptions of the Mongol armies and administration with travellers' tales of wild fantasy. Even a mediaeval monk shouldn't have believed the stories he repeated of the *cyclopedes*, who had only one arm and one leg, hopped faster than a horse, and under duress proceeded on both in a sort of cartwheel; but some of Carpini's stories have a whiff of possible truth. Those of the Land of Burithabet, for example, where "whenever anyone's father pays the debt of human nature they collect all the family together and eat him." Far-fetched? But this cannibalism was practised by the Massagetae, those ancient Khoresmian nomads who had given Alexander so much trouble. Perhaps the memory - maybe even the custom itself - might have lingered somewhere?

So when Carpini spoke of people who lived underground, using secret passages to creep up on the Mongols and attack them, might he have been thinking of qanats? Could there have been a guerrilla movement, an *intifaada* of desperate men who struck at the Mongols before vanishing, like Harry Lime, into a maze of underground channels whose existence was unknown to the occupying force? I longed to see a qanat, but in vain.

I stopped where a ditch had leaked a puddle into a grass-filled hollow, for it might be the best grazing all day. Kaan, though, pulled away to grub in the sand. It was a moment before

I saw what attracted him. He was scoffing mulberries, fallen from the surrounding trees. Mulberry trees, host of the silkworm. It couldn't have been more appropriate; ambrosia of the Silk Road to feed my Celestial Horse.

And just ahead, waiting for us, a city older than the Silk Road itself: Merv, now close enough to fill the horizon.

*

I rode through a gap in the outer walls, as through the door in the Narnian wardrobe, and into the past; and the first person I saw was Genghis Khan.

Actually, his plate armour was cardboard and his sword wooden. I stuffed my overblown imagination back into its box and slammed the lid. By the time I'd gathered a few wits and looked about me, I was already expecting what I saw: a film crew.

In fact it wasn't a film, but a Turkmen historical soap, and rather more sophisticated than its costumes. Its hero, they told me, was Yusup Ahmed, a local warrior of the eighth century. The first Moslem here when the prevailing religion was Persian Zoroastrianism, he sided with the Arab invaders, trying with their help to unite the tribes under a single government.

"Exactly," added the actor, "as our president wishes to do now." Obviously a film with a message. There were more ways than one to get on in the embryonic Turkmen film industry.

"Come to lunch at our hostel. It's just over there. There's a garden with grass for your horse." If so, it must be the only grass in all this barren wilderness. I wouldn't get a better offer all day. The full tour could wait for the afternoon.

I had time, though, for a quick look at the nearby Kis Kala. The fluted walls of the small fort, built for his daughter by a sixth century Sassanian governor, made it look like an oversized pink wedding cake that had kept exceptionally well. Now besieged by a herd of goats, it had withstood the missiles of the real Yusup Ahmed and his Arab allies. Six hundred years later it was still in use, this time for Sultan Sanjar's famously

329

debauched parties. The meaning of its name, the Girl's Castle, would have served equally well at either end of its history.

At the hostel, swaggering warriors figures laid aside their cardboard helmets and swords to join the table.

Gulping down mouthfuls of stew, they outlined the plot. The budget didn't run to horses, and I soon realised why I'd been asked to lunch. "Can you come back tomorrow with your horse?" But the lorry back to Ashkhabad was booked, and my flight home was now only a few days away.

So I repaid the meal by giving a ride to Andrui and Marana, the director's children who had been giving Kaan his own lunch. They took me to watch the cameras at work in the mausoleum of Mohammed ibn Said, descendant of the Prophet Mohammed. Ibn Said, founder of a sect associated with the strictest Islamic codes, must have been turning in his grave today. For on his roof a scantily-clad starlet strutted her stuff for the television cameras, while technicians, sound engineers and cameramen stamped and swore in the tiny space about his tomb.

Andrui took Kaan's reins so that I could creep up, well away from the microphones, for a closer look. "Watch your feet!" I warned, as he stood inches from Kaan's own. For he went barefoot, careless of the sharp stones and last year's dry camelthorn spikes scattered over the sand.

Camelthorn and ditches - there was no escaping even here the twin curses of our journey. When at last I struck out for the castellated earth walls that marked Merv's third age, the city of the Seljuk Turks, I was continually frustrated by the need for detours. A wide canal ran parallel to the walls, and I ground my teeth as I followed it for half a mile on the wrong side. A lad on a donkey, spotting my problem, led me to a ford, driving his goats across and back to make sure I understood. But with only two steps the water came up to Kaan's hocks, and he stopped in confusion. After having come so far he had a right to his opinions, and I didn't press him.

At last the canal burrowed under a road through a massive concrete pipe. Within a few steps we were inside the ramparts.

If I'd hoped to catch some lingering scent here of the people who had once lived, worked, dreamed and died within these walls, I was disappointed. Vainly I searched my imagination to catch the curse of the camel driver, the ring of the blacksmith's hammer, the hubbub in the bazaars. But the sterile plain held no echoes; no ghosts whispered to me among the sage brush.

With Kaan stepping delicately through the thorn, we made our way through a herd of browsing camels to one of Central Asia's biggest monuments. Sultan Sanjar's mausoleum, over a hundred feet high and once covered with blue tiles, could be seen from the distance of a day's march.

Poor old Sanjar wasn't looking too well. The square block at his base was sound enough, the five arches down each side having benefit of restoration. But his dome appeared to be collapsing inwards, despite the scaffolding that was meant to support it, and his surroundings were disfigured by mounds of bricks, heaped together and merging with other piles of cement, sand, or building rubble.

Nothing, though, could diminish the statement made by its size: that the man whose bones lay beneath your feet was a very important man indeed. Grandson of the all-conquering Alp Arslan, Sanjar was heir to one of the greatest empires even Central Asia has ever known; and he set his own mark on it by re-founding its capital, building his new Merv alongside the Seleucid walls that had served for fourteen hundred years.

On the far side, the walls rose to impressive height. Like O'Donovan, I climbed to a summit for a commanding view. Immediately before me lay the Seleucid Merv, its vast enclosure empty of all but tamarisk. On the horizon, tiny by comparison, was the outline of a smooth oval: Margiush, early settlement of the Zoroastrians, seed of future empires. Camels grazed about its base.

It must have been about a mile away. No great distance, after we had come so far. But I could see more canals, more drifts of camelthorn. I glanced down at Kaan who stood, reins looped carefully about his neck, chewing in disgust on a piece of desiccated sage brush. No, enough. We had nothing left to prove. I had seen Margiush; and was well satisfied.

As we finally left Sanjar's ruined city - by the tourist road this time, for I'd had quite enough of canal-dodging - the sun was coming out from the behind the clouds. The late afternoon light softened the landscape, deepening the pink of the tamarisk along the road, giving a glow to the mud walls and reducing bitter desolation to a gentle melancholy.

Following a trail of ruined citadels, mausolea and a strange beehive-shaped tomb, I came back into farmland on the edge of Bairam Ali. Here, beside the last two of Merv's five fortresses, labourers were cutting evening feed. Trailers of bees stood in the shade of more earth ramparts, there to milk the hateful camelthorn of its one benefit. Once more grass grew beside the road, and Kaan took his first meal since lunchtime.

The Turcoman fort known as Bairam Ali Khan Kala, Prince Bairam Ali's fortress, lay hard by Shah Rukh's earlier walls. Bairam Ali gave Merv its last flowering two centuries ago, repairing the Murghab dam and rebuilding the fort. It was a tragically brief last gasp. Bairam Ali was fatally ambushed by an emir of Bukhara who broke the dam, flooded the city and carried its people off to slavery. When Captain Abbott visited fifty years later, Merv had followed the Murghab on its new course ten miles further east, and was now little more than a village.

I followed Bairam Ali's walls, complete with gradually deepening moat, round two sides of a square, until they vanished under the modern town which bears his name. The transition to the twentieth century was abrupt, and jarring. Jarring also for Kaan, for we were back on tarmac. From now on I must walk.

Stopping at a drinks stall, I sank two large glasses rapidly, and put down a fistful of manats. But the girl refused to take them.

"You're our guest!" she protested. I argued, but she was adamant.

"No," she declared firmly; then added something that I seemed to have heard before.

"This is Turkmenistan," she said.

XVII

Kaan travelled from Kolkhoz Chkalova back to Ashkhabad in the truck Djuma had arranged, his legs thickly padded in the striped curtain material from the Mari department store.

There aren't any horse boxes in Turkmenistan. The truck was open, with steel bars over Kaan's head to prevent him from jumping out. To load him, it was reversed into a pit alongside a carefully levelled earth ramp, so that Kaan could walk from the ramp across the tailgate, which was spread with rugs of felt, into the body of the lorry. He went straight in with his usual aplomb, having first said his own goodbyes to Chkalova with another athletic aerial display as he passed the mares' corral.

There was scarcely time to take my own leave of Djuma's lads. I left my brush and meagre veterinary supplies with the head lad, noticing that this morning there was yet another youth with only one arm. Then we were off, bouncing over the rough kolkhoz tracks with lurches that made me wince on Kaan's behalf. But I needn't have worried for, leaning out of the window and screwing my head round to watch him anxiously, I saw him ride the bumps like a cyclo-cross star, the superb Akhal-Teke balance finding yet another expression.

I had mixed feelings about going back at this speed along the way we'd come. It was hard to decide whether I was glad to be seeing the familiar scenery from the comfort of a lorry's cab, or whether I would rather be back on horseback. On the whole, the first reaction won; I have never liked "there-and-back-again" journeys, and if I'd ridden further, it would have been on, not back. And the comparison was interesting. I had thought that, by truck, each day's march would have been ticked off with depressing speed. But it was not so. On the contrary; each section, though repeated by the shortest route and under power, seemed to take for ever.

From the other side of Tedzhen, the mountains stood out in the distance like old friends; I hadn't realised how much I'd missed their company while travelling the dreary plains. Of the road itself I recognised little, for after all I hadn't followed it that much; it had only seemed like it at the time.

So there were new things to see. The large dry river bed on an otherwise featureless stretch; yet another Turkish-built cotton factory, gaudy in green and yellow, near Kaakhka; the number of old city mounds, even more numerous than I'd realised. Near one was a long bank that might have been part of the Merz: it was in the right place, and topped by what looked like the remains of castellations. For some miles after Kaakhka oily black silt covered the road, lying in slimy pockets at the foot of the embankment. "Flash floods," explained Djuma's brother, Sukhan. "It often happens after heavy rain or a sudden thaw in the mountains." Recalling the parching, desiccated lands Kaan and I had crossed, I could hardly believe I was in the same country.

We sped past Aina's, too far away even to pick out her house; and stopped briefly at Yalya's, to exchange greetings and pick up the few things I'd left. We stopped less briefly and with increasing frequency at every town, for the truck was developing radiator trouble, and needed to be constantly soothed with cool water. So the day was already nearing its end when we passed under that gloomy mountain ridge which had watched over my path for so many days. The crimson sun at its far end sank almost imperceptibly, as we pursued it west, down on to Ashkhabad. By the time we got to Anau it was quite dark, and I was glad of it; for I knew that last stretch too well.

Kaan bellowed his greetings as we came into the Hippodrome, knowing himself back home even in black night. But the journey had one last horror to throw at us.

Here at the Hippodrome, gathering place of the best bloodstock in Turkmenistan, there was no carefully dug pit, no earth ramp for unloading, as at Djuma's well-run yard. Instead, directed by Shokrat and the rest of Rep's lads, the driver backed the lorry up to a pile of building rubble, stopping at an angle to the slope. When the tailgate came down, one end landed on sand mixed with lumps of concrete and rusty bits of metal, while the other hung suspended in mid-air a couple of feet off the ground. Kaan took one look and very sensibly refused to come out, huddling at the far end of the truck with his ears back.

In vain I begged the driver to find a better place; or at least to reverse into this one a bit straighter. He couldn't be bothered. The stable boys agreed that I was making an unnecessary fuss. Good lads, all of them, they loved their horses; but this was the way things were always done, and they couldn't conceive of any other.

After an unsuccessful blend of cajoling and coercion, during which Kaan crashed his head on the bars but made no positive move, another horse was brought to try and lure him out. The results were chaotic. Both horses ended up on the floor, Kaan on the ramp with his front legs wrapped round an iron bar and his back ones dangling over the void. Yet he somehow emerged unscathed, and I thanked my stars for his gaudy leggings.

As he was led off, I was shaking more than he was. Perhaps the lads felt sorry, though; for instead of being stabled he was turned out in an earth paddock... with a filly for his comfort.

And he was duly comforted; in thought, at any rate, as he nuzzled up to her with obvious delight. Whether in deed, only the stars knew.

*

As I lay on top of the railway truck, wide awake and looking up at a sky glittering in the moonlight, the Hippodrome at last was a friendly place.

It was far too late to phone Olga. Shokhrat and his friends pressed me to share their supper, then made me a comfortable bed alongside their own on the roof of the truck that was their home. "We always sleep up here when it's hot," they said. So after scrumping a great armful of hay for Kaan from Rep's store, I climbed up the rickety ladder and lay under the stars, enjoying at last, now that Kaan was home and dry, the memories of the trip.

It hadn't turned out as I had envisaged it. Journeys seldom do. But I wouldn't have had it differently. I may not have searched the depths of Kaan's speed and stamina, for conditions hadn't allowed it. But his limits had been tested in other ways. He had proved over and over the courage, patience and gentleness of the Akhal-Teke horse, as well as its unique adaptation to travelling the various landscapes of Central Asia. I could have had no finer companion on the road.

And it had turned out to be a voyage of discovery about more than just the Turcoman horse. I had learned at first hand the full meaning of Turkmenchilik, that blend of hospitality, generosity and honour that has survived intact the transition from a harsh, semi-nomadic self-sufficiency on the edge of the desert to the uniformity of twentieth-century Soviet life on the kolkhoz. Tamara Feodorovna had been right: these were the best of people. I felt deeply privileged to have made so many friends among Turcomans, Russians, and all in Turkmenistan.

Conolly, I thought, would have agreed. "...So frank and kind... (I am) inclined to think them a much maligned people." A generous comment from a man who was almost taken as a slave? Or a recognition that basic human values transcend social practices? For he, like me, came from a different culture, from an environment ready to condemn the unfamiliar. Yet, although we may not all do things the same way, in the end it is the same basic human needs, and the sharing of them, that is important to and unites us all.

From immediately below me came the sound of Kaan crunching hay. If I sat up I could see him, busily reducing the pile of feed with the willing help of his filly. Where else in the world, I wondered drowsily, would anyone half kill a horse through carelessness, then recompense him thus?

But, I reminded myself, this is Turkmenistan. They do things differently here.

POSTSCRIPT

He stood at the far end of the barn, head low as if it was too heavy to hold up. The skin was stretched tautly over the emaciated ribs, and the hip-bones stuck out obscenely from concave flanks. A raw wound ran half a saddle's length along the sharp spine, and a scattering of white-haired scars showed that it was just the most recent of many. The marks of a cruelly tight headcollar scarred the once-aristocratic face, and wariness and disillusion had dulled the lustrous eyes. Sweat caked the staring coat, sweat that had poured out of him during the long truck journey under a blazing sun. Even as I wept to see him brought so low, I was conscious of a miracle in that he was still alive.

At the end of our journey Rep had agreed to sell me Kaan, and I had travelled home naïvely believing that he would soon be following. But this was Turkmenistan; no means then existed for exporting horses. After one fax, communication from Rep dried up. Impotent on the end of a phone, I trawled every option: from Louise Firouz - breeder of Turcoman horses in Iran - who generously offered to transport Kaan from border to border if I could find a way to get him to Syria for quarantine; to the Estonian black marketeer who fantasised about shipping him out to Russia on a military transport plane. It was two years before a window of opportunity opened a crack, and by then - still no answer from Rep - I feared he was dead. Ex-racehorses don't live very long in Turkmenistan. The inevitable career change to life on the kolkhoz is a life-and-death lottery.

A month after my departure Rep, doubting my determination, had swopped Kaan for a cow. He was dismayed, then, when I turned up on his doorstep looking for my horse. Tied by his promise to sell him to me - and nagged by his redoubtable Armenian partner, Aida - he made the long journey to find him on a kolkhoz near, of all places, Merv. And so the pitiful shambles that now represented Kaan finally came back to Kolkhoz Makhtum Kuli, just a mile from the yard of Akhrana the camel breeder.

*

How do you build a horse up in a country where you can't go to a corn merchant and buy a bag of feed? I gave Kaan the best I could get - carrots, corn oil and sugar on a basis of shredded bread. Following local advice, I put sugar in his drinking water - another way of getting up to an extra kilo of carbohydrate into him daily. When it comes to rehabilitating a starving horse few, I thought sourly, can have more experience than the Turcomans. Later I managed to buy a sack of barley, and from then on there was always a bucket simmering on the stove of Rep's family at Kolkhoz Makhtum Kuli.

The first job on my list - that of taking a blood sample to screen for disease that might preclude Kaan's entry to Britain - had to wait. I couldn't believe that this shrivelled creature could even contain a test-tube-full of blood, let alone spare it. At last after five days Lena, Hippodrome vet and Geldy Kyarizov's sister-in-law, took the sample. At the same time I ventured a small dose of wormer. I returned to him with trepidation on day six, but needn't have worried; far from being set back, Kaan felt well enough to break his headcollar and challenge another stallion over a nearby mare. Cursing fluently as I and several boys tried to break up the scrap, I spared a corner of my brain for admiration: this horse was unbelievably tough.

In just over a week I was riding him. The mare had to be passed every day on the walk to the edge of the kolkhoz for grass, and I had more control from on top. His razor-sharp backbone almost cut me in two - especially when we had to jump the drainage ditches which criss-crossed the irrigated land. It was even more fun coming back, with one arm wrapped around the biggest sheaf of grass I could carry, and the other trying to restrain Kaan as he bucked for fun over the ditches, or plunged lecherously towards the mare. Two days of this and I began using a saddle, placed over a foam mat with holes cut for the fast-healing wounds.

Meanwhile, there was paperwork. And paperwork. And more paperwork...

Taking a horse out of Turkmenistan is a fraught business which few foreigners ever take on. Although hundreds of horses die every year without a bureaucratic ripple, no horse may depart alive without a document signed in quadruplicate by six learned experts testifying that it does not possess "significance to the breed", and topped off by a presidential signature. Plus, of course, veterinary, customs and export documents.

The Horse Ministry knew no more about the procedure than I did, and most of its lesser mandarins were in no hurry to learn. But the Brits weren't exactly dynamic, either. It took a month for the Central Veterinary Laboratory at Weybridge to certify Kaan free of the Big Four: Dourine, Glanders, Equine Viral Arteritis and Equine Infectious Anaemia. Not until I had those results could I buy him and get on with the papers.

I would have fallen at the first fence of this obstacle race, but for the most important part of my Window of Opportunity. The latest Horse Minister had been sacked. Appointed in his place was... Geldy Kyarizov.

For the first time, the office was held not by a faceless bureaucrat but by a real horseman. Geldy recognised the motives which drove me to export a thousand-dollar reject, rather than megabucks of horseflesh which would earn worthwhile export taxes. He personally took both me and Kaan under his wing, driving his reluctant deputy to cut through Gordian knots of bureaucracy. It was Geldy who solved the problem of transport that had vexed me for two long years, promising a place for Kaan in the box that was to take two of his own horses to Sasha Klimuk's prestigious Stavropol Stud in Russia. Finally, with enormous generosity - and true Turkmenchilik - he installed Kaan in his own yard so that, the huge file of documents finally complete, I could leave him behind in Turkmenistan without worrying.

Even so, the journey out was beset with problems. There were two routes to Stavropol: unsurfaced roads across several

339

hundred miles of the Kara Kum, or by the Caspian Sea to Baku and through the anarchic Caucasus - including Chechnya. Neither could even be considered. But Fate smiled, for later that summer a new trans-Caspian ferry route opened up to Astrakhan, well north of the war zone. On the last day of August, Kaan arrived at the Stavropol Stud for what should have been a few weeks' quarantine.

Now he was on the map; on the far edge of the range from which import to Europe was feasible. But my choice of transporter - an Englishman - was disastrous. There followed eleven months duplicity, a bout of Strangles - one of the most dangerous and virulent infections in the veterinary manuals - and a journey shockingly planned and executed which killed one of Kaan's travelling companions.

Yet when, the final stage completed, I took him out to graze in my field, as I had done so many times in Turkmenistan, he knew - despite thirteen months separation from me, and after countless stables and countless journeys and countless handlers - that he was home.

*

It's hard to believe what Kaan went through. He relished each day of his new life with the joy of the reprieved, taking nothing for granted; except, perhaps, hay, over whose type and quality he became tyrannically fussy. He raced round his field at enormous speed, exulting in full power and strength for perhaps the first time ever. He slobbered endlessly into his water bucket, celebrating the disappearance from his life of frequent thirst.

In many simple daily things, old traumas pursued him. Sometimes, as I prepared to mount, he would remember the grind of a bare saddle tree against a raw wound; then his eyes would glaze and panic consume him for a moment. But such instances became rarer; for in time the bad experiences disappeared under the growing weight of good ones.

For he learnt voraciously. New lessons, such as the mysteries of dressage. He found in himself a particular aptitude for jumping, and thrilled at his own power, becoming a multiple winner. He raised money for charity, and sired many foals. His family of descendants stands at eighteen, and growing. He, and I, explored at last together - as I had dreamed of doing in Turkmenistan - a small part of the versatility and talent of the Akhal-Teke.

But all that is another story.

GLOSSARY
of Turkmen and Russian vocabulary

Administrator hotel receptionist

Ark citadel

A'ul village

Babushka grandmother

Bashlik village headman

Chai-khana tea-house

Char fermented camel's milk

Dapochki slippers

Devushka girl

Divan wooden platform

Ferma kolkhoz dairy unit

Hakim town mayor

Iwan vaulted arch

Kara Kum Black Sands

Khalat knee-length Turkmen coat

Khauz cistern or reservoir

Kolkhoz collective farm

Konzavod stud (lit. "horse factory")

Kumiss fermented mare's milk

Kyzyl Kum Red Sands

Lepioshki round loaves

Madrasa Islamic theological college

Manat Turkmen currency

Mikhmankhana guest house

Militsianer military policeman

Nas a narcotic powder

Oblast province

Obo sacred cairn

Pelmeni meat dumplings

Piroshki small round buns

Pogranichnik border guard

Pishtak façade of a madrasa

Rinok market

Shashlik skewer-grilled meat

Skatchki races

Sukhoi dry, dryly muscled

Sum Uzbek currency

Turkmenchilik Turkmen code of honour

Zapovednik nature reserve

BIBLIOGRAPHY

Abbott, Capt. James, *Narrative of a journey from Heraut to Khiva*, Wm H. Allen & Co., London, 1843.

Atamuradov, Kh.I., Gorelova, T.G., Tsellarius, A.Y., *Badghiz*, Magarif, 1984.

Arrian, *Life of Alexander*, books 3 & 4.

Brent, Peter, *The Mongol Empire*, Book Club Associates/ Weidenfeld & Nicolson, 1976.

Berezikov, Evgeny, *Veliki Timur*, Ukitubtchi, Tashkent, 1994.

Burnaby, Capt. Frederick, *A Ride to Khiva*, Cassell, Petter & Galpin, 1876/Oxford University Press, 1997.

Byron, Robert, *The Road to Oxiana*, MacMillan & Co., 1937/Pan Books 1994.

Conolly, Lt. Arthur, *Journey to the North of India via Russia, Persia and Affghaunistan*, Richard Bentley, London, 1838.

Curzon, George N., *Russia in Central Asia in 1889*, 1889, Rep. Frank Cass & Co. 1967.

Dawson, Christopher, *The Mongol Mission: Narratives and letters of the Franciscan Missionaries in Mongolia and China, trans. by a nun of Stanbrook Abbey*, London/New York, 1955.

Edwards, E. Hartley, *Horses - Their Role in the History of Man*, Willow Books, Collins, 1987.

Franck, Irene M. & Brownstone, David M., *The Silk Road - a History*, Library of Congress Cataloguing-in-Publication Data, 1986.

Glazebrook, Philip, *Journey to Khiva*, Harvill (Harper Collins) 1992.

Herodotus, *The Histories*, Books 1, 4, 7, trans. Aubrey de Selincourt, ed. Penguin Classics, 1954.

Hopkirk, Kathleen, *Central Asia*, John Murray Ltd. 1993.

Hopkirk, Peter, *The Great Game*, Oxford Univ. Press, 1990.

Hyland, Ann, *The Endurance Horse*, J.A. Allen, 1988.

Krist, Gustav, *Alone Through the Forbidden Land*, trans. E.O. Lorimer, Readers' Union Ltd. (Faber & Faber), 1939.

Lawton, John, *Samarkand and Bukhara*, Tauris Parke Books, London, 1991.

Lister, R.P., *The Secret History of Genghis Khan*, Peter Davies, 1969.

MacLean, Fitzroy, *All the Russias*, Flint River Press/Penguin 1992.

   To the Back of Beyond, Jonathan Cape Ltd., 1974.

   Eastern Approaches, Jonathan Cape Ltd. 1949.

   A Person From England, Jonathan Cape Ltd. 1958.

Maillart, Ella, *Turkestan Solo*, reprinted Century, 1985.

Marshall, Robert, *Storm From the East*, BBC Books, 1993.

Maslow, Jonathan, *Sacred Horses*, Random House, 1994.

O'Donovan, Edmond, *The Merv Oasis*, London, 1882.

Phillips, E.D., *The Royal Hordes*, Thames & Hudson 1965.

Plutarch, *The Lives of Illustrious Men*, trans. & ed. The Spencer Press.

Shtorkha, A., *Veter Vgrive Horses*, A. Gklirimskovo, Moscow, 1975.

Teague-Jones, Reginald, *The Spy Who Disappeared*, Victor Gollancz Ltd., 1990.

Thubron, Colin, *The Lost Heart of Asia*, Heinemann, 1994.

Trippett, Frank, *The First Horsemen*, Time-Life International (Nederland), 1974.

Van Der Post, Laurens, *Journey Into Russia*, Island Press, 1964.

ARTICLES:

Abercrombie, Thomas J., *Ibn Battuta, Prince of Travellers,* National Geographic, Dec 1991.

Akhal-Teke Society of GB, Newsletters.

Bond, Michael, *Desert Melting Pots*, New Scientist, Jan 1997.

Edwards, Mike, *Searching for the Scythians*, National Geographic, Sept 1996.

Institute for Ancient Equestrian Studies, Newsletters.

Kuznetsova, Y, *Akhaltekintsoi v Probegakh,* Konevodstbo i Konnoi Sport, Issue 0023 - 3285.

Lawton, John, *The Cradle of the Turks*, Aramco World, Mar/Apr 1994.

Polosmak, Natalya, *Siberian Mummy Unearthed,* National Geographic, Oct. 1994.

Extract from Eastern Approaches by Fitzroy Maclean
reprinted by permission of Peters Fraser & Dunlop
on behalf of the Estate of Fitzroy Maclean

Peters Fraser & Dunlop
Drury House 34 - 43 Russell Street London WC2B 5HA
Tel: 020 7344 1000 Fax: 020 7836 9539

www.petersfraserdunlop.com
permissions@pfd.co.uk

The Peters Fraser & Dunlop Group Limited Employment Agents
VAT 503209687
Registered in England 218 5448

INDEX

346

347

Between the Desert and the Deep Blue Sea

A Syrian Journey

Gill Suttle

An Equestrian Travel Classic

To those for whom the name of Syria conjures up images of George W. Bush's "Axis of Evil", or who picture the Middle East in general to be a place of endemic unrest or squabbling religious factions, this book will come as a revelation. Here they will discover a nation where all clans and creeds live in enviable harmony, their goodwill towards each other exceeded only by the warmth of their welcome to an eccentric foreigner.

Syria's people represent the top layer of a multi-dimensional mosaic; for few countries possess such a diversity of culture, religion, topography or historical legacy. This is the story of a journey into more than one landscape.

A passion for Arab horses and a long acquaintance with Syria inspired the author to travel on horseback into the backwoods of this fascinating land in 1998. Here is an account greatly differing from those of most recent equestrian travel books, which usually describe heavily organised expeditions complete with logistics team, back-up lorry, spare horses and all the latest equipment. In contrast, this traveller enjoyed a relaxed, spontaneous ramble, living out of home-made saddlebags, enjoying the hospitality of local people and often sleeping rough. Best of all, her companion was that of her wildest childhood fantasies: an Arab stallion.

Together horse and rider traversed the gorges and cornfields of the Orontes valley, where Roman water wheels still work alongside modern irrigation; lost themselves among the ridges and passes of the Alawi Mountain, whose various minority sects live happily together and whose ruined castles recall the times of the Crusades; briefly touched the Mediterranean shore, before crossing the western reaches of the Badiat ash-Sham, or Syrian Desert, on the way down to the Damascus Oasis. They trod where the Egyptian Pharaoh gave battle, supped with descendants of Biblical Assyrians and mediaeval Assassins, and visited the Jebel-ad-Din, or Mountain of Faith, where villagers still speak Aramaic, the language of Christ.

While briefly informed by history, Islam and its offshoots, geography and - where absolutely unavoidable - politics, this delightful book is principally an account of the people of Syria - and of a gallant and memorable horse.

Illustrated with maps and a fine selection of photographs.

ISBN 1-59048-246-8
www.classictravelbooks.com
www.horsetravelbooks.com

STEPPE BY STEPPE

A SLOW JOURNEY THROUGH MONGOLIA

GILL SUTTLE

Four good legs are better than two lousy ones. So if you have an incapacitating illness, incurably itchy feet and an affinity for horses, what better country to make for than Mongolia, where horses outnumber people and have supported the nomadic lifestyle for 3,000 years?

In this country of contradiction and paradox, though, live horsepower may still be more elusive than the mechanical sort... if rather more reliable. Making the best of whichever's available, Gill Suttle sets out to discover whether, for some at least, there *is* hope of a life after - even during - the destructive illness ME.

But what of life after Communism? Is this land, from which the Mongol hordes of Genghis Khan once exploded to conquer empires, faring better or worse under the new lesson of democracy than the many other satellites of the former USSR? Exploring the diverse layers of Mongolian society together with the immense and varied landscapes, the author encounters a tough and resilient people making the best of hard times. From Yuppie wannabes in the capital, Ulaan Baatar, nomads of the ancient reindeer culture on the borders of Siberia, Titans in the wrestling arena and others come many stories of determination and success - such as the dramatic resurgence of the Buddhist faith, and the reintroduction of the endangered, prehistoric Przewalski Horse to its native land.

ISBN 0-9534536-1-8

www.scimitarpress.co.uk

JAILBREAK

A SLOW JOURNEY ROUND EASTERN EUROPE

GILL SUTTLE

A former British modern pentathlon team member, three-day-event rider and the first woman to win a full Oxford Blue for running, Gill Suttle found not just her sport but every significant part of her former life wiped out by the disabling condition ME.

Some years on, she breaks out of the prison of illness by travelling,in a van complete with bed, to Eastern Europe. Sometimes exchanging the driving seat for the saddle, she enjoys some fascinating glimpses behind the scenes of eight former Communist countries struggling to throw off their recent past; and in the process manages to shed at least part of her own.

From the heights of Berlin's biggest big wheel in Europe to the depths of a Czech pothole... mummies in a Slovakian crypt to nudists on an Estonian beach... watching Polish wild beavers to eating Lithuanian elk... riding among Hungarian cowboys to midnight arrest by gun-toting Soviet-style police - this is a wide view of Eastern Europe at its best (and worst), as well as a personal journey.

"A stimulating and lively read from a promising new travel author who vividly conveys the joys and difficulties of her journey across Eastern Europe in the early years of freedom from Communism."

"Excels when she talks about the views and the countryside... Her descriptions are evocative but concise"

"This book must be an inspiration to anyone suffering with ME."

"If you are addicted to horses, travel stories... and chocolate... Then this is the book for you!"

ISBN 0-9534536-0-X

www.scimitarpress.co.uk